Advance Praise for *The Art and Science of Sword Fighting*

Master Joe Varady's "The Art and Science" collection of martial-arts-related works has become among my most valued reference tools, and this latest work, *The Art and Science of Sword Fighting,* is a true masterpiece. As a long-time student and practitioner of the martial arts and with a particular interest in the weapons of various martial arts and cultures, and perhaps above all other weapons, I have come to fully appreciate the history of the sword, its evolution in design, and its use within the various cultures that have advanced it. *The Art and Science of Sword Fighting* provides a concise yet thorough encyclopedic-level knowledge of the sword, its history, the various designs and attributes, and the great masters who wielded them. But more significantly, this work serves as an instructional guide for anyone, at any level, who desires to understand the use of this weapon. Covering crucial topics such as how to properly hold the sword, footwork and movement, balance, and energy transfer when using the sword, this book provides you with every detail. The ingenious training aids along with the workouts and drills enhance your use of the weapon and will significantly improve your sword-fighting skills, will broaden your overall techniques, and will provide a solid foundation from which to develop a universal approach to modern-day sword fighting. Master Joe Varady's *The Art and Science of Sword Fighting* reflects his many years of study, practice, and implementation and serves as the perfect reference manual and instructional guide for both the beginner and the most advanced practitioner.

—**Master Michael J. Gallagher**, USA Taekwondo national weapons champion, owner of Generations Taekwondo, executive board member for Universal Systems of Martial Arts, board member and trustee for the Pennsylvania Karate Hall of Fame, board member of the Philadelphia Historic Martial Arts Society Hall of Fame, 2015 inductee of the Philadelphia Historic Martial Arts Society Hall of Fame, 2018 inductee of the Pennsylvania Karate Hall of Fame, Pennsylvania state officer for the World Taekwondo Masters Union

As a martial artist who has been training since 1985, and when I read or watch martial art instruction, I can usually tell if the person is authentic and if what they are showing would work effectively for self-defense. Master Joe Varady is one of the best examples of this.

His newest book, *The Art and Science of Sword Fighting*, is a fountain of knowledge for sword fighting. If you want to know more than just basic sword techniques and want to learn how to actually fight with the sword, this is the book for you.

Master Varady shows techniques with several different lengths of swords, is a great teacher, and is able to break things down and make them learnable.

I have collected all of Master Varady's books and videos. What's nice is how they all tie together through similar techniques and strategies, yet each book/video gives you new gems of knowledge. I have learned a lot through Master Varady's teaching and I'm sure you will too.

—**Paul Peterson**, Shihan, founder of Kingdom Karate, 4th degree black belt Hapkido, 3rd degree black belt Naha te Karate, 1st degree black belt Taekwondo

Joe Varady has once again written a comprehensive instructional guide, this time for the art and science of sword fighting, that beginners can easily understand and experts can respect. He provides detailed instruction not only on how to use the sword in training and fighting (both long sword and short sword), but also on selecting safety gear and making your own training equipment. In addition, he includes quotes and references from a variety of historical sources on this ancient art. It will become obvious to any reader that Joe Varady's knowledge and skill comes from both extensive study and practice. No matter if you are an expert fencer or just have a passing interest in swords and sword fighting, this book is well worth your time. It is so full of information that even a long-term practitioner may learn about something they didn't already know.

—**Sifu Brian William Jewell**, author of *The Wisdom of Wing Chun* and *Life Lessons Learned Through Sparring*

Drawing from a wide range of martial arts, Varady distills universal principles to create a style-neutral guide to mid-length and long blade. Whether your interests lie in modern sport fencing, HEMA, or kendo, this manual demonstrates the essential techniques that form the foundation of attack and defense across disciplines. While it is perfect for beginning and intermediate level students, advanced practitioners will also find it useful for both the analysis and breakdown of techniques and to learn some tips and tricks to put into their own game.

One added bonus for the beginner is Varady's guidance in selecting appropriate protective gear and in obtaining or constructing training equipment to meet your particular needs.

—**Bernie Mojzes**, Shodan, Chang's School of Martial Arts, student Live Steel Fight Academy and Modern Gladiatorial Arts

The Art and Science of Sword Fighting is yet another home run from Grandmaster Joe Varady, and an excellent complement to the three Art and Science titles. As with those previous books, the *Art and Science of Sword Fighting* distills its subject into the core principles regardless of historical lineage, martial style, or geography, and presents the reader a master class in learning to fight with the sword. Grandmaster Joe's background as a professional educator shines through as he takes the student on a logical progression of lessons, drills, and skill challenges. With a variety of solo and partner activities as well as sample workouts for each of the nine skill levels, it's like having Grandmaster Joe in the room with you. Whether you've studied sword fighting before or are a complete novice, this book should absolutely be part of your personal curriculum.

Astute readers of Grandmaster Joe's earlier books will almost certainly see common principles, skills, and scenarios rear their heads—short sword and single stick, long sword and the staff, close fighting, and self-defense. This is no accident and is another testament to the research, experimentation, and dedication that Grandmaster Joe brings to all his martial endeavors. Miyamoto Musashi, the famous Japanese swordsman Joe is fond of quoting, once said, "Know one thing, know 10,000 things." With this new book, Grandmaster Joe once again proves how true those words are.

—**Sensei Seth Clearwater**, instructor Satori Dojo

A comprehensive look at the history of sword fighting with step-by-step instructions on how to successfully train in swordsmanship. Complete with illustrations, this well-written book details methodical training steps to ensure proficiency through disciplined practice. Highly recommended!
—**Master Terri Giamartino**

Having read Master Joe Varady's excellently crafted volumes on staff fighting, stick fighting, and self-defense, I was looking forward to reading *The Art and Science of Sword Fighting*. Once again, Master Varady has created a comprehensive training system. *The Art and Science of Sword Fighting* is the *complete* instruction manual. The book wastes no time, diving straight into techniques while providing sufficient introduction and history. Master Varady explains and supports the techniques with the physics of sword fighting, research from historical master swordsmen of Europe and Asia, and his years of real-life experimentation.

Learn about the unique structure of one-handed short swords, two-handed long swords, and master swords. The training lessons cover footwork, defense, and attack angles, all illustrated with quality photographs that are easy to follow. As a master instructor, Varady provides mental preparation, safety, and the gritty but fair spirit of competition. He draws from his years of extensive experience in actual combat competition to produce an excellent training source.

Using illustrations, Master Varady describes how to build your own training targets and equipment and recommends the best professional armor and swords for training and competition.

The principles in *The Art and Science of Sword Fighting* can apply to all forms of self-defense and combat. All martial artists, whether beginner or expert, whether weaponless or armed, will benefit from reading this training guide. I did.
—**Michael A. Ponzio**, Shichidan, Cuong Nhu Martial Arts, author of martial arts weapon instructional manuals on Tambo (short stick), Bo (long staff), Sai, and Tonfa. Author of adventure and military historical fiction "Ancestry Novels" of ancient Rome and medieval Europe

Joe Varady has written an excellent and cogent synthesis of swordsmanship across multiple historical traditions. For someone who is a beginner in sword fighting such as me, *The Art and Science of Sword Fighting* provides a comprehensive introduction to handling one- and two-handed swords that I have seen nowhere else. The book has explicit instructions on all the standard guards, stances, attacks, and defenses used in sword fighting world-wide, plus some more advanced versions of these techniques that are highly effective for surprising your opponent. All examples are backed by an abundance of high-quality pictures illustrating proper body mechanics and footwork during practice and sparring. Joe has also developed a systematic set of solo and partner workouts that build on one another and will develop your body and mind, and dare I say heart, to make you a better swordsman. Joe also provides a lot of practical advice on the importance of using and buying the right protective and training equipment and building your own. I especially like his more user-friendly take on the traditional Meyer's square. I highly recommend this book for any beginner swordsman to start their journey, but I feel that even more experienced swordsmen will get something out of this book.

—**Anthony Peterson**, student of Joe Varady

Sensei Joe has put in the thousands of repetitions and many hours of hard work in trial and experiment. He has combed the history of so many cultures. And he has blended all this with personal application to formulate this common-sense instruction. The technical details are awesome.

After a hard-work dojo session, this is a must-have book to compare to your own practice. It's a great reference to filter all the advice that flows in a busy dojo. Not all dojo banter is accurate!

The easy-to-understand information and excellent illustrations will answer questions as they arise and inspire experiment for your next workout. I wish I had this back in the day, but I'm really glad to have it now!

This book is a great tool to achieve the requirements laid down by my own teacher, Professor Ernie Cates. Throughout the years, he would quote from Leonardo Da Vinci: "The student who does not surpass his master, fails his master."

—**Moose Cates**, Soke, Neko Ryu Goshin Jitsu, 4th dan Kodokan Judo. Student of my father, Professor Ernie Cates, 8th dan Kodokan Judo and founder of Neko Ryu Goshin Jitsu

JOE VARADY

The Art and Science of Sword Fighting
A COMPLETE INSTRUCTIONAL GUIDE

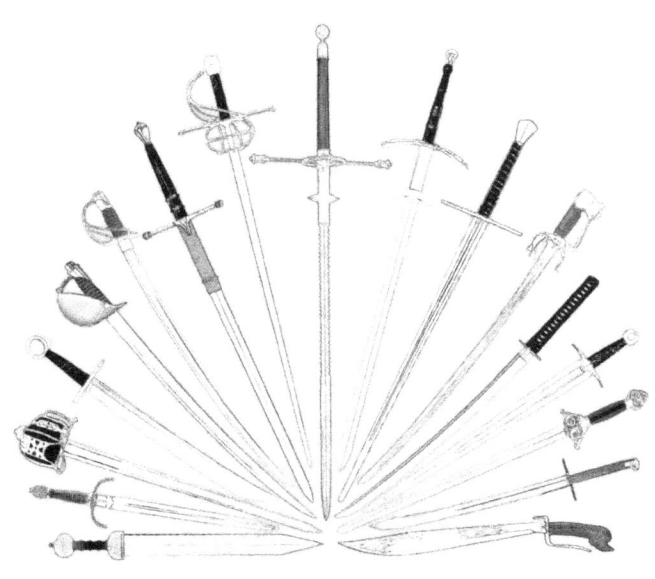

YMAA Publication Center
Wolfeboro, NH USA

YMAA Publication Center, Inc.
PO Box 480
Wolfeboro, NH 03894
800-669-8892 • www.ymaa.com • info@ymaa.com

ISBN 9781594399879 (print)
ISBN 9781594399886 (e-book)
ISBN 9781594399893 (hardcover)

Copyright © 2024 by Joe Varady
All rights reserved including the right of reproduction in whole or in part in any form.

Cover design by Axie Breen
Photos by Andrea Hilborn
Edited by Doran Hunter
Illustrations provided by the author
20240523

Publisher's Cataloging in Publication

Names: Varady, Joe, author.
Title: The art and science of sword fighting : a complete instructional guide / Joe Varady.
Description: Wolfboro, NH USA : YMAA Publication Center, [2024] | "9 levels, easy to expert"--Cover. | Includes bibliographical references.
Identifiers: ISBN: 9781594399879 (paperback) | 9781594399886 (e-book) | 9781594399893 (hardcover) | LCCN: 2024935151
Subjects: LCSH: Swordplay--Training--Handbooks, manuals, etc. | Swords--Handbooks, manuals, etc. | Fencing--Training--Handbooks, manuals, etc. | Fencing, Oriental--Training--Handbooks, manuals, etc. | Self-defense--Handbooks, manuals, etc. | Martial arts--Handbooks, manuals, etc. | BISAC: SPORTS & RECREATION / Martial Arts / General. | SELF-HELP / Safety & Security / Personal Safety & Self-Defense. | SPORTS & RECREATION / History. | SPORTS & RECREATION / Fencing.
Classification: LCC GV1143.4 .V37 2024 | DDC: 796.86--dc23

The authors and publisher of the material are NOT RESPONSIBLE in any manner whatsoever for any injury which may occur through reading or following the instructions in this manual.

The activities physical or otherwise, described in this manual may be too strenuous or dangerous for some people, and the reader(s) should consult a physician before engaging in them.

Warning: While self-defense is legal, fighting is illegal. If you don't know the difference you'll go to jail because you aren't defending yourself. You are fighting—or worse. Readers are encouraged to be aware of all appropriate local and national laws relating to self-defense, reasonable force, and the use of weaponry, and act in accordance with all applicable laws at all times. Understand that while legal definitions and interpretations are generally uniform, there are small—but very important—differences from state to state and even city to city. To stay out of jail, you need to know these differences. Neither the authors nor the publisher assumes any responsibility for the use or misuse of information contained in this book.

Nothing in this document constitutes a legal opinion nor should any of its contents be treated as such. While the authors believe that everything herein is accurate, any questions regarding specific self-defense situations, legal liability, and/or interpretation of federal, state, or local laws should always be addressed by an attorney at law.

When it comes to martial arts, self-defense, and related topics, no text, no matter how well written, can substitute for professional, hands-on instruction. **These materials should be used for academic study only.**

Printed in USA.

Dedication

When it comes learning any martial art, having knowledgeable teachers is obviously very important. However, it is equally important to have skilled training partners who share your drive and desire to learn. For the last twenty years, my main training partner with the sword has been Joe McLaughlin. I met Joe in 2003, when I started training at Live Steel Fight Academy (LSFA). He came with abundant previous experience in the martial arts, as did I. So, although we had very different martial arts backgrounds, we got along well right from the start. We worked hard to master LSFA's curriculum and worked our way up to becoming assistant instructors. In 2011, when the founder of LSFA, the late Dave Dickey, relocated to California, it was Joe who took over the school. Not too long after, in 2014, we joined forces to create a new program and cofounded Modern Gladiatorial Arts (MGA). Today, we continue to train together to deepen our understanding of sword fighting and to share that knowledge with others. This book is the culmination of our last twenty years of training and teaching together.

Table of Contents

Dedication — iii
Foreword — ix
Preface — xi
Some Notes Before We Begin — xii

Introduction: Swords and Swordsmanship — 1
    The Art and Science of Sword Fighting — 1
    Traditional versus Progressive Sword Fighting — 2
    What Is Swordsmanship? — 2
    A Brief History of the Sword — 3
    Anatomy of the Sword — 4
    Sword Classification — 6
    Which Is Better: A Short Sword or a Long Sword? — 8
    Longer Is *Not* Always Better! — 9
    Which Is Better: A Straight Sword or a Curved Sword? — 11
    Common Sword Types — 12
    Meet the Masters — 17

Part 1: Short Sword — 22

Level 1: Short Sword Offense — 23
    A Closer Look at Single-Handed Swords — 23
    Training Equipment: The Sword — 23
    Your Upper Body — 28
    Your Lower Body — 36
    Basic Striking Angles — 50
    Perfecting Your Lunge — 58
    The Importance of Isolation Training — 59
    Combinations and Patterns — 59
    Training Equipment: Meyer's Square — 60
    Free Flow — 63
    The Bubble Drill — 64
    Level 1 Workout — 65

Level 2: Short Sword Defense — 67
    Building a Solid Defense — 67
    Training Equipment: Gloves and Mask — 67
    Attack Zones — 72
    The Line of Combat — 73
    Evasion — 74
    Blocking and Parrying — 76
    Static Blocking — 76

Blocking/Riposte Drills	81
Block with the Edge or the Flat?	84
Jamming Blocks	86
Dynamic Blocking	87
Tres-Tres Drill	90
Training Equipment: The Pell	94
Level 2 Workout	97
Level 3: Short Sword Fencing	**99**
Training Equipment: Body Armor	99
Fencing versus Hack and Slash	101
Center, Centerline, and the Line of Combat	102
Engagement and the Bind	103
Gaining the Opponent's Blade	104
Glide	105
The Cone of Defense	106
Press	109
Beat	110
Change of Engagement	111
Double Change	111
Cut Over	112
Parry	113
Optimal Learning Zone	115
A Sample Bout	115
Level 3 Workout	117
Level 4: Advanced Short Sword	**119**
Training Equipment: Lower Body Protection	119
The Outside Game	119
Baiting and Drawing	121
Feinting	122
Trick Guards	123
Fancy Footwork	127
Master Cuts and Thrusts	128
In-Fighting	131
Foot Sweeps	138
Sparring	140
Salute	141
En Garde!	142
Types of Matches	143
Understanding Timing	144
Examples of Types of Timing in Sparring	144
Strategy and Tactics	145
The Seven Principal Rules	147
Level 4 Workout	148

Part 2: Long Sword — 150

Level 5: Long Sword Offense — 151
- A Closer Look at Two-Handed Swords — 151
- Training Equipment: Choosing a Sword — 152
- Training Equipment: Protective Gear — 153
- Gripping the Long Sword — 154
- Stances — 155
- Guards — 156
- Distancing and Footwork — 159
- Targeting — 160
- Basic Strikes — 161
- Edge Alignment — 163
- The Four Thrusts — 164
- Patterns and Combinations — 165
- Meyer's Square Training — 165
- Freestyling — 168
- The Pell Revisited — 169
- Level 5 Workout — 169

Level 6: Long Sword Defense — 171
- Building a Solid Defense — 171
- Evasion — 171
- Blocking — 173
- Counterattacking — 177
- Blocking/Riposte Drills — 178
- Block with the Edge or the Flat? — 181
- Jamming Blocks — 181
- Dynamic Blocking — 183
- Parrying — 184
- Tres-Tres Drill — 185
- Level 6 Workout — 188

Level 7: Long Sword Fencing — 189
- Controlling the Centerline — 189
- Engagement and the Bind — 189
- Gaining the Opponent's Blade — 190
- Glide — 191
- The Cone of Defense — 192
- Press — 194
- Beat — 195
- Change of Engagement — 195
- Cut Over — 196
- Double Change — 197
- Parry — 197
- A Sample Bout — 200
- Level 7 Workout — 201

Level 8: Advanced Long Sword	203
Long Range	203
The Three-Step Rule	205
Feinting	206
Programming	207
Trick Guards	209
Middle Range	212
Master Cuts (and Thrusts)	214
Half-Swording	216
Attempted Murder!	218
Murder Stroke	218
In-Fighting	219
The Bind	219
Kicking	223
Foot Sweeps and Takedowns	226
Sparring	229
Level 8 Workout	230
Level 9: Great Sword	231
Anatomy of a Great Sword	231
Grip	232
Stances and Footwork	233
Guards	233
Basic Strikes	234
Double Strikes	239
Defense	242
Cone of Defense	243
Trick Guards	243
A Hard-Learned Lesson	244
High Rear Guard	245
Low Rear Guard	245
Close-Range Techniques	246
Pommel Strikes	247
Level 9 Workout	248
Acknowledgments	*249*
Appendix 1: Sword Fighting Equipment Suppliers	*251*
Appendix 2: Instructional Resources on YouTube	*252*
Appendix 3: Test Cutting	*253*
Appendix 4: Make Your Own Padded Swords	*256*
About the Author	*261*

Foreword

by Chris Hall

The sword has a long history. It was one of our earliest weapons, no doubt at first simply a sharpened version of the club, but as humans have gone through a long process of refinement, on and off the battlefield, the sword changed to fit the circumstances. From changes in armor to deployment to an evolution in strategies and tactics, the sword became a specialized tool. Swords that cut, swords that stabbed, swords with range, swords with shapes to amplify their effectiveness, and swords that needed to be used in specialized ways show up throughout the arc of history.

All of these have been wielded by people who had similar physical forms and mental capabilities, and thus the evolution of sword technique: we developed ways to use our tools effectively and efficiently according to our physical strengths and limitations, the needs of the situations we found ourselves in, and the fullness of our lives on and off the battlefield.

In the process, we ourselves were refined.

As a thirty-year student, teacher, and researcher in the martial arts, I've come to realize how vital these particular arts are to achieving a full set of capabilities and capacities in the world. The art and science of the sword represent one element of what used to be called the common art of armament. The common arts in general are the ways that people meet their basic, embodied needs in the world: growing food, crafting homes and tools, navigating, healing, making clothes, and more. Defending one's self and others constitute one element of this larger set of skills, and since the sword and the way that it is used are so universal—almost every culture in the world has its parallel—then the art and science of the sword form a baseline set of competencies and vantages into the heart of what would rightly be called the common art of armament.

As a teacher, leader, and researcher in the Classical school movement, I've had the opportunity to speak and to write about these arts, including my book *Common Arts Education*, for the past decade. From that vantage, I would call to mind that even as the term is defined, it is important to note that training in the common arts is not simply for survival. It could be so at a primitive level, but when the notion of refinement enters the picture, the common arts become the arts of "thrival." We practice these arts to not only live, but to live well. This is the essence of the "lifegiving sword" mentioned by our forebears: not only do the capabilities developed through diligent training allow one to defend one's self and others, but the mental frameworks of strategies and tactics, plus the formation of prudence, temperance, justice, and fortitude in a student contribute to a refinement of the practitioner, a fullness of capability in the world that benefits not just the swordsman, but everyone.

Grandmaster Joe Varady has done much to propagate the arts of armament in virtuous ways through the past thirty years. He has refined his personal practice in a variety of realms, from empty-handed self-defense to the arts of stick, staff, and sword. As such, he understands not only each art in itself, but the connections and synergies between these arts that lead to sound practice and perspective. His command of the arts of strategy and tactics, physical and mental training, and achievements in the arena testify to his proficiency. Best of all, his students testify to the same: in addition to his personal cultivation of martial skills, his school, Satori Dojo, represents both a flowering and fruiting of a deeply-rooted tree of virtuous practice, shown by the achievements, attitudes, and growth of his students through time.

I highly recommend this book, *The Art and Science of Sword Fighting*, to you, practitioner. If you seek a well-balanced, well-informed, well-written introduction to the common arts of armament, you have found it here. In the spirit of our arts, and the inherited spirit of our forebears who encouraged us to grow in virtuous practice, I encourage you to make this volume a gateway not simply to the art of survival, but to the art of thrival. Let the formation of practice, drill, and refinement work on you as much as the information and enter into the stream of learning that spans the millennia joyfully, and with all seriousness of study.

—**Chris Hall, MEd,** founder Always Learning Education, author of *Common Arts Education* (Classic Academic Press), Shodan, Cuong Nhu Oriental Martial Arts, Master of Arts in teaching elementary education, thirty-year practitioner of martial arts, twenty-four years as an instructor, National-Level Alcuin Fellow, thirty-year veteran educator

Preface

My entire life I have enjoyed the challenge of training and fighting with weapons, including the sword. Like many kids, every stick I picked up, from twigs and branches to my mother's yard stick, became a sword in my hands. My first "real" sword was part of an old fishing rod that I found in the attic when I was less than ten. About three feet long, it made a good improvised rapier, and I still have it to this day. Since then, I have learned from multiple teachers and trained with many sword fighting groups. My unique and wide-ranging experiences, from heavy armored combat with members of the SCA (Society for Creative Anachronism) to historical fencing at Live Steel Fight Academy, to crossing swords with the graceful fighters of the Taiji Fencing League, have given me an unconventional perspective of sword fighting as a whole. Without the constraints of style or affiliation, and in conjunction with my background in the Asian martial arts, including kobudo and eskrima, I strive to discern the many universal principles common to all sword fighting. While my personal style may be a melting-pot of techniques, my ultimate goal is always to distill techniques down to their universal elements, combining the best and most effective ones into an integrated whole.

> Of no use to the world are those men who study to do exactly as was done before, who never understand that today is a new day.
>
> —Ralph Waldo Emerson

Some Notes Before We Begin

The terms beginner, intermediate, and advanced are relative and can vary between different schools of sword fighting. Techniques categorized as "advanced" here may be taught earlier in other systems. In this guide, I classify techniques as advanced using the lens of a beginner with no experience. Experienced practitioners of historical fencing will no doubt recognize many of the techniques in this book from training in their chosen styles. Rather than adhering to the traditional names of techniques, which vary from style to style and can be confusing, especially to the novice, I chose to use simple modernized terminology to describe the techniques.

It is important to note that practical understanding and proficiency in sword fighting require hands-on training and instruction from experienced practitioners. While this book and video series can go a long way toward expanding your sword fighting skills, whenever possible, it is recommended that you study and train under the guidance of a qualified instructor to ensure safety and properly learn the techniques and concepts.

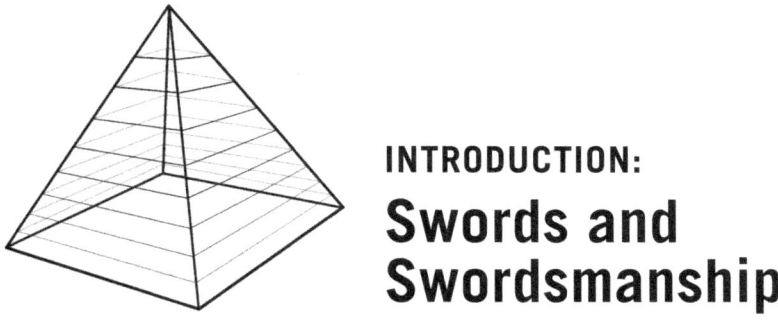

INTRODUCTION:
Swords and Swordsmanship

The Art and Science of Sword Fighting

The Art and Science of Sword Fighting is not promoting a style in the traditional sense of the word. It is a progressive, eclectic collection of sword-fighting techniques borrowed from many diverse sources. Most are universal concepts that can be applied easily to fighting with a wide variety of swords. It is, admittedly, a "country doctor" approach to swordsmanship, aimed at creating a general practitioner who is comfortable fighting with different types of swords. I chose this approach for two main reasons. First, it provides a solid foundation in the general art of fighting with swords, a necessity for beginners and experts alike. Later, once you have determined what your strengths are and where your personal interests lie, you may choose to specialize in a particular brand of swordsmanship. Regardless of what style that may be, a strong foundation will serve you well. Second, by not focusing on the historical context of any one particular style, it is my hope that advanced practitioners, regardless of personal style or affiliation, might transcend differences in styles and come together as swordsmen to examine the plethora of available techniques. In the short run, such collaboration will serve to improve our individual and collective understandings of sword fighting. In the long run, such study might lead to a modernized, universal system of swordsmanship, not unlike the development of today's Mixed Martial Arts (MMA).

The Art and Science of Sword Fighting is divided into two sections. Part 1 introduces the one-handed sword. Part 2 teaches how to use a sword that requires two hands to wield effectively. Each part is further subdivided into offense, defense, fencing, and advanced techniques. The material in Part 2 is presented in a similar fashion as Part 1 in that proficiency is built step by step upon skills learned in previous sections. By training diligently in this intentional manner, your swordsmanship will develop in a smooth methodical fashion.

Traditional versus Progressive Sword Fighting

Traditional sword fighting systems exist all over the globe, each with its own unique history and method of formal training. Established schools and styles offer many benefits, such as a formal curriculum, the community created by a group of students learning together, and exposure to advanced practitioners that possess a deep knowledge of their art. However, most sword-fighting styles focus on recreating one particular style of sword fighting as it is represented in historical documents, often requiring its students learn the techniques in the native language of that particular tradition, such as Spanish, German, Japanese, and others. I have the greatest respect for those dedicated to recreating, practicing, and preserving historical traditions. While historical sword study has its place, the fact is not everyone is interested in recreating history. Some just want to learn to fight with a sword. Historical European Martial Arts (HEMA) provides a strong foundation that should not be discounted, nor constrain modern development. This book takes a bold and progressive approach to next generation fencing. While there is still a good deal of history presented within it, this condensed course of study is designed to teach you how to wield just about *any* sword using an eclectic approach to swordsmanship aimed at ferreting out the universal concepts. This novel approach is, admittedly, a very ambitious task because swords come in so many shapes and sizes. However, by taking a fresh and methodical approach to the topic, I think that any student, including you, can quickly and successfully learn the art and science of sword fighting.

What Is Swordsmanship?

Swordsmanship, or fencing, is an art as much as it is a science. Art and science, like the yin and yang, are two halves of a larger whole that speak to the dual nature of combat. On the one hand, art finds its roots in human instinct and displays itself through self-expression, while on the other, science draws from empirical observation, analysis of data, and the identification of patterns. Each of these, both art and science, plays a crucial role in successful combat.

Sword fighting is a vigorous activity that develops strength, speed, agility, and overall physical fitness. It also promotes mental acuity and quick thinking. Once you have developed the requisite skills to the point where you no longer have to think about them to perform them properly, you can focus your attention on outwitting your opponent in an exciting game of physical chess...with swords!

Like the words *human* and *mankind*, the word *swordsman* applies equally to all genders. That said, it is also correct to use swordswoman to describe a female fencer. Using your swordsmanship is called fencing, swordplay, crossing swords, or, more plainly, sword fighting. Fighting is a general term that is used to describe everything from light, friendly sparring to uncontrolled mortal combat.

A Brief History of the Sword

The sword has been around for about 4,000 years. In that time, it evolved and changed in form, material, and use as new cultures and technologies emerged. The forerunners of the sword developed in Egypt during the early Bronze Age, around 3300 BC. These short blades were only about two feet long and little more than large daggers. It took about 1,500 more years before advances in metallurgy allowed later swordsmiths to create true swords that exceeded three feet in length, during the late Bronze Age, circa 1700 BC. These early swords had long, leaf-shaped blades that were good for both cutting and thrusting, with hilts that were merely an extension of the blade in handle form.

By 1000 BC, the Iron Age had arrived and with it came new sword designs. In Europe, Asia, and Africa, swordsmiths forged many new and unique blades. The development of the crossguard and pommel helped to make the sword a more effective weapon because it provided better balance and protection for the user's hand.

Carbon steel appeared first in India around the year AD 500, and it was a great improvement over iron for making swords. In particular, Damascus steel swords were prized for their exceptionally sharp edges and sturdiness compared to other weapons of the era. The composition of these swords, a secret since lost to time, was very similar to that of modern high-carbon steel. Additionally, the Indians and Persians were among the first to recognize the advantage of a curved blade, long before its introduction to Europe by the Turks.

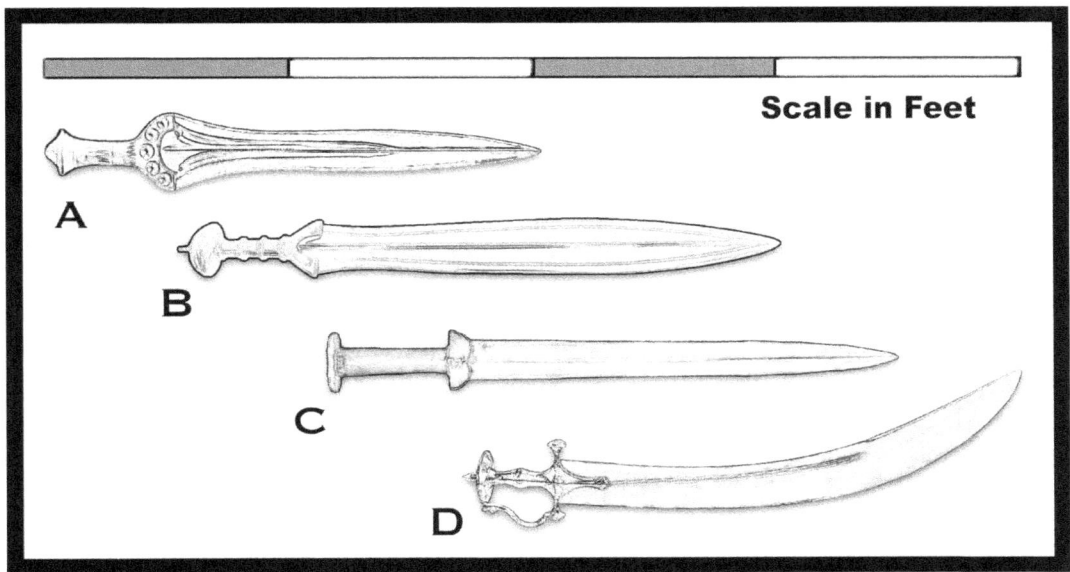

A) A late Bronze Age sword, Aegean c. 1700 BC; B) an Iron Age Greek xiphos c. 1200 BC; C) a steel Viking Age sword, Norway, AD 500; D) a curved Damascus steel tulwar, India, AD 1200.

In each culture, the most effective sword designs would flourish for a time but eventually be replaced as technology changed. Carbon steel allowed for the development of new swords that were longer, lighter, and stronger, giving their wielders both a figurative and literal edge over the less technologically advanced weapons of their opponents. These swords were more maneuverable, and their use required greater skill and finesse. By the 14th century AD, sophisticated styles of swordsmanship had developed and were taught in elite fight academies in Europe, as well as in the Near and Far East. It is from these schools of swordsmanship that the oldest surviving fencing manuals originate.

As firearms became more widespread in the 16th and 17th centuries, sword fighting began to decline in importance as a military skill; however, it continued to be practiced as a sport and as a form of self-defense. In the 19th century, fencing emerged as a popular competitive sport, with standardized rules and equipment to ensure the safety of its competitors.

Today, sword fighting remains a popular sport and martial art, with practitioners around the world studying various styles and techniques. While the use of swords as a weapon in warfare is now mostly obsolete, the art and sport of sword fighting continues to fascinate and inspire people of all ages the world over.

Anatomy of the Sword

The focus of this book is fighting with swords and not about the weapons themselves; however, it will benefit you to have a general knowledge of the parts of a sword, the major types of swords, and their intended uses. Swords come in many shapes and sizes, but all share the same basic anatomy. So, let's start with the parts of the sword.

At their simplest, all swords are composed of two parts, a hilt and a blade. The hilt consists of the grip, or handle, as well as the hand guard. Hand guards protect the user's hands from injury and can take on many forms, including cruciform crossguards, basket hilts, knuckle bows, and tsuba. The extended arms of the crossguard are termed quillons. The larger the quillons, the more protection they give your hands and arms. Some quillons angle toward the blade, as in the Scottish claymore, and some sweep back to cover the hand, as seen in the Italian rapier. The butt end of the handle is called the pommel. Often heavy, the pommel helps to counterbalance the weight of the blade. Between the handguard and the pommel, running the length of the handle, is an extension of the blade called the tang. You can't see the tang, however, because it is normally covered by the grip, which can be made of various materials including wood, bone, or leather, and can be wrapped with cord or wire.

A sword's blade can have one sharpened edge or two. When holding a double-edged sword, the edge of the blade that is aligned with your knuckles is referred to as the true edge. Since strikes with the back edge of the blade are generally not as strong, it is termed the false edge. In the case of a single-edged blade, the back of the blade, also called the spine, can be partially sharpened to create a short false edge at the end. The distal end of the sword is referred to as the point or tip. On some swords, especially long swords, there is often a non-sharpened area called the ricasso where the blade meets the crossguard. On a short sword, the ricasso allows the user to curl a finger over a quillion, allowing for better point control. Long swords, on the other hand, have an extended ricasso that can be used as an extension of the hilt to get more leverage.

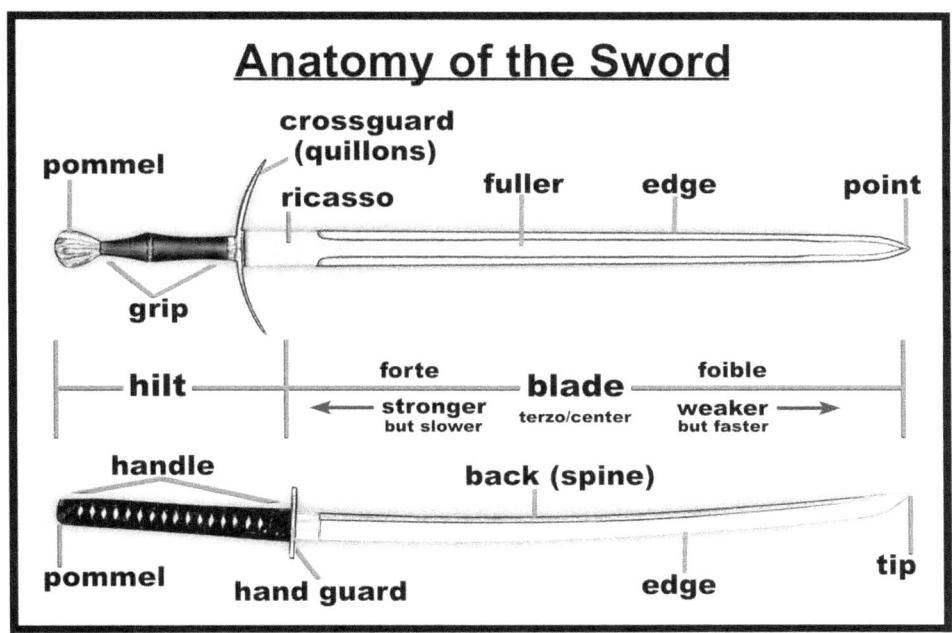

The arming sword pictured on top is an example of a double-edged blade with a cross guard. The bottom sword, a katana, is an example of a single edged, curved blade with a smaller, disc-shaped hand guard.

While some traditional sword systems go into excessive detail, dividing the blade into as many as twelve distinct sections, at first it is sufficient to know that a sword blade is stronger closer to the hilt and weaker toward the tip (stronger and weaker in terms of the blade's ability to resist pressure). The blade can therefore be divided into two parts, the strong "forte" and the weaker "foible."

Some blades have grooves or a depression running along the length of the blade. It is a common myth that these grooves or depressions are "blood grooves" intended to prevent suction from holding your blade in an opponent's body after stabbing. In fact, these grooves or depressions are called fullers, and their purpose is to lighten the sword, while the remaining flanges running along either side keep the blade from bending, similar to the way an I-beam girder functions.

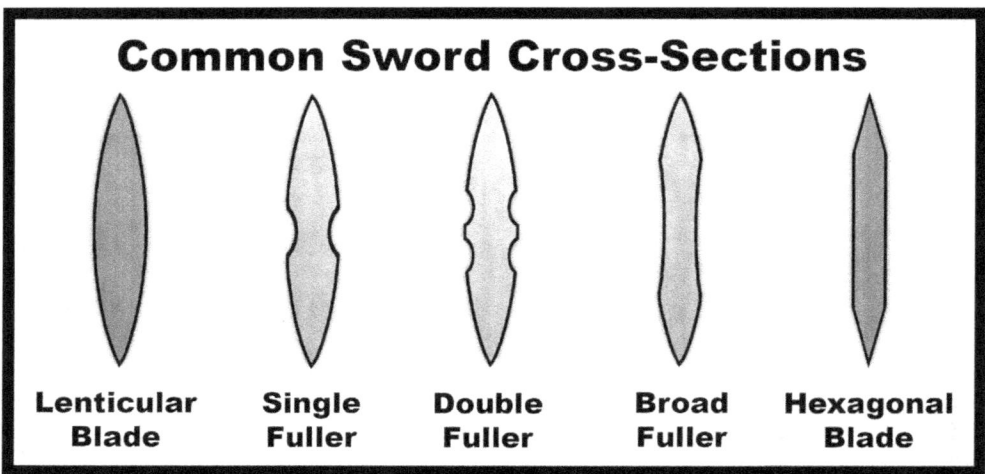

Examples of common sword blade cross-sections. Note that the center three have fullers.

Sword Classification

Sword sizes and shapes have varied widely throughout time and across distance, so much so that scholars have created elaborate classification systems based on ethnography and physical characteristics to keep track of them all. Some sword aficionados live to study swords down to their smallest details. These learned experts will argue, and perhaps rightly so, that a specific sword's particular characteristics classify it as a *this*-sword or a *that*-sword. While there is a place for these kinds of discussions, generally, they fall outside of the scope of this book. It is enough to know that every sword has its own unique set of strengths that can be exploited and weaknesses that need to be mitigated. Victory, therefore, depends as much, or perhaps even more so, upon the skill levels of the individual fighters as the particulars of the weapons they wield.

For me, it is more rewarding to *fight* with swords than to *talk* about swords. That said, while it is, of course, quite feasible to win a sword fight without any knowledge of the history or evolution of the weapon you are using, you will find it useful to have a working knowledge of the different types of swords and the terminology used to describe them. Keep in mind that this is a general overview to be taken as a guideline only; there are always exceptions and standouts.

Two Main Types of Swords

While oversimplified, the most practical classification for our purpose here is by their hilt type and usage. Swords basically fall into one of two categories: short swords and long swords. The terms short and long are used to describe the hilts of the swords, not their blade lengths. The term short sword describes a sword with a small handle, or hilt, only large enough for a single hand, marking it as clearly intended to be wielded as such. Short swords are also called side swords since they can be worn hanging from a belt at your side. Long swords are usually heavier and therefore equipped with longer hilts to accommodate two hands. Ironically, some short swords, such as the rapier, have blade lengths rivaling those of a long sword; however, they are much lighter and still intended to be wielded in one hand.

The Bastard Sword

Hand-and-a-half swords, also called bastard swords, fall somewhere in between short swords and long swords because they could be used effectively in one hand or two. (The moniker originated because the bastard sword was a sword without a family; one not easily classified as either a single-handed short sword or a two-handed long sword.) Of course, much depends upon the size and strength of the person wielding the weapon. One man's bastard sword may be another man's long sword, since a larger or stronger fighter may be able to swing a heavy sword very effectively with only one hand while a smaller or weaker fighter may require two hands to manipulate the same weapon effectively. In addition to many European long swords, the Japanese katana is usually regarded as a bastard sword.

Small Blades

Even though their short length restricts their usage to close-range combat, small blades are essentially diminutive swords, and there is as much variety in them as there is in swords. However, most of these short weapons can be classified as either knives or daggers. Knives have single-edged blades, and their primary purpose tends to be utilitarian as opposed to daggers, which are double edged and designed for combat. Knives and daggers are commonly used as secondary weapons when paired with a sword.

Great Swords

The distinction between long swords and great swords is not always clear. Like the bastard sword, the final decision about whether a sword is a long sword or a great sword ultimately depends upon the size and strength of the wielder. Long swords and great swords both require the use of two hands to be wielded effectively, yet the two are different. Long swords are light and nimble enough to stop and change direction mid-swing, allowing for feints and complex engagements, whereas great swords cross the line between sword and polearm, making them more akin to a staff or spear. Therefore, great swords are typically swung in large, flowing strikes that conserve momentum so that the weight and inertia of the sword become a benefit, not a detriment. Examples include the English great sword, Italian spadone, Spanish montante, German zweihänder, Chinese zhanmadao, and Japanese ōdachi.

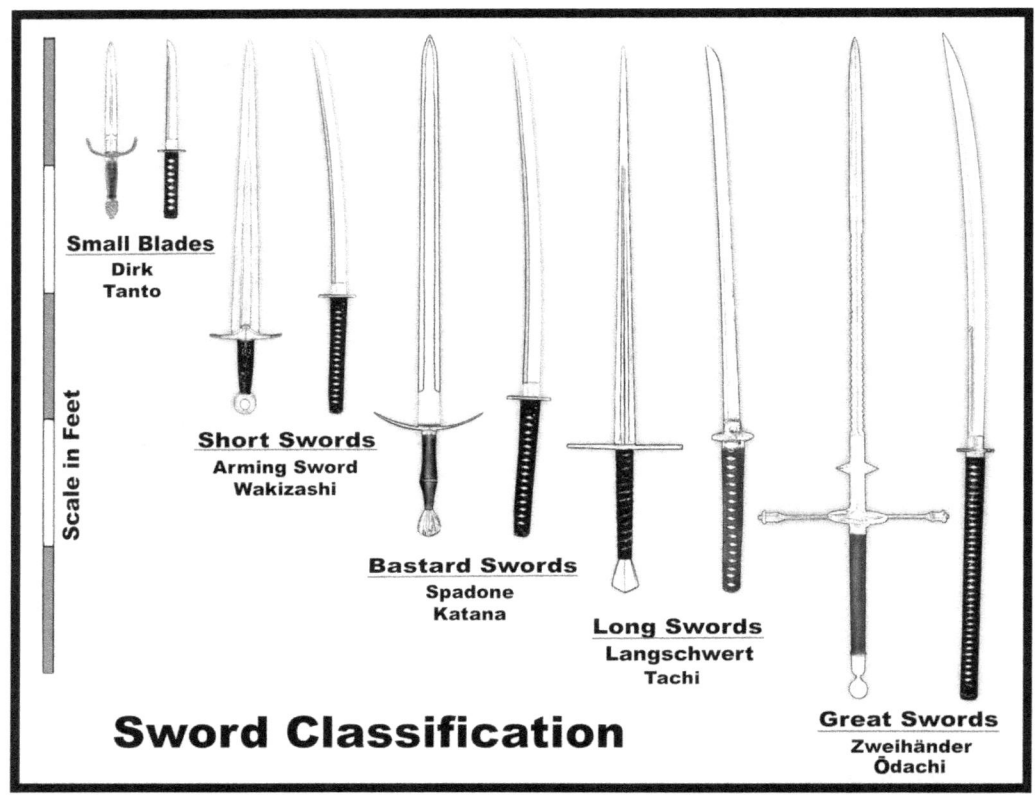

Sword Classification

Which Is Better: A Short Sword or a Long Sword?

The question of optimal sword length is actually a debate over trade-offs. On the one hand there is speed and control, while on the other, power and distance. Naturally, there are always exceptions. The general rule is that, in the hands of equally skilled combatants and on open ground, the weapon with the greater range should win. Using that logic, it can be said that short sword beats dagger, long sword defeats short sword, great sword overcomes long sword, spear trumps great sword, and bow defeats spear.

Short swords have greater accessibility in unexpected situations. Because short swords can be carried more places and more easily than a long sword, short swords were often considered civilian weapons. Not only are short swords easier to carry, but the shorter the blade, the faster it can be pulled from its sheath. When caught by surprise, this factor could be the difference between life and death. It is why the Samurai practice Iaido, an art entirely dedicated to quickly drawing the sword and responding to sudden attacks. Since long swords were too large to carry around conveniently and more difficult to draw and deploy, they were employed mainly as heavy battlefield weapons.

In close quarters, such as indoors, a short sword is generally easier to wield and is thus more desirable to use. The long sword's larger movements will be restricted in confined spaces, reducing its effectiveness. Short swords are good in one-on-one combat; however, on open ground or when fighting in a mass melee, longer blades have the clear advantage of range and power. When it comes to power, having two hands on the hilt greatly increases the amount of leverage that can be generated with the sword. The longer and heavier the blade, however, the more effort it takes to start and stop, which makes heavier swords slower and less wieldy in comparison to short swords that, because they weigh less, can attack, feint, and change direction more quickly and effectively. It should be noted, though, that "effective" power has a lot to do with proper edge alignment, a skill that can take time to master. For a newer student, it's a lot easier to keep a single-handed sword's edge aligned, which helps them transfer more power to the target with less effort.

Today, firearms have replaced swords for self-defense and as weapons of war. However, the comparison between short swords and long swords and their modern counterparts shows that they fill very similar niches. Handguns, like short swords, are light, small, and designed to be easily carried, making them suitable for everyday self-defense. Long swords and long-barreled guns, such as rifles and shotguns, on the other hand, are heavier, less portable, and generally require both hands to handle effectively. Though short swords and handguns can both be lethal and effective for self-defense, long swords and long-barreled guns are capable of delivering a greater amount of kinetic energy into their targets, which results in increased stopping power. On the other hand, handguns excel in situations where portability, maneuverability, and quick access are essential. This feature is why short swords and handguns have been and are the weapons most commonly used for self-defense, law enforcement, and as backup weapons. On the other hand, long swords and long-barreled guns have been and are the heavier-duty weapons employed in military operations. It is important to note, though, when paired with a shield, the short sword was very much a battlefield weapon.

So, what is more important to surviving a sword fight: speed or power, maneuverability or distance? Or is it best to try and balance all elements? In reality, there are no right or wrong answers; the best sword for the situation is determined by the totality of the circumstances and one's personal preference.

Longer Is *Not* Always Better!

When I was training at Live Steel Fight Academy in the early 2000s, our instructor, Dave Dickey, came up with the brilliant idea to have random mixed weapons matches. He had two cloth bags, one filled with the names of the fighters, the other filled with the names of different weapons. It went like this: each fight consisted of three rounds. Two names were chosen from the fighter bag, then each of those fighters drew from the weapon bag. Whatever weapon they picked would be the weapon they fought with in the first round. In the second round, the combatants switched weapons with each other and fought again. In the third round, each fighter got to choose, without knowing their opponent's choice, which weapon they wanted to use in the third and final round.

When my name was picked, I reached into the weapons bag and drew out a small wooden disk about the size of a silver dollar. I read the word written on it aloud for all to hear, "Spear!" My opponent then reached into the bag. He looked at his token and mumbled dejectedly, "Dagger." A collective sound of pity arose from other fighters, like you might hear when you see someone take a particularly nasty shot. Everyone was thinking about the general rule which is, as we mentioned, short sword beats dagger, long sword beats short sword, and spear beats long sword. Applying this logic, my opponent's puny dagger did not stand a chance against my six-foot spear. We put on our helmets and gloves, armed ourselves, and squared off. I figured this was going to be like shooting fish in a barrel.

At that time, Live Steel Fight Academy met at a karate studio in a room perhaps twenty feet on each side, complete with mirrors and heavy bags. It was plenty of space for most sword matches, but it didn't leave much room to maneuver with a long spear. Still, I scored the first few points with ease. However, as I did, my fight brother was quietly and simultaneously collecting and processing new data. Soon, he was passing the tip of my spear *before* I could stop him. In the confined space, I was unable to maintain an effective range, and, once inside it, he was able to grab my spear with his free hand, effectively immobilizing it, while he slashed and stabbed me mercilessly with his dagger. Our fight had started out quite well; however, in the end, I lost the first round.

I couldn't wait for the second round so that I could get my revenge! Since my opponent had just shown me how to cross the gap effectively without getting stabbed, I was able to use his own tricks against him. While it is never easy getting safely past the tip of an opponent's spear, the room was just confining enough that I pulled it off more often than not and won the second round.

Then came round three. We started back-to-back in the middle of the floor, while our seconds each stood before us holding a dagger and spear. At Dave's command, I reached for my choice of weapon and spun around to face my opponent. Everyone laughed, including us, when we all realized that we had both chosen the daggers. Neither of us wanted to go another round wielding a cumbersome long spear in such close quarters.

The moral of the story is that there is no "best" weapon. Whereas the spear would normally decimate a dagger-wielding foe on open ground, it was not so when fighting indoors. The same applies to a long sword. In cramped fighting conditions, a short sword would be more desirable since it is shorter, more maneuverable, and thereby more effective in close quarter's combat.

Which Is Better: A Straight Sword or a Curved Sword?

Each style of sword comes with its own unique set of advantages and disadvantages. Both straight and curved swords are capable of slicing off the limbs or head of an opponent with a single swing. In general, it can be said that straight blades evolved to be used in conjunction with a shield against armored opponents. Curved swords, on the other hand, tend to be more effective against unarmored opponents. For this reason, curved blades were more common in Asia and the Middle East where it was often too hot to wear heavy armor. They later gained popularity in Europe as armor became less common due to the advent of firearms.

As we just mentioned, when comparing short swords versus long swords, in a self-defense situation, you need to be able to access your weapon quickly, which means having to free your sword from its scabbard as fast as possible. Given two swords with the same blade length, one straight and one curved, the curved sword can be drawn more quickly since it moves with the natural arcing motion of your arms. Therefore, the curved sword can be brought into play faster, effectively attacking while being drawn. The straight sword, on the other hand, requires your arm to make a far less natural linear motion to pull it from its scabbard, and then, once free, the blade needs to be reoriented before attacking.

Straight swords tend to be better for thrusting since the handle is in a direct line with the tip. Curved swords, however, allow you to thrust from a greater variety of angles, allowing you to stab around an opponent's weapon or shield. The more dramatic the curvature of the blade, the more difficult it is to thrust with accuracy. Curved swords can also be used to land cuts that could not be scored with a straight edged blade, such as utilizing a false edge to attack behind the opponent's neck or leg or curving around their guard. When it comes to swinging, having a backward curvature on a blade preserves the sword's length while shifting its center of mass slightly toward the hilt. This shift in the weight of the sword sacrifices some power, but results in increased speed and handling. The curve allows for more mass above the center of percussion, a sword's strongest striking point, and naturally draws more edge surface over the target. The result is a longer, deeper cut. This is one reason that curved swords, such as the calvary saber, are preferred weapons for use on horseback.

A straight blade impacts the target at a relatively perpendicular angle, which concentrates the power of the strike. This ability maximizes power. Think about chopping wood with an ax; all the energy goes into the wood and the ax stops. On the other hand, a curved blade intersects its target at a steeper angle, more closely following that of the cut, allowing the strike to draw through the target more easily than a straight blade. Think about how you would cut a steak; you draw the knife along the meat to slice it cleanly as opposed to hacking at it. Additionally, a curved sword slices better than a straight sword of equal weight and sharpness because both ends of the blade are curving away from the target, concentrating the power of the cut into a smaller section of the blade. This is why a serrated knife cuts better than a straight edge. Each serration helps concentrate its force. A straight blade, though it connects with more of its target, distributes the force along a greater surface area, lessening the effectiveness of the cut.

A) A curved blade makes impact with less surface area, concentrating the amount of pressure exerted while allowing the blade to continue moving and drawing through the target.

B) A straight blade impacts a broader surface area, dispersing the amount of pressure per square inch but releasing all of its energy directly into the target, bringing the blade to a stop.

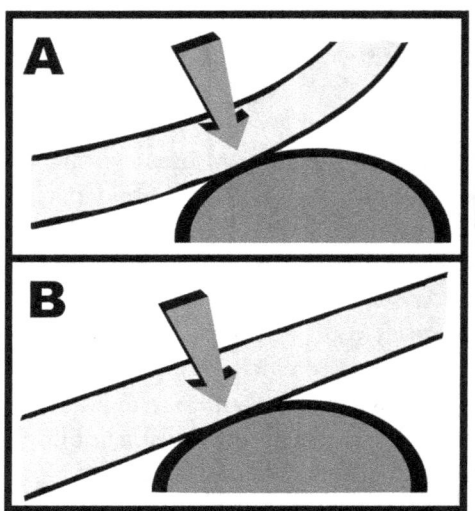

Common Sword Types

The following assemblage, while by no means an exhaustive list, provides a quick index of some of the major types of swords with which you will want to be familiar as a sword student.

One-Handed Swords/Short Swords (1–10)

1. **Roman Gladius**

    Overall length: 24–33 inches

    Historical period: c. 300 BC to AD 300

    The gladius is a short sword with a wide, double-edged blade used for slashing and stabbing. It was designed to be used in conjunction with a large rectangular, semi-cylindrical shield called a scutum.

2. **German Messer**

    Overall length: 30–40 inches

    Historical period: c. AD 1300 to AD 1500

    The messer, German for "knife," is essentially just that, a very long knife with a single sharp edge. Messers were commonly carried as sidearms in medieval Germany.

INTRODUCTION: SWORDS AND SWORDSMANSHIP 13

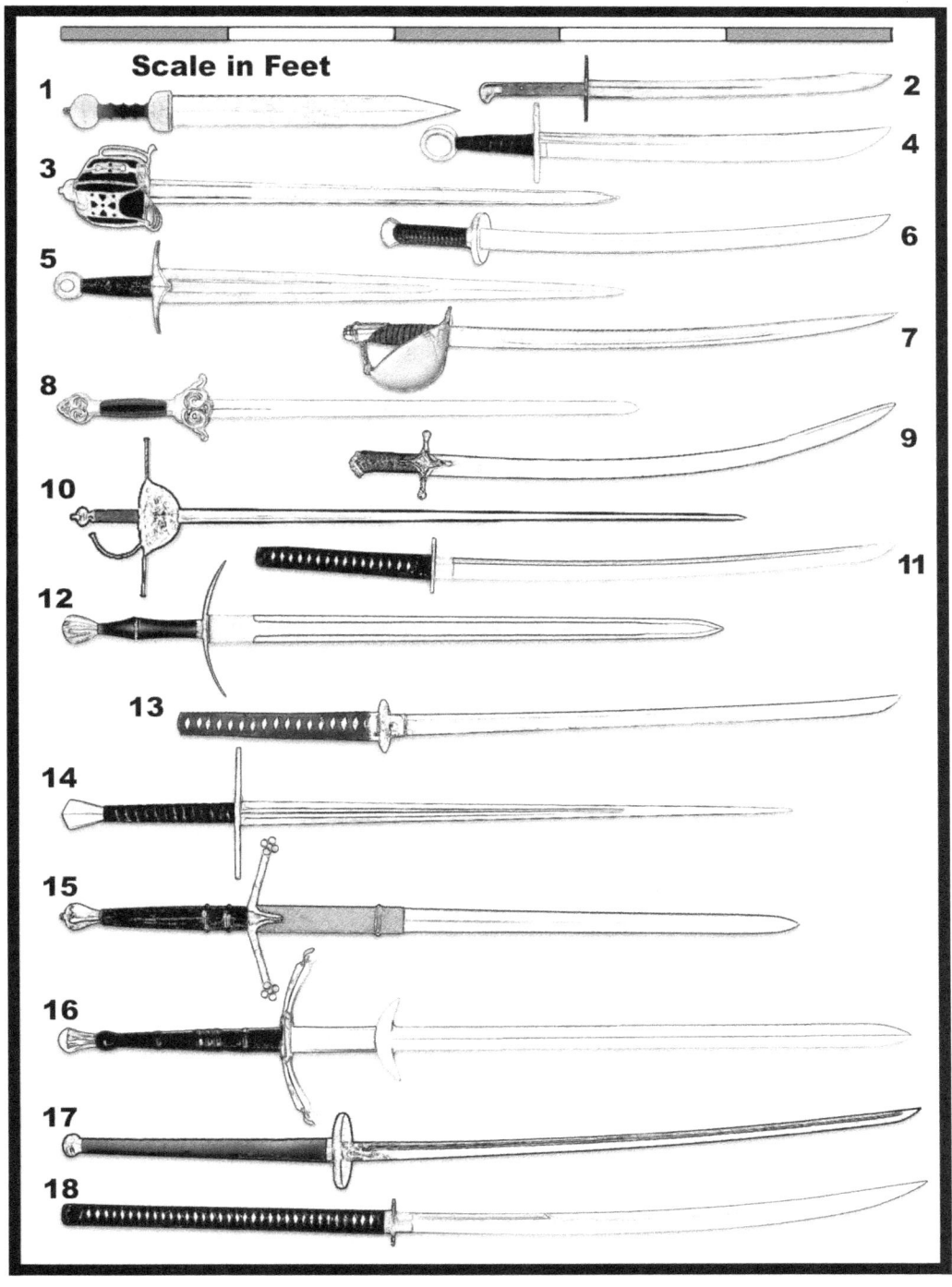

3. **Scottish Broadsword**

   Overall length: 28–32 inches

   Historical period: c. AD 1500 to AD 1800

   The broadsword has a wide, straight, double-edged blade. The handle is equipped with a basket hilt that provides almost full coverage for the hand, protecting it against cuts.

4. **French Falchion**

   Overall length: 30–40 inches

   Historical period: c. AD 1300 to AD 1600

   The falchion is a broad-bladed, slightly curved sword with a flare-clipped tip. The falchion was popular in England, France, and Italy during medieval times.

5. **Medieval Arming Sword**

   Overall length: 28–40 inches

   Historical period: AD 1000 to AD 1600

   The arming sword, often called a knightly sword, was a single-handed sword with a straight, double-edged blade; it was typically used in conjunction with a shield or buckler. It evolved over time from the earlier Viking age sword, specifically with the addition of a large cruciform crossguard. A medieval knight always wore his arming sword in public, even when not in full armor, as he would be considered "undressed" without it.

6. **Chinese Dao**

   Overall length: 33–44 inches

   Historical period: c. 1500 BC to AD 1900

   The dao is an Asian sword with a wide, single-edged blade. The dao was in use for over two thousand years, during which it took on many forms. Daos with wider blades are often referred to as Chinese broadswords while a dao with a straighter blade might be called a Chinese saber.

7. **English Backsword**

   Overall length: 36–40 inches

   Historical period: c. AD 1500 to AD 1900

   The backsword has a single-edged blade and is named for its flat spine. Since backswords were cheaper and easier to make than double-edged swords, the backsword became a common infantry and naval weapon. In sport, backsword is synonymous with single stick.

INTRODUCTION: SWORDS AND SWORDSMANSHIP

8. **Chinese Jian**

   Overall length: 28–36 inches

   Historical period: 700 BC to AD 1900

   The jian is a single-handed sword with a narrow, double-edged blade. Sometimes referred to as a Taiji sword, the jian has been used in China for over 2,500 years.

9. **Persian Scimitar**

   Overall length: 30–36 inches

   Historical period: AD 1500 to AD 1900

   The English word scimitar (derived from the Persian word shamshir, meaning sword) has come to be used to describe all manner of curved swords from the Middle East. The scimitar is usually used to slash and cut at unarmored opponents.

10. **Spanish Rapier**

    Overall length: 38–46 inches

    Historical period: AD 1500 to AD 1700

    Rapiers sport distinctive, elaborate hand guards. They were the principle sidearms worn by civilians living in Western Europe during the Renaissance. The rapier has a long, slender double-edged blade designed for cut-and-thrust fencing against unarmored opponents.

Hand-and-a-Half Swords/Bastard Swords (11–12)

11. **Japanese Katana**

    Overall length: 36–48 inches

    Historical period: AD 900 to AD 1900

    Made famous by the Samurai of feudal Japan, the katana has a curved, single-edged blade. Although it can be wielded with one hand, the katana has a long grip that can accommodate two, making it a true bastard sword.

12. **Fiore-Pattern Long Sword**

    Overall length: 36–48 inches

    Historical period: AD 1400 to AD 1600

    Named for Italian swordmaster Fiore dei Liberi, these long swords are light and short enough to be used effectively in one hand yet feature a hilt that can accommodate both hands comfortably. This type of sword was referred to as an epée bâtarde or "bastard sword."

Two-Handed Swords/Long Swords (13–15)

13. Japanese Tachi

Overall length: 48–60 inches

Historical period: AD 900 to AD 1600

A single-edged blade, the tachi is longer and straighter than a katana. A battlefield weapon, the tachi was not typically worn by the Samurai who used them. The tachi requires two hands to wield effectively, categorizing it as a long sword.

14. German Langschwert

Overall length: 48–60 inches

Historical period: c. AD 1100 to AD 1700

The quintessential Medieval long sword, the langschwert has a distinctive double-edged blade with a wide cruciform handguard. Too cumbersome for carrying every day and too expensive for most people to afford, long swords were weapons for tournaments, duels, and battlefields. Too heavy to be wielded in just one hand, the long handle provides for good leverage and quick handling with two.

15. Scottish Claymore

Overall length: 48–60 inches

Historical period: c. AD 1400 to AD 1700

This Scottish long sword featured a unique cross hilt with forward-sloping quillons topped by quatrefoils, ornamental designs of four lobes and symbols of good luck (like a four-leaf clover). The word claymore can be confusing as it is also used to describe later 18th century Scottish basket-hilted broadswords.

Great Swords (16–18)

16. German Zweihänder

Overall length: 60–80 inches

Historical period: c. AD 1500 to AD 1600

Great swords like the Zweihänder and Spanish Montante signal the ending of a long trend of increasingly larger and larger swords that started in the 14th century. The large size and weight of these swords gave them increased range and striking power, so much so that they were employed more like polearms than swords.

17. Chinese Zhanmadao

Overall length: 60–80 inches

Historical period: c. 200 BC to AD 1600

The zhanmadao, or "horse butchering saber," has a long, single edged blade, straight for most of its length, then curving in the last third. These swords were known for their ability to kill both a horse and its rider in a single swing.

18. **Japanese Ōdachi**

    Overall length: 60–80 inches

    Historical period: c. AD 1600 to AD 1900

    The ōdachi, or nodachi, is an anti-cavalry sword used mainly by infantryman to attack the legs of enemy horses while staying out of the reach of their riders. As with the European great sword and Chinese zhanmadao, ōdachi swordplay necessarily differs from that used when employing other, shorter Japanese swords.

Meet the Masters

Throughout history there have lived many famous swordsmen, warriors who achieved astounding feats of courage and skill. The best survived to become sword masters, knowledgeable instructors who earned their living teaching their sword fighting skills to others. Those with the means recorded their wisdom and experience in illustrated texts. Unfortunately, relatively few of these early fencing manuals have survived to the present day.

Students of the historical martial arts, such as HEMA (Historical European Martial Arts), use these documents as the primary source material for their practice. These manuals were written by people who survived actual life-or-death duels and battles using swords, experiences that no living man can claim. Their lives are interesting, and their perspectives are especially valuable because they are uniquely qualified to point out the idiosyncrasies unique to actual combat with sharp swords. Here is a brief overview of ten of history's most influential sword teachers.

Johannes Liechtenauer (1300–1389)

Liechtenauer was a German sword master who greatly influenced fencing. While he never recorded his teachings, after his death, his students formed The Society of Liechtenauer to preserve his lineage of swordsmanship. Members of this group, such as Sigmund Ringeck, later expounded upon Liechtenauer's theories to write some of the most significant fencing manuals of the 15th century.

Liechtenauer depicted sitting alone in his room playing with his swords, image from a fight book compiled by Peter von Danzig in 1452.

Fiore dei Liberi (1350–1410)

Fiore was an Italian weapons master. His book, the *Flower of Battle* (c. 1400), is one of the oldest manuals on fencing to survive to the present day. In it, Fiore covers dagger, sword, spear, axe, and armored combat.

Hans Talhoffer (1420–1490)

Talhoffer was a German sword master who wrote at least five manuals, among the most popular being *Fechtbuch*, or *Fight Book* (1440s), which expounds upon all sorts of weapons such as dagger, short sword, long sword, mace, spear, and poleaxe.

Achille Marozzo (1484–1553)

In 1536, Italian fencing master Achille Marozzo authored an extensively illustrated five-part treatise on swordsmanship titled *A New Work* (*Opera Nova*). In it, he addresses fencing with a wide variety of bladed weapons, from dagger to great sword.

Camillo Agrippa (1510s–1595)

Agrippa was a true Renaissance man. An Italian architect and engineer, he applied his knowledge of geometry and physics to swordsmanship. His manual, *Treatise on the Science of Arms, with a Philosophical Dialogue* (1553), changed the way people looked at sword fighting. Agrippa focused on the rapier, including rapier and dagger, double rapiers, and rapier and shield.

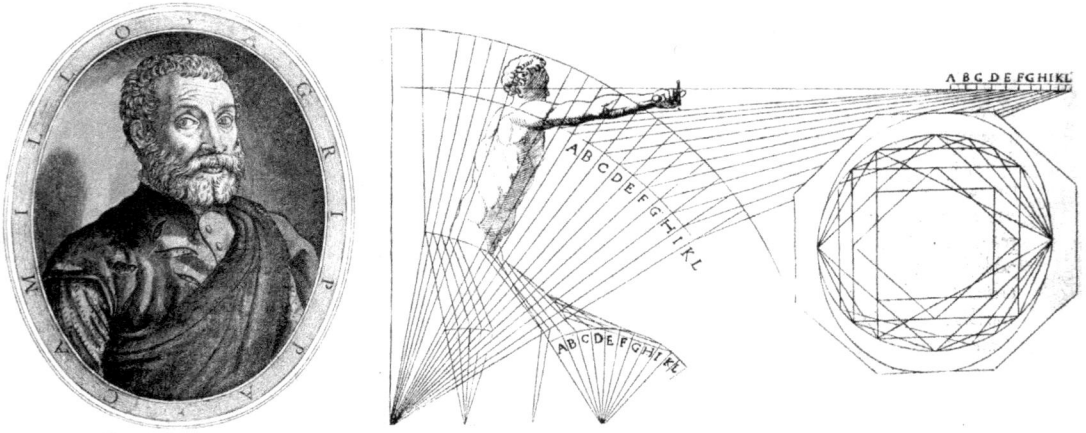

Camillo Agrippa in 1553 (left) and a page from his *Treatise on the Science of Arms* (right).

Joachim Meyer (1537–1571)

Joachim Meyer was a German sword master and the author of *A Thorough Description of the Free Knightly and Noble Art of Fencing, in All the Typical Guards, Adorned and Arranged with Many Beautiful and Useful Figures*. First published in 1570, this sophisticated treatise purported to teach the entire art of fencing.

Ridolfo Capo Ferro (late 1500s–early 1600s)

Capo Ferro was an Italian fencing master who wrote a treatise called the *Great Representation of the Art and Use of Fencing* (1610). In it, he covers single rapier, basic sword grappling, rapier with dagger, rapier paired with a cloak, and rapier use with a rotella (small round shield).

George Silver (late 1500s–early 1600s)

In 1599, English fencing master George Silver wrote a manual explaining why he believed that the short sword was superior to other weapons, especially the rapier. He titled it *Paradoxes of Defence, wherein is proved the true grounds of fight to be in the short ancient weapons, and the short sword hath the advantage of the long sword or long rapier, and the weakness and imperfection of the rapier fight displayed*.

Gérard Thibault (1574–1629)

In 1628, Dutch fencing master Gérard Thibault wrote *Académie de l'Espée* (*Academy of the Sword*), hailed as one of the most detailed and elaborate manuals ever written on fencing with the rapier. Thibault's style was considered unorthodox as it was based on high stances and small, economical motions.

A plate from Thibault's Academy of the Sword describing how to fight a left-handed swordsman.

Miyamoto Musashi (1584–1645)

Musashi was a Japanese swordsman and a master of dual wielding. In fact, he became renowned for his unique style of double swordsmanship. Over the course of his life, Musashi fought sixty-one duels, losing only one, and that to a man with a short staff. Just before he died, Musashi recorded his thoughts on swordsmanship, including strategies and tactics, in *The Book of Five Rings* (1645).

Miyamoto Musashi wielding two bokken. Woodblock print by Utagawa Kuniyoshi.

Donald McBane (1664–1732)

McBane is considered one of the most prolific duelists of all time. This Scottish sword master fought over one hundred duels over the course of his career. He recorded his accumulated fencing wisdom in *The Expert Sword-Man's Companion* (1728).

Alfred Hutton (1839–1910)

Alfred Hutton was a British fencer and army officer who authored many manuals, including *Swordsmanship* (1862), *The Swordsman* (1891), and *Sword Fighting and Sword Play* (1897). He was one of the first advocates of learning from the old masters and therefore could be considered the grandfather of Historical European Martial Arts (HEMA).

Inigo Montoya: You are using Bonetti's Defense against me, ah?

Man in Black: I thought it fitting considering the rocky terrain

Montoya: Naturally, you must suspect me to attack with Capo Ferro?

Man in Black: Naturally, but I find that Thibault cancels out Capo Ferro. Don't you?

Montoya: Unless the enemy has studied his Agrippa…which I have.

—*The Princess Bride*

Part 1: Short Sword

Part 1 of *The Art and Science of Sword Fighting* will help you develop the basic skills required to wield a one-handed sword effectively. It is divided into four parts. In Level 1, you will learn how to attack with the sword, how to stand, hold the sword, and move your feet as you cut and thrust. In Level 2, you will develop a strong defense by learning how to block and parry your opponent's weapon. In Level 3, you will learn the ins and outs of fencing using scientifically based techniques to vie for the center. Finally, in Level 4, you will round out your single-handed swordsmanship skills with some more advanced fencing concepts.

While it is natural for there to be some variation of technique between individuals, the basic skills of swordsmanship are universal. It is essential that beginners take the time to build a strong foundation through diligent and consistent practice. Moves must be repeated until they can be performed automatically, without conscious thought. While this may seem like a difficult and daunting task, I assure you that dedicated and focused practice is the only path to success.

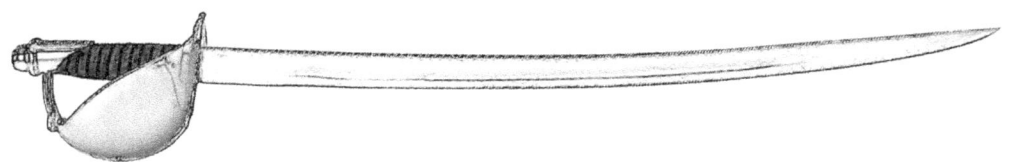

A properly balanced sword is the most versatile weapon for close quarters ever devised. Pistols and guns are all offense, no defense; close on him fast and a man with a gun can't shoot, he has to stop you before you reach him. Close on a man carrying a blade and you'll be spitted like a roast pigeon, unless you have a blade and can use it better than he can. A sword never jams, never has to be reloaded, is always ready. Its worst shortcoming is that it takes great skill and patient, loving practice to gain that skill; it can't be taught to raw recruits in weeks, nor even months.

—Robert Heinlein
Glory Road

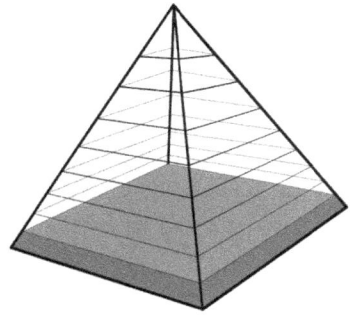

LEVEL 1:
Short Sword Offense

A Closer Look at Single-Handed Swords

We've already examined some of the advantages of a short sword over a long sword, namely accessibility and maneuverability. Short swords are generally more accessible than long swords as they are easier to carry and deploy quickly. They are also more maneuverable since they are small enough to be used effectively in close quarters as well as wieldy enough to feint, faking your opponent out by suddenly changing directions mid-stroke. The disadvantage of the short sword is usually its shorter range; however, remember that "short sword" refers to the length of the handle, not the blade, so there are some exceptions to this rule. The great equalizer when it comes to single-handed swords is that they can be used with a shield or second weapon, allowing you to check an opponent's longer weapon in order to close into striking range, but dual wielding is the topic for another book.

Training Equipment: The Sword

Before you can start training, you are going to need a sword. There is a plethora of swords available on the market and choosing the right one is not merely a matter of personal preference. It is important that you know how to choose a sword that fits your body size and feels good in your hand. It must also be of appropriate construction for the type of training you will be doing.

Materials

Do NOT buy a sharp sword! At least, not yet. A sharp sword can be as dangerous as a loaded gun and should never be used for any kind of partner work. Even at Live Steel Fight Academy, although we occasionally test cut with live blades, we NEVER fought with sharp steel. Buying a sharp sword would be like playing airsoft or paintball with real guns. Keep your sharp swords reserved for test cutting. In fact, you don't even need to buy a metal sword at all.

Since wooden swords are far cheaper and usually safer than their metal counterparts, every culture that has employed the sword has used wooden substitutes in training. In Japan, samurai practiced with the bokken, while in England soldiers trained with wooden swords called wasters. Wooden swords maintain the weight and heft of a real sword but are far less likely to inflict serious injury. They are also durable enough to withstand the wear and tear of hard training without needing to be replaced very often. They do have to be checked regularly, however, for cracks and splinters. Minor damage can usually be fixed with wood glue and sandpaper.

Swords made from polypropylene or other plastics, commonly referred to as "synthetics," are a modern-day contribution to sword training. Keep in mind, though, that you get what you pay for. Cheap swords are usually either too heavy and stiff or too light and flexible. Well-made synthetics, on the other hand, are designed to be as close to real swords in weight, balance, and size as possible so that they help develop proper form and technique in solo practice, partner drills, and sparring. The disadvantage of synthetics is that they do not simulate real blades when pressed together, an action referred to as a "bind." Sharp metal blades tend to catch, unlike synthetics that slip when pressed against each other, making it difficult to execute many techniques with realism. Like wooden swords, synthetics are generally less expensive than metal swords, as well as much safer to train and fight. Unlike wood, synthetic swords are extremely durable and do not crack or splinter. Since they can be used for a long time without needing to be replaced, they make a cost-effective investment. Overall, synthetic swords are a great option for regular training.

This is not to say that wooden or synthetic swords are not dangerous. While they are generally regarded as safer than their metal counterparts, wooden or synthetic swords can still hit hard enough to cause serious injury, especially if you are not wearing protective equipment suitable to the intensity of the activity. A waster or bokken, swung with intent and no control, can snap a femur. When thrusting, flexible plastic or modern spring steel swords are safer than a wooden sword because they are designed to bend.

Foam padded swords are good for light sparring with minimal protective gear. However, they generally lack the weight and heft of a real sword and therefore do not make very good trainers. Not only do they lack the feel of the genuine article, but most padded swords are not designed to hold up to intensive training against anything but another padded weapon. Their weaker, often hollow, plastic cores can't stand up to hard collisions against denser and heavier wooden or synthetic swords. The one advantage of foam swords is that they tend to stick together in the bind like sharp blades would, making them good for developing skills for that particular instance.

Training with blunt steel blades is very exciting and most closely replicates using a live blade. However, blunts are costly in comparison to wood and synthetic trainers. They also require more substantial protective gear to be used safely, especially in sparring. Nicks or bends in a blunt sword require maintenance and, even when fixed, can create weak spots where the blade may be subject to future breakage under stress.

Unsharpened training swords made of light, soft metals such as aluminum, are often intended for solo demonstration only and will not hold up under any sort of contact drill.

Likewise, "fantasy" swords, and other swords created for display purposes, lack the structural integrity required for safe training and likewise should not be used. And, let me say it one more time, just to be clear: DO NOT use a sharp sword, even for solo work. Sharp swords, sometimes referred to as "sharps," require the utmost attentiveness and should only be used for test cutting under very controlled conditions (see Appendix 3 at the end of this book).

A Precautionary Tale

In 1989, I was a twenty-year-old college student and a member of a fraternity at Gettysburg College. I was also the senior student of the karate club, and as such I was in charge of ordering supplies. One day, my big brother, Smitty, was in my room and started thumbing through the catalogue. His eyes lit up when he saw the swords. "Buy me a sword!" he said excitedly.

"No way," I responded, "you'll cut yourself, or worse, someone else."

But that wasn't the end of it. Over the next few days, Smitty kept bugging me about ordering a sword. "If you won't order it for me, I'll just call the number and buy it myself," he sulked.

Eventually, to avoid him being mad at me, and against my better judgement, I added a sword to the next order.

When the shipment finally arrived, Smitty rushed into my room. "Where is it?" he demanded.

I reluctantly handed him a long, slender cardboard box. "I'm still not sure I should be giving you this."

"Whatever, worry-wort," Smitty taunted as he unceremoniously tore open the box and removed the three-foot katana that lay within. Grasping the handle in one hand and the shiny black scabbard in the other, he drew the blade half way out of its sheath. "Wicked cool!" he uttered, turning the blade slightly and watching in awe as the light reflected off the oiled steel.

"Please be careful," I warned, "this isn't a toy."

"Yeah, yeah," he chided me, snapping the blade back into the scabbard, and added, "I'm not stupid, you know." He turned on his heel, shut the door behind him, and was gone.

It wasn't more than a few minutes later that my door burst open once again. This time it wasn't Smitty, it was his roommate. His eyes were huge, and he spoke way too fast. "Smitty just stabbed himself! We're taking him to the hospital!" he shouted, turned, and was gone, leaving me staring at an empty doorway.

As soon as I realized he wasn't kidding, I rushed out after Smitty's roommate, catching up with him as Smitty was being loaded into a car in front of the fraternity house. Smitty, though on his feet, was clamping a bunched-up t-shirt to his left thigh. Blood was leaking out from underneath, running down his thigh, and soaking his blue jeans red. I was in shock as I asked him, "What the heck happened?"

Smitty didn't answer. In fact, he wouldn't even look at me as he got into the car. His roommate was more than happy to fill me in. "Smitty gave us a little demonstration with his new sword," he explained excitedly, "but, when he went to put it away, he missed the sheathy-thingy completely and stabbed himself right in the leg!" He could barely contain his laughter.

Smitty shut the door and rolled down the window. He looked at me and finally spoke. "It went right in," he said, his voice filled with amazement, "like a hot knife through butter." Then he suddenly snapped back to his old self, "When I get back, I don't want to hear any 'I told you so's,' okay?!"

By the time Smitty returned from the hospital a few hours later, with seven stitches closing the wound in his thigh, I had secured the katana and placed it back in its box. As requested, we didn't talk about it. By dinner that evening, however, the entire fraternity had heard the story, and the brothers all had a good laugh at Smitty's expense. In the end, I gave Smitty back his money and kept the sword for myself, taking it home with me on the next break. A fraternity house was no place for a live blade!

Length

As previously discussed, short swords come in a great variety of shapes and sizes. The specific sword type does not matter as much as its capabilities. Long, thin blades make effective thrusting weapons while short, thick blades are more suited for cutting and chopping at close range. While there are advantages and disadvantages to all swords, the most versatile sword is a medium-sized, general-use sword that is good for both cutting and thrusting.

A typical single-handed sword has an overall length between thirty inches to thirty-six inches from tip to pommel. To properly measure a sword for you, stand normally with the sword in your dominant hand and let it hang loosely at your side. The tip should come close to the floor, but not touch the ground. This length is good for a beginner, as a longer sword may be more cumbersome to wield and a shorter sword may not have the required reach.

Once you have gained competence with the basic techniques using a medium-length sword, you can try fencing with a longer sword. The Italian fencing master Capo Ferro recommended a long rapier that, when the tip is resting on the floor, has quillons level with the user's navel, resulting in a sword with an overall length somewhere between thirty-nine inches and forty-five inches. He thought, and I quite agree, that this length provided the optimal balance of speed and reach, allowing the swordsman to cut and thrust from a safe distance. However, it takes time to develop the strength and coordination required to wield such a sword effectively. It is far easier to learn with a more manageable, medium-length sword. George Silver recommended a sword that was short enough that, if you were to grab your opponent with your off hand, you could still easily stab him with your sword.

Other than that, what appeals to you? Do you lean more toward Eastern swords or Western? Your sword can have a single or double edge. It can also be straight or curved. Keep in mind that, as I mentioned in regard to longer swords, those with a very dramatic curve have special characteristics that require a certain degree of experience to be used effectively, and, as such, should be avoided during the early stages of training.

After you have mastered the basics of sword fighting, you may choose to specialize in one type of sword or another. Always remember that the sword is just a tool, a means to an accomplish a goal. Therefore, the most effective sword is the one that is best suited to the situation. In the end, though, it can be said that victory is determined as much by the skills of the swordsmen as the types of swords they wield or armor they wear.

Balance

More important than the particular type of sword you choose is the sword's balance. The balance of a sword is an important aspect of its design because it affects the sword's handling and how it feels in your hand. An unbalanced sword, even a light one, is going to feel more awkward and move less efficiently than a well-balanced blade.

The exact location of the point of balance will vary from sword to sword depending on the design, dimensions, and materials used in its construction. To find a sword's point of balance, also known as its center of gravity, balance the sword horizontally on your finger. The farther forward this point is located on the blade, the more tip-heavy the sword, making it better suited for thrusting attacks. A sword that is tip-heavy may feel more agile and maneuverable but may also require additional effort to control when cutting. Conversely, a sword with a point of balance closer to the hilt is more blade-heavy and may feel more stable and controlled in cutting strikes, while perhaps also feeling slower and less maneuverable.

Different styles of swordsmanship have differing preferences for sword balance based on what works best with the majority of techniques taught in their specialized curriculum. Ultimately, the best point of balance is the one that feels most comfortable and effective for you, the individual wielder.

A common guideline is that the point of balance should be located about one-third of the way from the crossguard toward the tip of the blade. Having the point of balance in this location allows for an equal amount of maneuverability and control. The sword will feel light in your hand, making it easier to change direction quickly or to recover from a missed attack. At the same time, it will still have enough weight in the blade to deliver powerful cuts and thrusts.

Your Upper Body

Swordsmanship begins with awareness and body control, specifically in regard to proper alignment and structure. Your whole body will have to work in concert. Since there is a lot to examine, we can divide up the material into what your upper body and lower body should look like and do. Let's start with your upper body. How should you hold your sword? And, what should you do with your free hand?

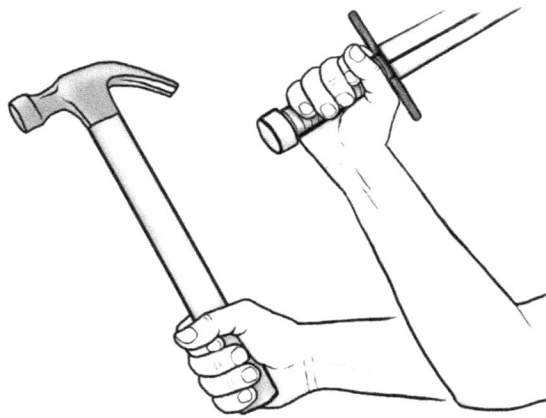

Holding the Sword

The natural way to hold a sword is in a firm *hammer grip*. In the hammer grip, all four of your fingers wrap fully around the handle, and your thumb is locked over the top of your fingers, making a fist around the handle for a secure grip. The fulcrum is the webbing between the thumb and forefinger at the top of the hand. Most of the time, the sword is held in a relaxed grip, but not so loosely that it can be knocked out of your hand.

If you loosen your grip slightly, you are in a *handshake grip*, where your fingers hold the handle loosely in an extended position. This grip adds range to your strike but lowers the control of your sword slightly in comparison to the hammer grip because it places the fulcrum lower down on the hilt, at the pinky finger side of your hand, and farther from the sword's point of balance. For maximum range, straighten your wrist into a full *extended grip*.

While your reach is longer, your wrist structure is weaker than in the hammer grip, meaning that you generally can't hit as hard.

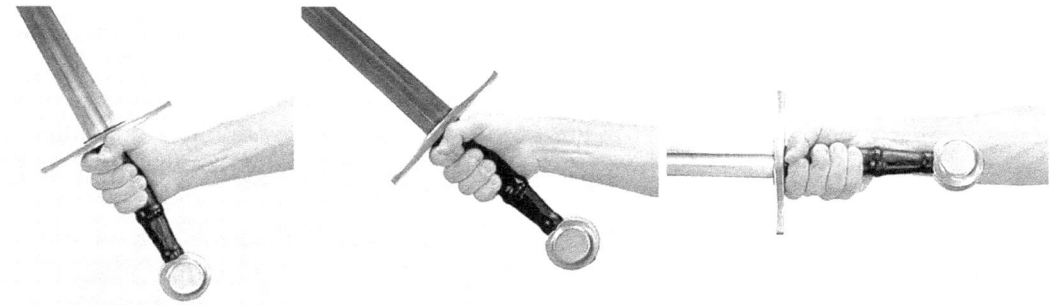

Hammer grip (left), handshake grip (center), full extended grip (right).

There are other variations on these basic grips that can increase the power, control, and range of your sword. However, be aware that there are some downsides to these variations. In the *thumb on grip* variation, your thumb is placed along the top of the grip adding power to your strike, but moving your thumb this way not only sacrifices sideways stability, it exposes you to the dangers of an insecure grip. In the *thumb on blade* variation, your thumb is placed over the crossguard and pressed against the side of the blade for greater stability. For increased control of your weapon, you can snake your index *finger over* the crossguard. With both these variations, however, you expose your fingers to getting cut if your sword is not equipped with protective finger rings. For swords with protective rings, though, the finger over is usually the default grip. It gives you better tip control and mechanical stability, especially when thrusting with your sword.

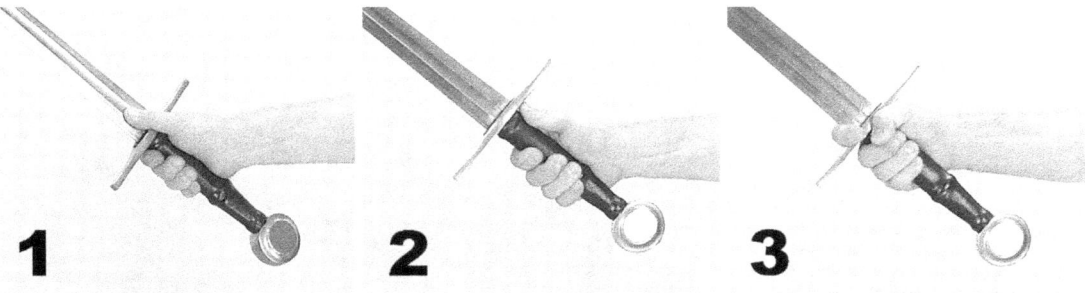

Grip variations: Thumb up on blade (1), thumb on grip (2), and finger over (3).

It is important to flow between grips in a fight as needed, so you need to train to be able to switch between grips effortlessly. For example, you might use a hammer grip to block an opponent's attack, then shift into a handshake grip as you riposte (counterattack), only to momentarily shift into a thumbs-up grip for a particularly powerful attack, before shifting back to the hammer grip for another block. Maintain a relaxed grip when you are not immediately engaging the opponent or his sword. At the exact instant you strike or block, you must tighten your hand, flexing at the moment of impact to provide the proper alignment, structure, and force necessary to transfer the energy from your body into the sword and vise-versa.

An important aspect common to all of these grips, whether standard or variations, is a strong, straight wrist. Hyperextending your wrist backward or forward into what is called a "broken wrist" position results in poor alignment and structure, and hence, weak cuts and thrusts.

Your Free Hand

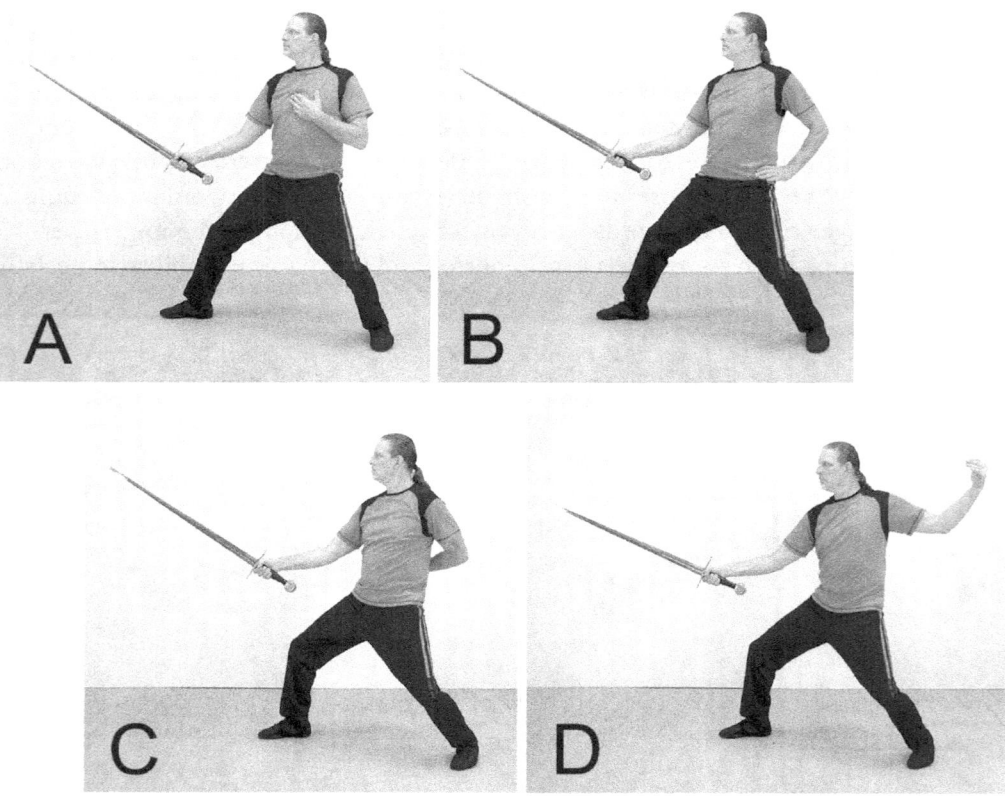

There are a wide variety of positions for your free hand. Each position depends on your personal preference and the weapons involved. Your free hand is usually held in front of your body, putting you in a good position to quickly grab and grapple (picture A). This placement of your hand can prove crucial in a fight, as George Silver noted: "All other things being equal, the superior grappler is going to win." You can do little about a cut with your free hand held in front of you other than provide an additional layer of protection over your torso, akin to "sacrificing a wing," but it is possible to parry or sweep away thrusts that manage to get past your sword when you hold it in front. Placing your free hand here also allows you to block objects thrown at your face.

When use of your free hand is prohibited, such as in sport fencing, it is usually placed on the back hip (B) or held behind the back (C) to keep it out of range of the opponent's sword. Holding your free hand extended behind you (as commonly seen in Olympic-style fencing) can provide a counterbalance to your sword arm (D). This redistribution of your body weight can help you quickly withdraw your front foot after a deep lunge.

In the end, the proper position for your free hand, like many other aspects of wielding a sword, is a matter of personal preference, the skill level of the user, the weapons involved, and situation.

Your Eyes

Your eyes provide you with crucial information, so it is important that you know where *and* where not to look. The hand is quicker than the eye, so don't attempt to follow your opponent's sword with your eyes; it moves too fast. Avoid staring into your opponent's eyes as well, since you make yourself vulnerable to manipulation and being misled by your opponent. Instead, keep your gaze general, centered around your opponent's throat, specifically where his neck meets his body. Looking actively here allows you to see subtle body movements that telegraph an attack. Keep alert for any shoulder motion that might indicate he is cocking back an arm to strike you.

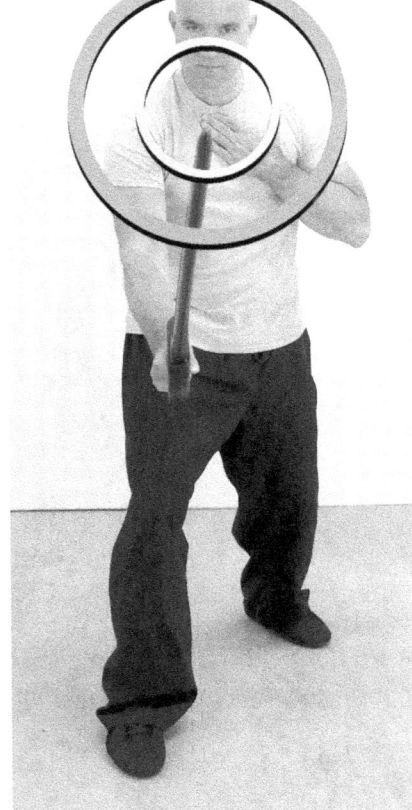

Keep your gaze general and centered on your opponent's throat. This will allow you to see subtle body movements that telegraph when he is about to attack.

Guards

En garde, French for "on guard," is the term commonly heard in fencing that commands the combatants to prepare to fight. Showing you are prepared usually entails raising your sword and assuming a defensive posture, also called a guard. Defensively, guards offer you protection; offensively, they serve as the initial launch positions for your attacks. True guards are positions where your sword is held in front of you where it can be used to keep the opponent at bay. Loaded guards, on the other hand, keep your sword retracted, cocked, and ready to strike. Loaded guards offer less in the way of defense but compensate with their offensive cutting potential. Trick guards, which will be presented in Level 4, are bait positions that deliberately leave you seemingly vulnerable as a means of inviting an opponent's attack.

True Guards

There are only two true guards used in single-handed sword fighting: middle and hanging. The middle guard is the posture that usually comes to mind when you hear "En garde!" In this position, your sword is held at waist level with your thumb rotated up and your blade pointing toward the opponent's face. This guard offers a good balance of both defensive and offensive qualities. Defensively, the middle guard offers good body protection. To block most strikes, you need only move your hands a few inches. Offensively, your sword is chambered for the most economical of strikes, the straight thrust.

A right middle guard.

The hanging guard is so named because the tip of your sword hangs down, as though being worn in a belt. In the hanging guard, the hilt of your sword is held high with the blade extending diagonally downward in front of your body and the point aimed at your opponent. The hanging guard is a combination of a true guard and a loaded guard because, while the tip is still pointed at the opponent allowing you to "hide" behind your sword, by lifting the hilt of your sword you expose your body. The trade-off is, offensively, you are already chambered for a quick, powerful downward attack.

A right hanging guard.

Loaded Guards

A loaded guard is a ready position that aligns your body and sword to deliver your strike with the most effective mechanics possible. Initiating your strike from a position conducive to the angle in which you intend to cut allows you to maximize the amount of mass and momentum you put into the strike. Ready positions, or loaded guards, are not considered true guards because the sword is held to the side of your body with the tip facing somewhere other than the opponent. Loaded guards also sacrifice much of your defensive capability in favor of a strong offense.

Not only do your cuts originate from a ready position, they should finish in a ready position as well. By finishing each strike in a ready position, you are immediately prepared to strike again, maximizing the speed and efficiency at which you can deliver consecutive strikes. In this way, ready positions facilitate smooth transitions between your strikes.

When you hold the sword in your right hand, with the blade on the right side of your body, you are in an open ready position. When you hold the sword in your right hand with the blade on the left side of your body, you are in a closed ready position. The closed and open positions can each be further subdivided into high, middle, and low guards depending on the level of your sword.

In a high guard, you hold the sword with the tip pointing upward. This guard loads your sword for a strong downward cut. You can assume a high guard holding the sword directly over your head (1), outside, on your right (2a), or inside, on your left (2b).

Likewise, a middle-level loaded position can be chambered to the outside (3a), or to the inside, with your sword arm crossing your centerline (3b).

A low loaded position is one in which the tip of your sword is lower than the hilt. Your sword can be held to either the open right side of your body (4a) or to the inside (4b). A low loaded position prepares you for strong upward diagonal cuts.

Although there is a most efficient cut that can be delivered from each position, it should be noted that ready positions do not limit the choice of strikes that you can deliver. Theoretically, you should be able to deliver every attack from every guard. While unexpected, other cuts will follow a longer line of attack to the target.

The Best Guard

Ultimately, the best guard for you will depend on the situation, which brings to mind another important distinction between true and loaded guards. It boils down to a compromise between range and protecting your weapon hand. In a true guard, your weapon is held close to the opponent, but so is your hand. Swords with an enclosed hilt allow you to hold your sword well forward of yourself without unduly endangering your weapon hand. Conversely, if you are wielding a sword with little or no built-in hand protection, it is probably best to choose to utilize a loaded guard, such as an outside guard, that keeps your hand safely withdrawn.

The Importance of Flow

Guarding and ready positions are sometimes interpreted as static ready positions. In actuality, sword fighting is a dynamic activity; you should always be in motion. Your guard should never be static, and instead should always be moving, smoothly and flowingly. Constant motion makes you less predictable and keeps your opponent mentally occupied trying to guess your next move. This unpredictability is why it is important to practice and become proficient with the different guarding positions; you need to be able to switch between them quickly and effectively when fighting. If you remain stationary for more than a few seconds, your opponent will have time to analyze your weak points and mount an effective offense putting you on the receiving end of the attack, making you respond to the opponent instead of what you want to be doing, namely dictating and controlling the action.

By no means do you always have to go on the attack, but you should flow smoothly between the guard positions every few seconds. Such flow will keep your opponent guessing, as he will need time to observe your change in position, mentally reorient himself to your new position, decide on a new course of action, and then act. *Observe, Orient, Decide, and Act*: these are the steps that anyone must go through each time they make a move. This concept, known as the "OODA Loop," was popularized by military strategist USAF Colonel John Boyd. While it may only take your opponent a second to go through this process, this gap should provide you with sufficient opportunity to retain the initiative in such a way that you are the one "leading the dance" and your opponent is the one who is consistently trying to respond.

It is best not to flow randomly from one position to another. Consider strategy and tactics. Defensively, you might want to keep your sword perpendicular to your opponent's weapon to make it harder for him to strike you. If your opponent's sword goes high or low, stay with him. Offensively, since it is easier to detect motion from stillness than it is to detect motion from motion, a flowing, ever-changing guard is a deceptive way to hide your strikes from your opponent until it is too late for him to block or evade them.

Your Lower Body

While your upper body appears to be doing most of the work in sword fighting, the truth is that your locomotor system, also known as the musculoskeletal system, is just as crucial to your success. Your weapons platform needs to be mobile in order to be effective. Let's take a look at ways you can stand and move to maximize your effectiveness with the sword.

Stances

Stances promote proper alignment and structure of the body. Keeping your body weight balanced over a stable base allows you to fight more effectively with your whole body. There are five basic stances that you will commonly employ: the neutral or ready stance, forward stance, lunge stance, back stance, and cat stance. As with your guard, stances should never be static but flowing in response to your opponent and the everchanging situation of fighting.

In order to move and strike powerfully, your upper and lower body must move in concert. Since your spine acts as the center axis for your body, strive to keep it straight but relaxed. Moving this way is the most economical way to move because there is a minimum amount of rebalancing to be done before you can effectively strike again.

Neutral Stance

The neutral stance is a semi-crouched position that prepares you for fighting. Also called the ready stance, it is a good position because your weight is centered, which allows for quick movement in any direction. Stand with your feet about shoulder width apart and one foot ahead of the other the same distance as well with your weight distributed evenly between both feet. Crouch slightly by bending your knees and hollowing out your body. Stay light on the balls of your feet, which loads both legs for quick, springy stepping.

A right neutral stance with middle guard.

Forward Stance and Lunge

The forward stance and lunge are used to maximize your reach when attacking. To assume a forward stance, start from a ready stance and slide your front foot forward until your stance is about twice your shoulder width, from front to back, with most of your weight on your front foot. In the final position, your back leg is straight, while your front knee is bent.

A long forward stance is called a lunge. Although your weight is loaded on the balls of your feet, keep your feet flat on the floor and do not let your lead knee extend past the toes of your front foot. Keep your toes and knees pointing the same way, so as not to put lateral stress on your knee. Take care not to overextend yourself or you will not be as stable or mobile.

A right forward stance (left) and right lunge (right).

Immediately after a lunge, you'll need to recover quickly to a more mobile, less exposed stance. You can recover forward or retreat back to a guarded position. To retreat, push off the ball of your front foot as you strongly contract your adductors (inner thigh muscles) to pull your feet back together quickly. To advance, bring your back foot to your front, either stopping in a guarded position or performing a half step into a second lunge (explained in the next section on footwork).

Be careful not to over-lunge, as this can leave you in an exposed position. Note how the lead knee is extended past the ankle. This will make it difficult to recover quickly.

Back Stance and Cat Stance

The back stance and cat stance are used to move your body quickly back and out of the range of an opponent's strike. To assume a back stance, shift your weight to your back leg. Always keep both knees flexed, with their energy spiraling outwards, and stay low in your back stance, coiled like a snake ready to strike.

When you pull your lead foot back farther into a very short back stance, it is called a cat stance. With only about 10 percent of your body weight on the front foot, the cat stance lacks the stability of the longer stances, but your legs are spring-loaded for quick movement in any direction. Since the cat stance does not provide a strong, stable base, it is not used at close range where your opponent can grapple and knock you over.

Use the cat and back stances to hover just outside of your opponent's effective striking range until you see an opportunity to spring forward and attack.

Back stance (left), and cat stance (right).

Footwork

Good footwork increases the effectiveness of your offense and defense. It is essential to hitting your opponent without getting hit yourself, which is really the whole point of sword fighting.

Offensively, footwork allows you to close distance on your opponent quickly without alerting your opponent. Defensively, your footwork should be reactive to the opponent. For example, when your opponent moves toward you, you can move backward the same amount to maintain the same safe distance between you and your opponent. More sophisticated footwork allows you to not only avoid your opponent's effective striking zone but also deliver your own attacks upon his undefended flank.

As with stances, the general rule on footwork is to keep your body weight balanced over a stable but fluidly mobile base. This begins with a straight spine. A straight spine with stacked vertebrae requires minimal energy to maintain because it divides your body weight evenly and distributes it between your feet. This allows you to pivot your body quickly from side to side without having to rebalance yourself. A straight spine is also needed in order to make quick movements in any direction. If you tilt your spine, you not only unbalance yourself in the direction of the lean, but you also make it harder to move in the opposite direction.

By keeping "on your toes," you stay spring-loaded for quick movements and powerful striking. This position does not mean your heels do not touch the ground, but the majority of your weight stays on the metatarsals, commonly referred to as the balls of your feet.

Smooth footwork is the result of not only pushing off with the ball of your supporting foot, but also landing on the ball of the receiving foot. Heel stepping is slower because your heel lacks the musculature required to strike properly or even move again until the ball of your foot comes in contact with the ground. By landing directly on the ball of the foot, you are simultaneously loaded to move and grounded to pivot and strike.

Take care not to make telegraphing movements that reveal your intentions before you step. Your natural inclination might be to shift your weight slightly onto your supporting foot to unweight your stepping foot, moving your body's weight away from the direction in which you intend to step. This motion is counterproductive because you must then overcome this initial inertia and bring your body to a stop before you can begin shifting your weight back in the direction you originally intended to move. It also makes you slow and telegraphs your movements to your opponent.

When possible, seek the advice of a training partner or, better yet, a qualified coach to help you refine your techniques. Use a mirror to watch yourself and set up a camera to video yourself training. Look for the small telltale signs you make before you move, then work to eliminate them. Your feet should glide lightly and smoothly across the floor, neither dragging nor losing contact. Don't just watch your feet; examine your head, shoulders, and arms for extraneous movements. Your head should not bob up and down but rather maintain a constant level. Not only does this exercise allow you to do a good deal of self-correction, it will teach you simultaneously how to start reading your opponent's movements.

Basic footwork with the sword comes in two types: the shuffle and the step. When you shuffle, you move the foot that is on the same side as the direction you are moving. When you step, you do the opposite; you move the foot that is farthest from your intended direction of travel.

Shuffling

When fighting with a sword, it is customary to hold your weapon in your dominant hand and lead with the same side foot. This position gives you the best reach with the weapon and makes it easier to keep it between you and your opponent. Since you are strongest with your sword in your lead hand, shuffling is an effective footwork that allows you to maintain the same guard and stance while you move in, out, and around your opponent.

Shuffling is performed by taking a small step in the direction you want to go, quickly followed by your trailing foot. Begin by pushing off the ball of your rear foot as you reach forward with your front and then land on the ball of your front foot. Immediately tighten your adductors, the inner thigh muscles that bring your legs together, to pull your rear foot back into a stable stance.

To move backward, take a small step back with your rear foot, followed by your front. Push off the ball of the front foot, not your heel. Reach with the ball of the rear foot, and, as soon as it touches the ground, contract your adductors strongly to pull your front foot back

LEVEL 1: SHORT SWORD OFFENSE   41

into a stable, grounded stance. Use this same method when stepping with your left foot to move left or your right foot to move to your right.

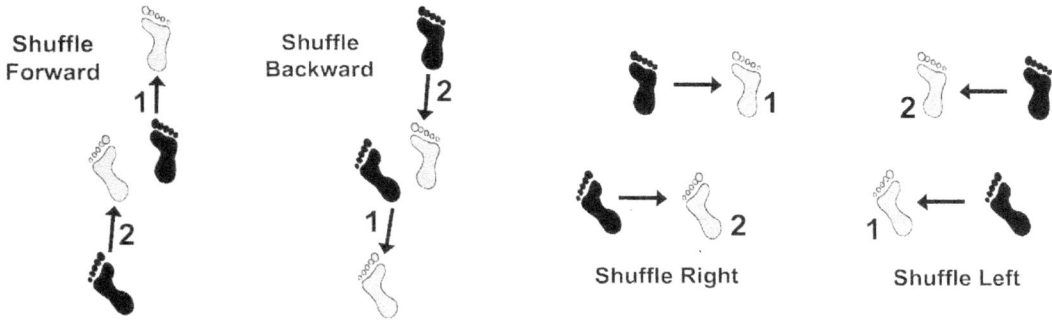

The black feet indicate the start position, while the grey feet indicate the final position.

Shuffle Forward: Begin from a stable, balanced neutral stance (1). Step forward approximately one shoulder width with your front foot (2). Immediately follow with your rear foot, recovering to a stable, balanced neutral stance (3).

Shuffle Backward: Begin from a stable, balanced neutral stance (1). Step backward approximately one shoulder width with your rear foot (2). Immediately follow with your front foot, recovering to a stable, balanced neutral stance (3).

Sideways Shuffle: When shuffling, you want to maintain a wide base of support without crossing your feet. To do this, step in the direction you want to go first with the foot on that side of your body, followed by your other, or trailing, foot. The top series shows a shuffle to the left. Starting from a neutral stance (1, top), step your left foot about one shoulder width to your left (2). Your right foot follows, recovering to a stable, balanced neutral stance (3). To shuffle to the right, you need only reverse the directions (bottom series).

Circling

Circling, also called angling, is a type of shuffle that helps you avoid an opponent's strikes while still being able to deliver your own. When your opponent is maintaining distance in front of you, you can circle him as though he was on the inside of a circle that you were standing on, facing inwards. To circle, or angle inwards, step forward on a diagonal to either your right or left side. Which side you circle to depends mainly on your opponent. Immediately adjust your angle to keep your opponent on your centerline, while moving off of his centerline, making it harder for him to hit you effectively.

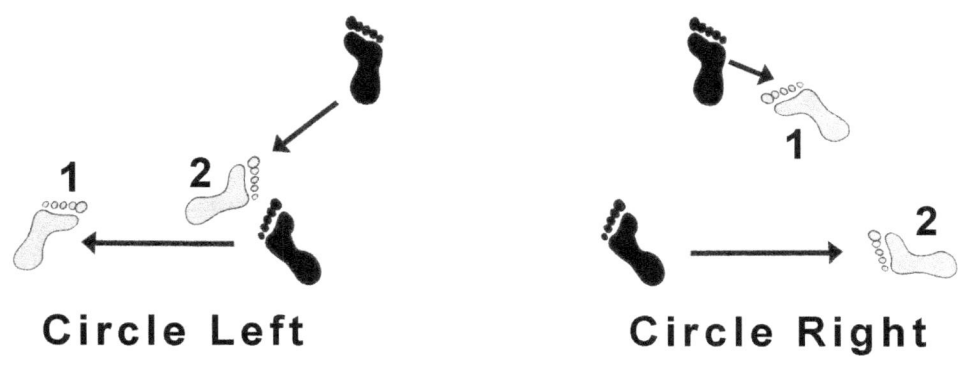

The black feet indicate the start position, while the grey feet indicate the final position.

Occasionally an opponent will charge in, usually in an effort to close the gap quickly from long range to middle or even close range. When the opponent charges, avoid moving straight backward in an effort to maintain your distance. Your body is moved by pressing off the ball of the foot, so you move faster moving forward and pushing off the toes than you can moving backward, especially if you push back off your heel. This gives a charging opponent the advantage as he can move forward faster than you can retreat, so it is often best to move laterally off the line of attack. Circling out is an effective method of giving ground to an advancing opponent, allowing you to avoid his strikes while still being able to deliver your own.

Visualize yourself retreating from an aggressive opponent. Instead of running straight backward, turn your body sideways as you retreat in a direction perpendicular to their incoming motion. Begin by sliding your rear foot backward on a diagonal to either your right or left side. Immediately adjust your angle to keep your opponent on your centerline, while moving off his centerline, making it harder for him to hit you effectively. This motion of "opening the door" is analogous to the actions of a matador in a Spanish bullfight.

Stepping

Stepping comes in three types: full steps, half steps, and switch steps. The first two are very useful when wielding a sword in one hand. The third type, the switch step, is more often used when wielding the long sword.

A full step, sometimes called a passing step, is when one foot passes by the other, forward or backward. In his classic treatise *A Book of Five Rings*, Miyamoto Musashi says that the most devastating strikes are performed with this type of footwork. This is because the stepping motion allows you to put more mass and momentum into your strike. Since you usually

LEVEL 1: SHORT SWORD OFFENSE   45

want to lead with your weapon foot, this is not footwork you normally do with a single-handed sword (unless you are using a shield, but that is a topic for another book). However, if you start a fight using typical shuffling steps, a well-timed full passing step can be a good way to quickly advance on an unsuspecting opponent. Stepping is a key part of certain strategies, such as the rear-guard defense taught in Level 4.

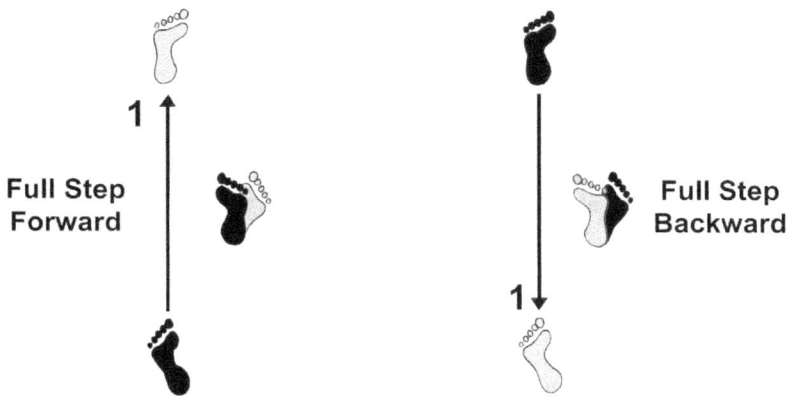

The black feet indicate the start position, while the grey feet indicate the final position.

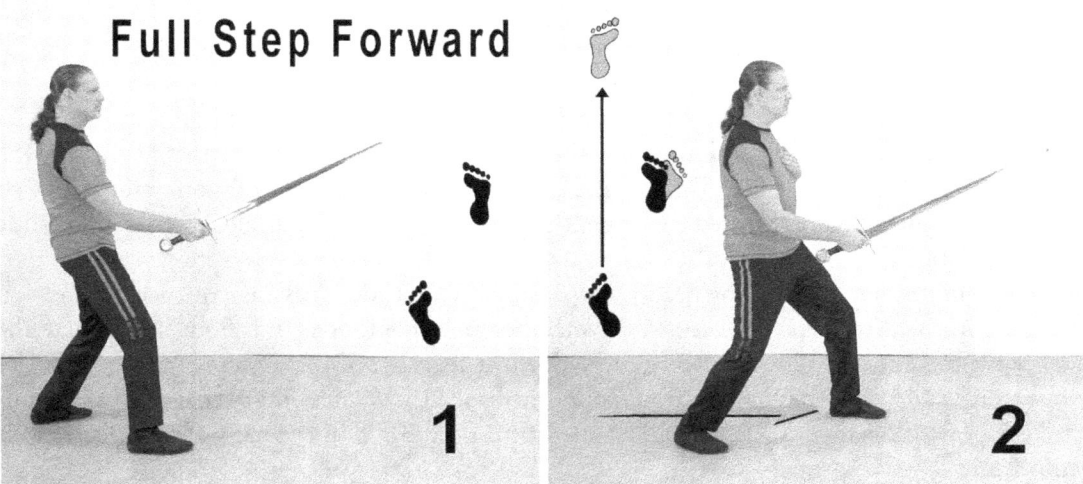

Full Step Backward

When moving sideways to your left or right, I recommend shuffling as opposed to full stepping. Taking a full step sideways crosses your feet, momentarily putting you in a vulnerable position where, if you are charged, you can trip over your own leg.

Aside from the shuffle, the step most commonly used in conjunction with the single-handed sword is the half step, also known as a gathering step. A half step is similar to a shuffle in that it allows you to maintain a same-side lead as you advance or retreat. To move forward, shift your weight to your front leg as you bring your back foot forward to your front foot. Then, transfer your weight to the rear leg so you can step forward with the lead leg. To step backward, simply reverse the directions.

The gathering step can be used to immediately continue an attack on an opponent who has just moved out of range and momentarily relaxed due to a mistaken sense of security. The weakness of the gathering step is that, like the cat stance, your feet are momentarily placed very close together. If performed in range, this can leave you susceptible to a quick low-line grappling attack.

A gathering step can also be used to move sideways without crossing your feet. Instead of stepping in the direction you want to go with the same side foot as in the shuffle, initiate the step with the opposite side foot, bringing your feet together. Quickly and smoothy transfer your weight and step out again with the opposite foot. Always remember that powerful, controlled footwork is the result of pushing off with and landing on the balls of your feet, never your heels.

LEVEL 1: SHORT SWORD OFFENSE 47

The black feet indicate the start position, while the grey feet indicate the final position.

Half-Step Forward

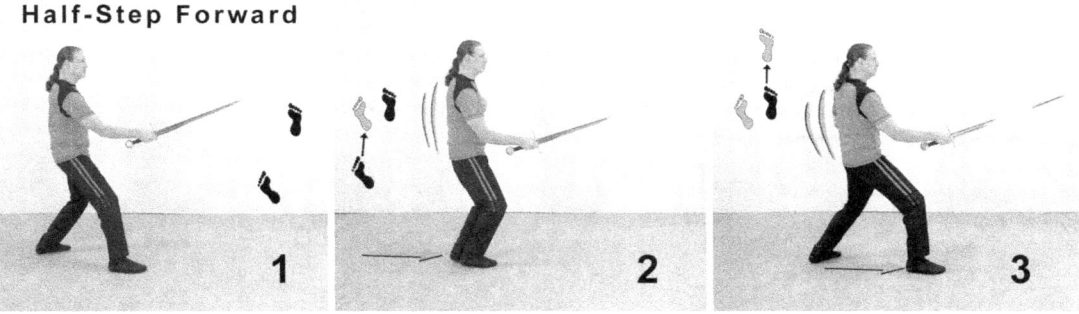

Retreating Half-Step

48 THE ART AND SCIENCE OF SWORD FIGHTING

Training Equipment: The Floor Pattern

There is a classic saying: "Footwork wins fights." So it should be no surprise that a wide variety of methods have been developed for training effective footwork. Of these methods, the floor pattern is one of the simplest yet most effective.

Floor patterns give you a framework with which to practice your footwork, helping you develop quick, sure movement. Understanding the different lines and angles allows you to respond quickly and appropriately to your opponent's movements. Drilling on a floor pattern becomes a game of physical chess as you explore how to move in relation to an opponent.

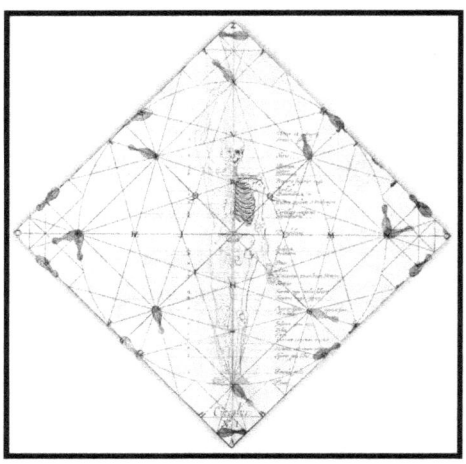

An example of a Spanish fencing circle.

One of the most elementary floor patterns is Marozzo's Star (named, of course, for Achille Marozzo), which was an asterisk-shaped star. The pattern taught how to step forward, backward, and side-to-side moving along the lines. Understanding the movements on this elementary pattern will help you unlock the combinations contained within the other, more complex patterns.

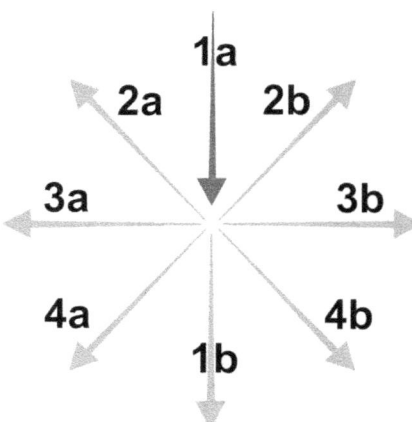

Marozzo's Star: Marozzo's Star is a simple floor pattern for developing basic footwork. Begin by imagining that an opponent is attacking you, with the topmost vertical line representing his incoming movement (1a). You could move straight backward (1b), but since this keeps you on the opponent's line of attack and he can move forward faster than you can backward, as well as the reality that your opponent probably has initiative and momentum on his side, this may not be the best option. You can angle forward to the left or right (2a and 2b), move laterally to the left or right along the horizontal lines (3a and 3b), or angle backward to the left or right (4a and 4b). These movements make up your basic responses to an incoming attack.

Range, Distancing, and the Circle of Death

To become a competent swordsman, you must develop a tacit understanding of different ranges and how to properly distance yourself from your opponent. Distancing is the space between you and your opponent, while range is how far you (and your opponent) can reach with your weapons. Range and distancing dictate what techniques you can apply effectively.

There are three general ranges: close range, middle range, and long range. Long range is the distance you can reach while lunging forward and thrusting with the tip of your sword. Middle range is the distance at which you can reach out and touch your opponent with your sword without stepping. When you can touch your opponent with your free hand, you are in close range. Each of these ranges has its own specific set of strategies, tactics, and arsenal of effective techniques that we will examine in more depth in later levels.

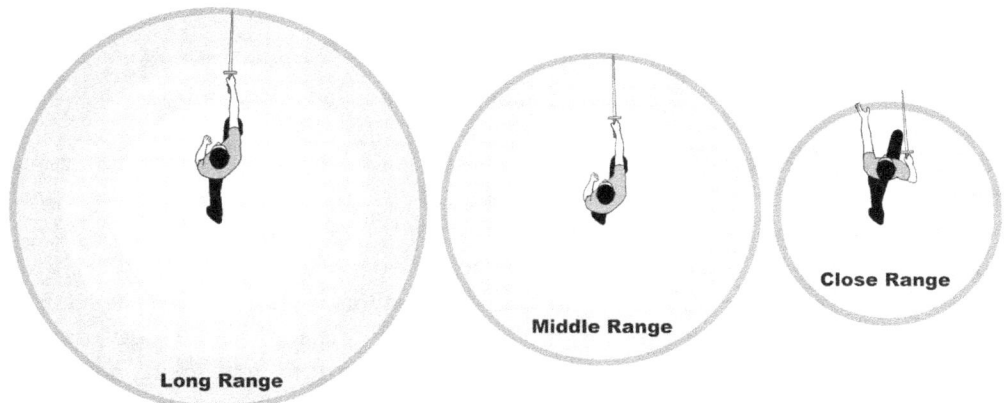

Footwork and distancing are interrelated skills that you must develop fully to fight effectively with the sword. A skillful sword fighter controls the fight by controlling the distance, which is accomplished by reading the opponent's movements and then applying the appropriate footwork to adjust his position relative to the opponent. It is helpful to visualize the "Circle of Death," an imaginary circle around you and your opponent that defines the effective ranges of your swords. Since thrusts made with the tip of the sword have the greatest range, it is just outside of this range that you will usually want to position yourself. Staying just outside of your opponent's effective striking range keeps you relatively safe as you look for the proper opportunity to close the gap and initiate your own attack. To hit anything outside of long range, your opponent will have to take a step forward. With training, you should be able to detect any foot movements early enough to maintain the distance between you and your opponent by stepping back yourself, and effectively staying outside of his striking range.

50 THE ART AND SCIENCE OF SWORD FIGHTING

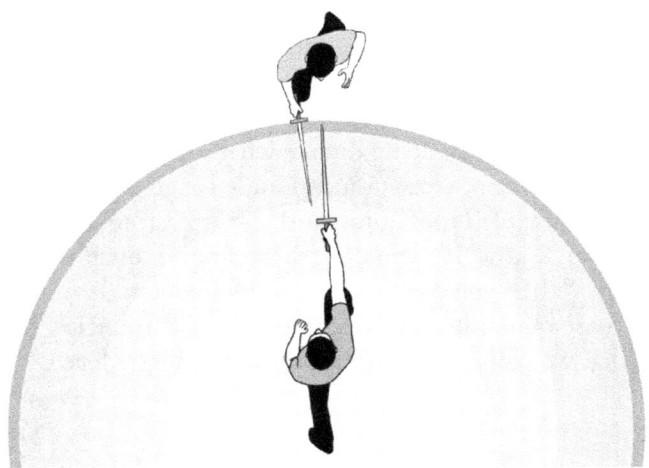

Hover just outside of your opponent's effective striking range.

As we have said, defensively, you want to stay outside of the opponent's longest range until you are ready to enter. Of course, you must stay at high alert, but since your opponent can't effectively strike past his maximum range, minimal energy should be expended on any opponent who remains outside of your circle. Once an opponent enters your circle, however, he should be engaged at the earliest opportunity. It is important to note that "engaging" the opponent also includes non-physical techniques such as feints and evasive footwork, as well as immediate direct physical confrontation. After all, you want to fight smart, not hard.

Offensively, you don't always have to wait for your opponent to enter your circle. You can always move your own Circle of Death forward by simply advancing toward the opponent.

Basic Striking Angles

To be an effective swordsman, you will need to learn how to become one with your weapon. Drilling these nine basic striking angles will begin your study of proper body mechanics, specifically your body's relationship to the sword, the floor, the space you occupy, and the space around you. Drilling in the fundamental strikes teaches you distancing, range, targeting, edge alignment, and tip control. You will also learn how to deliver power by moving from your center, or core.

There are nine basic striking angles. Practice each strike separately at first, checking to make sure you follow the same path each time you strike. Strive for precision as you swing the sword, slowly at first, gradually working up to hard, fast, whipping motions. Use a mirror or video camera to check and analyze your motions and movements, as well as how you flow between them. Remember, your whole body must be engaged.

Proper positioning of your body, weapon hand, and feet are vitally important for effective striking. Your body's mass and momentum should power your strikes, not just your arm and shoulder muscles. Pivot on the balls of your feet to get the power of your hips and shoulders into your strikes. However, do not turn your body so much that you expose your flank and leave yourself open to a counterattack.

The nine basic strikes can be practiced using the following pattern. It begins with an open ready position (open because the attacking arm is chambered on the same side of the body) and starts with a downward diagonal strike from right to left because that is the most common angle of attack.

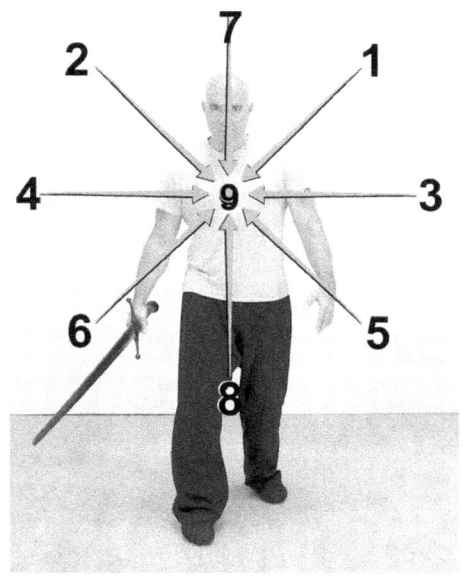

At first, begin each strike from a fully chambered ready position and fully commit to the delivery of each one, following through each strike completely, going through the full range of motion. Shorter strikes are faster and usually more practical for fighting, but you must first understand the mechanics of each swing on a large scale before you can begin to economize the overall motion, minimizing the preparatory and finished positions while still maximizing your speed and power.

There are three levels: high, middle, and low. High strikes target the head and neck, while low strikes target the knees and legs. At the middle level, all strikes should pass through a six-inch target at solar plexus level, and your diagonal strikes should be angled to cut through your opponent from shoulder to hip. Strive to make your horizontal strikes flat and your vertical strikes straight up and down. Forehand strikes originate from an open ready position, whereas strikes that start from a closed ready position are classified as backhand strikes. While cuts are usually made with the true edge of the blade, they can also be performed with the false edge as well.

There is a logical rationale behind this particular pattern of strikes. First, the strikes flow smoothly from one into the other, providing you with an example of how the strikes are used consecutively and in combinations. Strike 1 (diagonal downward from right to left) is the habitual method of attack that most people revert to when fighting with a weapon, and you will use and encounter it very often. The horizontal strikes are the next most common, followed by the less common diagonal upward and vertical strikes. The final strike, strike 9, is a thrust. The full pattern forms the shape of an asterisk that demonstrates how to flow smoothly between the nine different strikes.

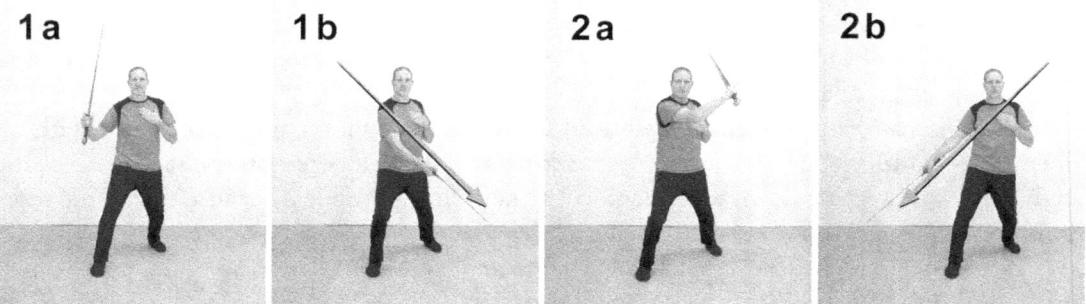

The nine basic strikes performed with the true edge: Start from an open ready position, your sword held in a natural grip in your right hand and the tip of the sword over your right shoulder (1a). Make a diagonal downward forehand strike from right to left (1b). Continue strike 1, following through to a high closed ready position with the sword over your left shoulder (2a). Make a diagonal downward backhand strike from left to right (2b).

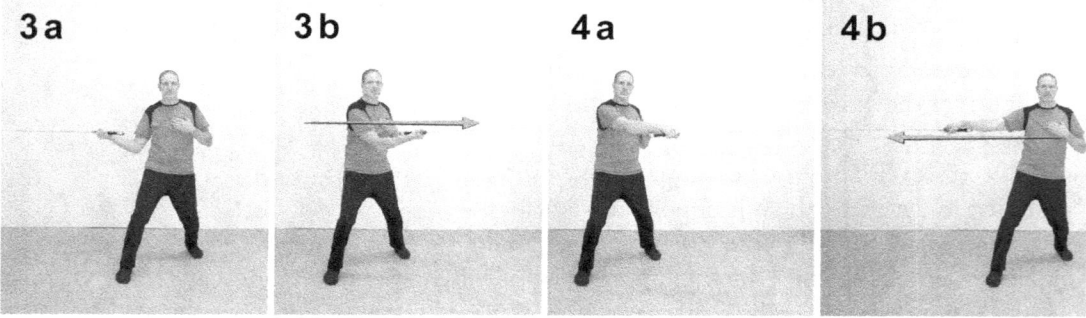

Continue your swing until you reach the middle-level open loaded guard (3a). Strike horizontally from right to left (3b). Continue through to the middle-level closed ready position (4a). Strike horizontally from left to right (4b).

After horizontal strike (4b), lower your sword into a low open ready position (5a). Strike diagonally upward from right to left (5b). Continue to a low closed ready position (6a). Strike diagonally upward from left to right (6b).

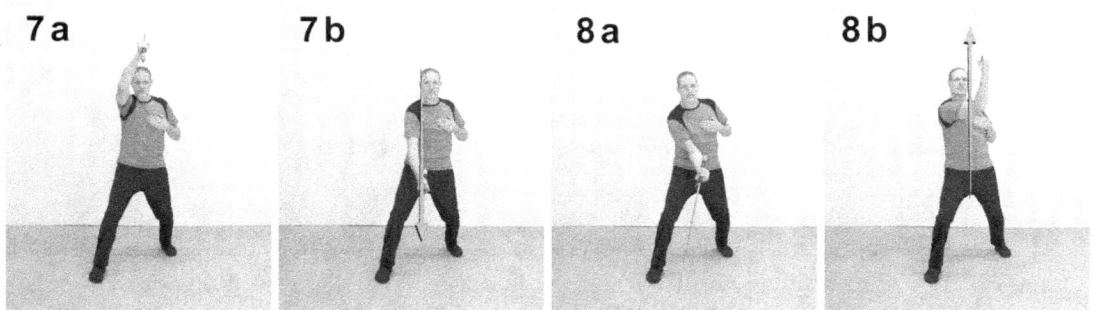

Continue your swing, bringing the sword around your head and into a high overhead ready position (7a). Strike vertically downward through the centerline (7b). Turn your hand over so your palm is facing up (8a) and strike vertically upward through the centerline (8b).

After completing strike 8, pull your right elbow back to your right side, continuing until you reach a middle-level open ready position with the tip of the sword aimed forward at your opponent (9a). Thrust to the center with the tip of the sword (9b).

This pattern is mainly used for learning the nine basic strikes. After you have learned how to execute each strike individually and how to flow smoothly between them, it is time to practice the strikes in different orders as well. For example, you could practice reciprocal diagonal strikes (paired strikes that cut back along the same angle). After performing strike 1 (diagonally downward from right to left), you could immediately cut back with a strike 6 (diagonally upward from left to right). This pattern is an effective combination because it attacks both sides of the body in quick succession and is therefore difficult to block.

Edge Alignment

Proper edge alignment is just as important as power generation. While edge alignment is pretty intuitive with a single-handed sword, it should not be taken for granted. A powerful strike will not cut well if your edge alignment is off by even a degree or two. To facilitate a clean cut, at the moment of impact your sword must be held firmly with the flat of your blade aligned perfectly with the angle of your strike.

The Brutal Effectiveness of the Sword

The Battle of Killiecrankie took place in Scotland during the Jacobite rebellion of 1689. Jacobites were Highlanders who fought for Scottish independence from Britain. During the battle, three thousand Scottish Highlanders faced off against four thousand British loyalists in the Killiecrankie Pass. Both sides suffered horrible loses. True to their aggressive tribal nature, the Highlanders charged the Loyalists, who, armed with the latest firearms, got off three rounds with their quick-loading muskets. Each time they fired, more and more of the Highlanders fell, yet they kept on. By the time they got to within fifty yards of the Loyalist lines, over five hundred of the Jacobites had already been killed or wounded. There, the

Highlanders paused to discharge a round with their own, more primitive firearms before tossing the guns aside and drawing their swords as they charged the loyalist lines. The Loyalists' muskets, which only a moment before had been such an asset, suddenly became deadly nuisances as the soldiers struggled to affix their bayonets. The Highlanders' swords, basket-hilted broad swords called claymores, tore into the unprepared Loyalist lines, slaughtering half their force before those who remained retreated in a rout. A description of the bloody battlefield written by Sir Ewen Cameron of Lochiel brings into shocking focus the brutal damage that a sword is capable of inflicting upon the human body:

> ... the enemy lay in heaps almost in the order they were posted; but so disfigured with wounds, and so hashed and mangled, that even the victors could not look upon the amazing proofs of their own agility and strength without surprise and horror. Many had their heads divided into two halves by one blow; others had their skulls cut off above the ears by a back-stroke, like a night-cap. Their thick buffe-belts were not sufficient to defend their shoulders from such deep gashes as almost disclosed their entrails. Several pikes, small-swords, and the like weapons were cut quite through, and some that wore skull caps had them so beat into their brains that they died upon the spot.

Types of Strikes

To add further variety and versatility, there are three different types of striking that can be applied to the basic strikes. Each type of strike serves a different purpose. All of the nine basic strikes can be performed as a half strike, full strike, or double strike.

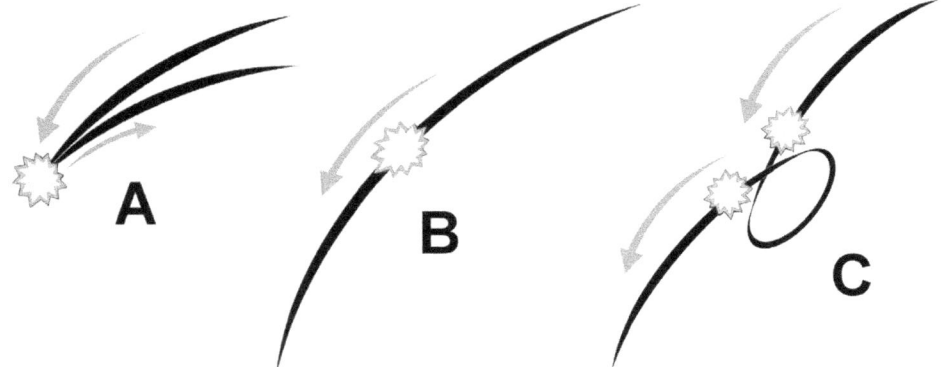

The paths of a half strike (A), full strike (B), and double strike (C).

Half Strikes

Half strikes are fast, but typically lack the power of a full strike. Half strikes hit their target then return back to a ready position without continuing through the target. Your finished position does not necessarily have to be the same ready position that the strike originated from, but it is usually on the same side of the body. The half strike is useful because it allows you to attack, then recover quickly should your opponent block and close the line. The half strike's weakness is that your sword has to come to a complete stop before it can change direction; starting the sword moving then stopping it each time takes time and energy, both to accelerate and decelerate the sword.

Half Strike: Begin from a loaded high guard (1). Strike forward, stopping just through the target (2). Snap back to a loaded, high guard position (3).

Full Strikes

The full strike focuses all of your body's mass and momentum into a single, committed attack. Not only are full strikes very strong, they are the instinctual way that most people attack with a sword. The basic strikes are usually performed as full strikes that follow completely through the target. At the end of the strike, you may choose to either stop your sword, or let the remaining momentum carry it through into a new loaded position.

LEVEL 1: SHORT SWORD OFFENSE   57

Full Strike: Begin from a loaded high guard (1). Strike forward, accelerating through the target (2). Abruptly decelerate, ending in a low guard position (3).

Double Strikes

Double strikes utilize a twirl to strike twice along the same angle with a single swing. Double strikes are deceptive as the sword passes the target twice in a single swing. Both passes could be used as strikes, or the first pass of the weapon could act as a feint or draw to create an opening to the target with the second pass of the sword, which is usually the more powerful of the two since it follows completely through the target, allowing you to fully commit to the strike. The difference between performing two consecutive strikes and a double strike is that, in a double strike, your wrist is held on your centerline until both cuts are completed.

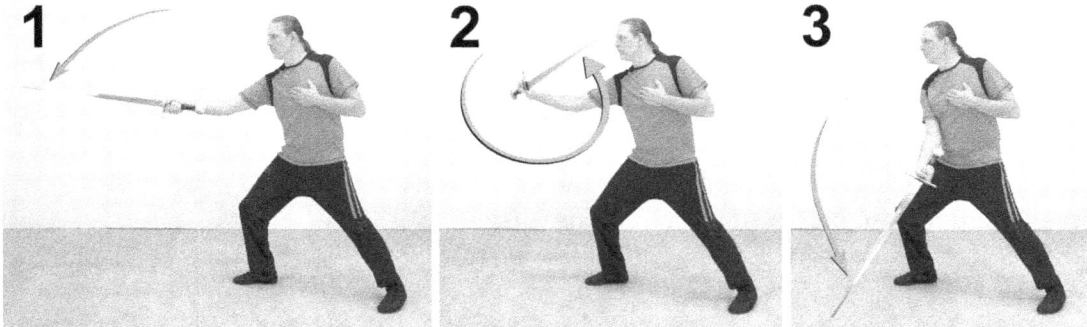

Double Strike: From a loaded high guard, strike forward, accelerating through the target (1). As your sword clears the target, pivot at the wrist to bring it around again (2). Strike through the target a second time on the same angle, ending in a low guard position (3).

Working from this basic concept, you could use a twirled double strike to attack from two slightly different angles, such as a right to left diagonal strike followed by a right to left horizontal cut.

Perfecting Your Lunge

It takes time to develop a strong, practiced lunge. Start by establishing your lunging range. Place the tip of your sword on a target hanging vertically in front of you. Then slide your rear foot backward into a full lunge until you have reached the maximum distance between your back foot and the target. Without moving your back foot, retreat your front foot into a neutral guarded position. This distance is your optimal fencing range, so you need to get accustomed to it. Practice lunging forward from this distance, touching the target with the tip of your sword until you gain an intuitive feel for your maximum range.

When performing the lunging thrust, it is important that all movement begins with the tip of your sword. Initiate your attack with your hand and wrist, aligning the handle and tip of your sword with the exact spot you are targeting (1). Next, extend your arm toward the target. Ingrain this quick movement before adding any footwork (2).

Your lower body is the last to move. Make sure that your sword always precedes any movement of your front foot. Reach forward with your lead foot as you forcefully extend your back leg and drive your sword straight into the target (3). Immediately recover into a coiled guarded position with a bent rear leg, ready to lunge forward again at a moment's notice (1).

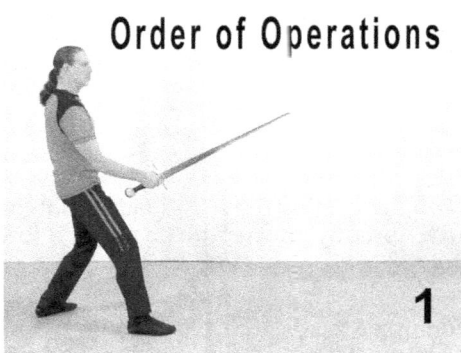

Order of Operations

The Importance of Isolation Training

I think we can all agree that, to be effective fighting with a sword, your techniques have to work. In order for your techniques to work, you must be able to perform them automatically, without thinking. The automatic use of effective techniques requires muscle memory. Muscle memory can only be developed over time through massive amounts of repetition that ingrains the necessary neural pathways in your brain. Only then is your brain ready and capable of sending the correct sequence of electronic signals to the appropriate muscles of your body, at just the right times, to consistently replicate and ultimately apply the techniques in a fight.

Isolation is the act of examining, practicing, and perfecting each strike, thrust, and footwork by itself, independent of other techniques. Every movement is actually comprised of many smaller motions. Once you know what the technique looks like when performed in its entirety, its smaller movements should be practiced individually also, starting with slow, short sequences, gradually working back up to the whole technique. It is important to take your time and not rush through this process. If you move too quickly through it, especially at first, you will be more apt to make mistakes, and mistakes will cost you time and energy, which is why moving more slowly can actually result in faster learning.

> Slow is smooth and smooth is fast.
> —US Navy SEALS

Practice performing every strike from each guard. This exercise provides you with a lot of good material to practice that will help you get better. For example, assume a middle guard and perform a number 1 full strike ten times, returning to your middle guard between each strike. Then, do ten repetitions executing a number 2 full strike. Repeat this exercise with all nine strikes. Next, perform the nine strikes from a hanging guard and then from a high guard. Besides the angle, you can also change the type of strike you deliver from each guard. Perform the exercise in each guard with half-strikes, full strikes, and double strikes. Before you know it, this type of practice will have helped you develop the important feeling that the sword is an extension of your body.

Combinations and Patterns

Patterns are prearranged combinations that are thought out and drilled into muscle memory in advance of using them. These sequences of coordinated techniques are designed to increase your odds of delivering a successful attack. By training and ingraining a few reliable combinations, you can keep your opponent guessing what you will do next, while simultaneously eliciting expected responses from them. For example, you may use a series of quick strikes designed to create a particular opening in your opponent's defense, which you can then exploit to deliver a finishing blow.

By having a ready arsenal of drilled combinations at your disposal, you reduce the amount of time and mental energy you spend figuring out the best ways to attack and defend. Fighting this way can help you conserve physical energy, as well, by letting you control the pace of the fight. Instead of trying to overwhelm your opponent with one single powerful strike, use a series of smaller, more precise attacks to gradually wear down your opponent's defenses. This tactic can help you maintain the initiative in the fight by forcing your opponent to constantly be on the defensive, while at the same time limiting their ability to launch an effective counterattack.

You already started learning combinations when you practiced the nine basic strikes. Now, it is time to take your swordsmanship to the next level with a time-tested method commonly known as the Meyer's Square.

Training Equipment: Meyer's Square

In his 1570 manual, *Art of Combat*, Joachim Meyer recommended using an ingenious visual aid to assist in the learning and practice of cutting patterns with the sword. His illustration consisted of a square divided into four parts, with the numbers one to four lined up in each quadrant. While Meyer never gave this diagram a name, it has come to be known as Meyer's Square.

While a Meyer's Square can look confusing to the uninitiated, the concept is simple. The numbers indicate the order and angle for your first, second, third, and fourth strikes. In all, it describes four separate combinations, each of which consists of four cuts.

You can create your own Meyer's Square using masking tape on a wall, or you can draw one on a piece of posterboard. Don't worry, it doesn't have to look pretty; it only needs to serve the purpose. If you wanted to get fancy, you might paint one on a piece of plywood. You could, of course, just purchase a commercially printed Meyer's Square. Printed on fabric, they can be temporarily hung for practice then taken down for easy storage between sessions.

Training on a Meyer's Square will help you develop accuracy, distancing, tip control, and blade orientation, among other things. Train for accuracy by tracing the lines as closely as possible. Develop perfect distancing by making sure that the tip of your sword comes within one to three inches of the target. Practice control by not touching the target; however, if you do, the target gives you great instant feedback so you can make the necessary adjustments.

Practice proper blade orientation by making sure that the edge of your blade is in perfect alignment with the arc of your swing. Practice the strikes using only the true edge of the blade before adding in false edge attacks. Once you are able to perform all these foundational elements consistently, add footwork into the drills, moving in and out of range between combinations, strikes, or between pairs of strikes. Be creative and you will begin to unlock not only the true potential of the Meyer's Square , but also realize your own potential as your swordsmanship skills increase.

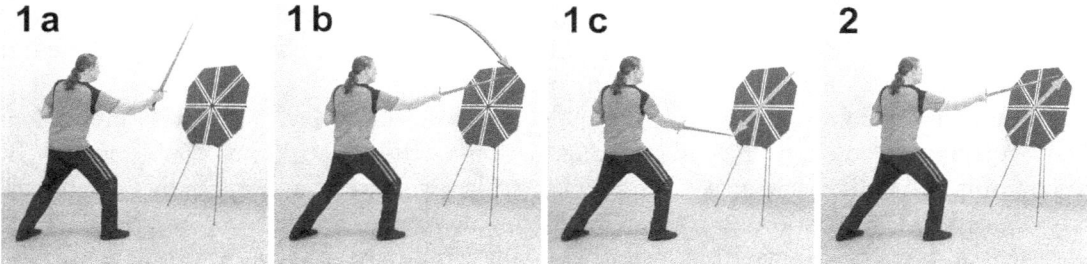

Performing the first pattern on the Meyer's Square: Start in a right open loaded position (1a). Move the tip of your sword to the beginning of the line running downward diagonally from right to left (1b). Perform the first cut, accelerating through the center, coming within one to three inches of the target, and stopping at the end of the line (1c). Immediately cut back along the same line. In this case I used the false edge because it was faster than turning the sword over to realign the true edge with the new line of attack (2).

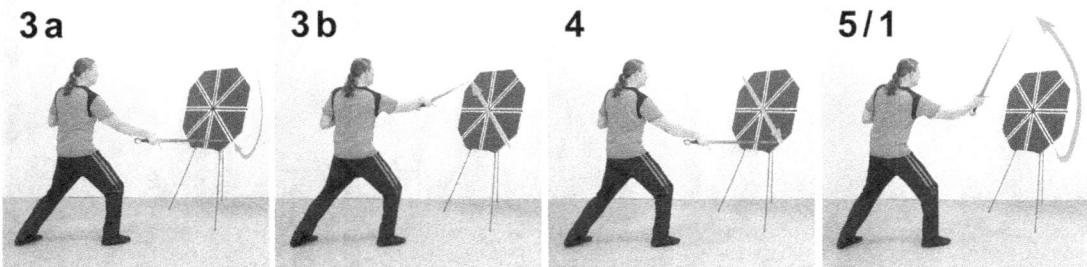

Line up your third cut by bringing the tip of your sword in a tight arc to the lower righthand corner of the target, to the beginning of the line running diagonally upward from right to left (3a). Cut upward along the line, coming within one to three inches of the target, accelerating through the center then stopping at the edge of the target. Again, I used the false edge, or back of the blade, for this cut, but it could have been made just as easily with the true edge (3b). Abruptly reverse directions, cutting back along the line with the true edge (4). Return to a right open loaded position, ready to repeat the pattern (5/1).

Training the patterns on the Meyer's Square may feel awkward at first since some cuts or combinations are likely to feel more natural to perform than others, but the more you practice, the more fluid and natural your movements will become. The goal is to make the sword feel like an extension of your arm. If you find you have problems memorizing these patterns, don't worry. Simply drilling them will give you the physical skills you need, and, later, you can deploy them in any order as situations dictate.

In my updated version of the square shown here, I made some improvements on Meyer's basic design. First, the numbers are oriented, resized, and color-coded for easy reading. Second, a diagonal line has been added to help you train your accuracy and blade orientation. Don't forget that you can always cut along the horizontal and vertical lines as well as thrust to the center. In this way, you can disregard the numbers and simply use the Meyer's Square to train all nine of your basic strikes in any order.

Once you are comfortable performing the basic strikes and Meyer's Square combinations with full strikes, you can practice the combinations with half strikes or double strikes. By combining full strikes, half strikes, and double strikes, you create an essentially endless variety of possible combinations to train, master, and add to your arsenal.

As if all these training options weren't enough, you'll want to spend time practicing with the sword in your off hand as well. Not only will using your off-hand result in more symmetrical muscular development but the coordination you develop with your off hand will be helpful should you choose to practice dual wielding later on.

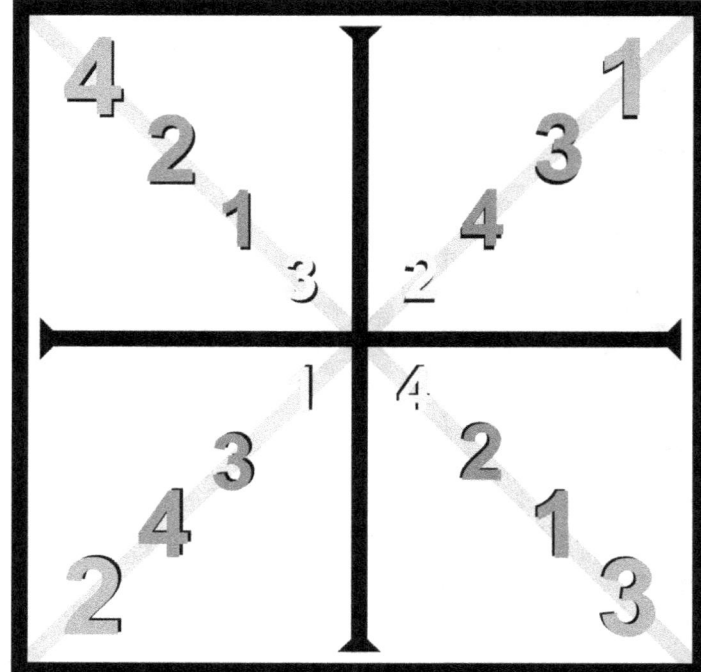

An Updated Meyer's Square: This more "user-friendly" version of the traditional pattern features numbers of different sizes and colors designed to help you easily recognize each combination.

Free Flow

Working your patterns on the Meyer's Square is an effective method to quickly develop your offensive sword fighting skills. However, training to the target has its limitations. Because the target is stationary and does not move, it is difficult to develop the smooth, flowing footwork that is required to execute your combinations effectively against a live opponent. Free flow is an important exercise that will remedy this drawback.

Free flow is the sword fighting equivalent of shadow boxing. Of course, you should do this practice with a wooden or blunt sword, NOT a sharp blade. Even so, one of the primary goals of this exercise is to teach you how to move with the sword without injuring yourself. So, always practice as though you were wielding a live blade.

Holding your sword, assume a guard and begin moving through your strikes and combinations using good footwork. Your goal is to teach your upper and lower body to work together in unison. Connecting your upper and lower body is important because your lower body not only supports your upper body, but it powers your strikes as well. Each time you step or redistribute your weight, there is an opportunity to transfer your body's momentum into a strike. Free flow practice will teach you how to coordinate your entire body with your sword.

Your next goal is to learn how to deliver a series of thoughtful, coordinated, properly executed attacks. When it comes to your upper body, combine everything you learned from your practice with the guards, the nine basic striking angles, the three types of strikes, and the Meyer's Square patterns. Meanwhile, your lower body is performing footwork, mainly shuffles and steps, that accentuate the movements of your upper body. Remember to have patience and move slowly enough that you can observe and develop an understanding of how your individual movements integrate to create natural and effective combinations.

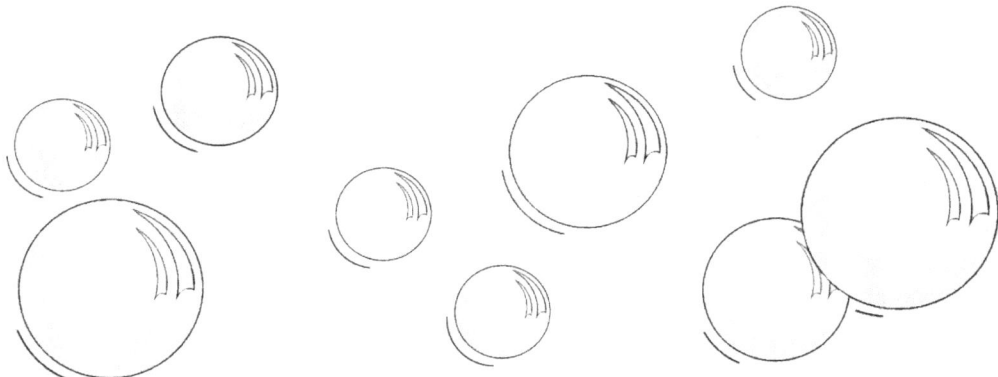

The Bubble Drill

A fun method for training speed and accuracy with your sword is the bubble drill. Use a bubble maker or have a partner blow bubbles for you to cut, thrust, and pop with your sword—before they touch the ground or you! Perform this exercise only outdoors, in a wide-open area where you will not hit anything accidentally or, worse yet, hit anyone in your zeal to burst the bubbles.

This exercise introduces a great deal of variables to your practice, so never perform this type of activity with a sharp blade. Some of you will still not heed this warning. For you, I recommend watching a YouTube video by Skallagrim entitled, "Sword Fails: Don't Do This! Showing Off Gone Wrong." The host's description reads, "This is my reaction and commentary to a number of blade related mishaps in videos. A good opportunity to discuss sword safety and analyze what went wrong when people cut themselves. In some cases, it's sheer edge-lord stupidity, in others it's simply lack of proper technique along with a bit of bad luck. Although I don't want to be a killjoy telling people they can't have fun with swords, obviously it's dangerous to mess around with sharp, pointy things recklessly. So here are some cautionary tales . . . " Don't worry, the video doesn't show any gore or blood. Again, save practice with sharp swords for test cutting under very controlled circumstances, which we will talk about in Appendix 3 at the end of this book. In the meanwhile, focus on building a good foundation by perfecting your basic techniques.

Level 1 Workout

This 60–90-minute workout is designed to help you develop the strength, proper body mechanics, accurate targeting, distancing, footwork, and power needed to wield the sword effectively.

1. Warm-Up: 15–20 minutes. Start with some light stretching. Follow this with five to ten minutes of cardio work such as jumping rope. Go until you feel tired and your heartrate is elevated, then do some more light stretching until your heart rate returns to normal. Next, grab your sword and work through some basic footwork (advancing, retreating, side-to-side, and circling). Use a footwork pattern while you practice your basic cuts (diagonal, horizontal, and vertical), first slowly then gradually speeding up. Remember to intersperse thrusts into your cuts. Cut, cut, thrust!

2. Targeting/Distancing/Control: 15–20 minutes. Perform the nine basic strikes to a a target board or Meyer's Square. Strike within one to three inches of the target. Practice each strike singly at first, then in combinations of two, building up to combinations of three to five techniques.

3. Power Training: 10–20 minutes. Practice the nine basic strikes to a heavy bag, pell, or tire dummy (see Level 2 for building instructions). Use a sturdy training sword and take care not to break it. Again, build combinations by performing the strikes singly at first, then in combinations of two, building up to combinations of three to five techniques. Include footwork by starting at a distance, closing the gap, entering with feints and combinations, then exiting on a new angle. Begin striking softly, gradually increasing the speed and power of your strikes only as your strength and confidence increases.

4. Variety: 15–20 minutes. Keep your workout fresh by switching things up. The nine basic strikes can be performed in many different combinations. Each of the nine strikes can be performed in three different ways (half, full, and double), making twenty-seven different strikes. Each could also be aimed high, middle, or low, bringing the total to eighty-one strikes. Adding in the twelve types of footwork expands the list to 729 strikes. Of course, you have two hands, so if you practiced every strike with your right and then again with your left, you would perform 1,944 different strikes. Whew, that's a lot . . . you'd better get practicing!

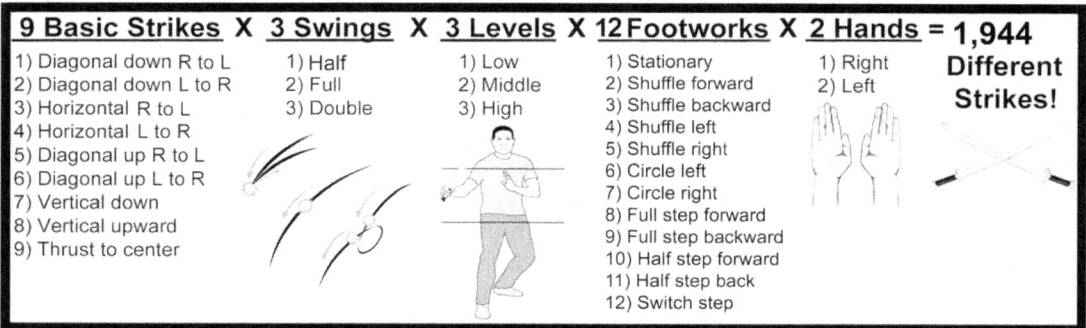

A regular training routine is important, but you also need to challenge yourself. As you get more comfortable with the basic strikes, try practicing in different conditions: in close quarters, in the rain, on uneven surfaces such as stairs, while sitting, or even lying on the floor. Develop reality-based self-defense skills by substituting your sword with improvised weapons that you find in your immediate environment such as an umbrella, tennis racket, etc.

5. Cool Down: 5–10 minutes. Take a few minutes to take your body from "Fight or Flight" into "Rest and Digest." Now is the time to use static stretching to increase your flexibility and break up the lactic acid that has accumulated in your muscles.

6. Follow-Up. When you are done, record each of your workouts in a training log. Include how long you trained and a short synopsis of the material you covered in the session. Set a goal for yourself, such as performing the above workout ten times before moving on to Level 2. Stay motivated, remain disciplined, be consistent, and work hard. With practice, you will continue to improve your skills and deepen your understanding of sword fighting. You're just getting started!

If you have not already done so, procure a copy of the companion video series to this book. It is well worth the money! The instruction augments what you are learning, breaking the material presented in each level into easy-to-follow lessons. Most importantly, video can show and teach you things that still photos cannot, despite the many arrows and motion lines I included throughout this book to help convey the proper motion of each technique.

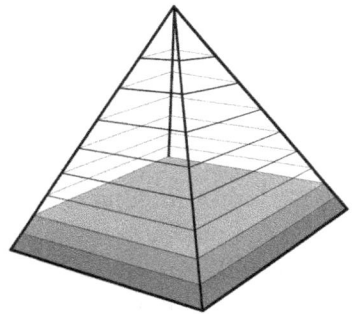

LEVEL 2:
Short Sword Defense

Building a Solid Defense

Whereas Level 1 used solo training to teach you the fundamentals of offense with the sword, Level 2 utilizes partner training to apply your newly acquired offensive skills to develop a solid defense. It is no secret that in many sports a good defense is critical to a good offense. Having a strong defense when sword fighting can have a helpful psychological impact on your opponent. It sends the message to your opponent that you are composed, confident, and not easily overwhelmed. A well-developed defensive posture can make your opponent more cautious and hesitant with their attacks, thereby giving you the advantage in the fight.

It's important to note that defense doesn't mean being passive or simply absorbing blows. It involves intentional, proactive techniques such as evading, blocking, parrying, and countering. By actively defending yourself at all times, you increase your chances of staying safe and gaining an upper hand in a sword fight.

Training Equipment: Gloves and Mask

In order to safely practice sword fighting with a partner, it is important to acquire and wear safety equipment appropriate to the activity. Light drilling and sparring require a minimum of protection to ensure against serious injury, while medium and heavy contact require substantially more. Don't worry, though, you don't have to go out and buy a suit of plate. In Level 2, you will be doing light drills with a partner, so you will only need to armor your most vulnerable targets, namely your hands and head.

Hand Protection

Your hands are one of the most vulnerable parts of your body during sword fighting. Therefore, hand protection is essential. There are several different types of hand protection that can be used for sword fighting. The type of hand protection that is best for you will depend upon the specific type of swords you will be using and the level of intensity you are engaging in. I recommend that you have two pairs of gloves: a pair of light gloves for controlled drilling and light sparring, and a pair of medium or heavy gloves for fighting.

Light gloves offer minimal protection and are only appropriate for controlled practice, such as during drills or when sparring with padded swords. When it comes to light gloves, you have several options. Welder's gloves, available at most hardware stores, are made of leather and are usually heavy enough to ward off the sting of most blows, making them suitable for light contact drills. Motorcycle gloves with plastic finger and knuckle protection also offer enough protection for light contact drills. The best option, however, are padded fencing gloves because they are designed specifically for sword fighting and, therefore, offer better protection. On average, light padded gloves will cost about $50–$100.

Medium gloves should protect you against strikes that could otherwise break your hand, but they are not designed to protect you against a sword swung with bad intent. In medium contact, such as in controlled sparring with wooden or synthetic weapons, lacrosse and hockey gloves provide decent hand protection. Though somewhat bulky, these gloves have good flexibility. Be aware, however, that there are gaps in their padding that can sometimes leave your fingers open to hard strikes. Goalie gloves are especially desirable since they are designed with more padding, in particular for the vulnerable thumb. Padded HEMA gloves are probably the best option of all as a medium glove because they are designed to address the weaknesses of the gloves already described. The vulnerable gaps in other glove designs are closed, and plastic plates are added to protect the most vulnerable parts of the hand. While I give some specific examples, when it comes to gear, it is always good to do your own research to see what products are available and highly recommended. Medium-level gloves will usually cost you between $100 and $150. If you are looking for better pricing, Red Dragon's sparring gloves offer a reasonable balance of overall protection and flexibility at a relatively inexpensive price, as do Purpleheart Armoury's Dragon Slayer gloves.

Full-contact sparring requires a higher level of protection. When engaging in any sort of competition, it is best to assume someone will lose control and that you will therefore need maximum protection. Heavy gear is meant to protect you against strong uncontrolled attacks or strikes delivered with intent. Heavy gloves should be able to withstand blows that would otherwise shatter hand bones. Clamshell gauntlets consist of articulated plastic or metal plates and offer full protection for your entire hand and wrist. While gauntlets offer more protection than gloves, they can be heavy and cumbersome, affecting your mobility. If you are sparring with long swords, this is the level of hand protection that you will need. Both Black Knight mittens by HF Armory and SPES Historical Fencing Gear's heavy "Lobster" gloves offer excellent protection with a starting price of about $200.

Once your hands are protected, you might consider armor for your forearms as well. Vambraces, or bracers, are forearm guards that are commonly made of leather, plastic, or metal. While some cover just your forearm, other designs extend to offer elbow protection as well. Vambraces can be worn alone or in conjunction with gloves or gauntlets. Vambraces, bracers, or forearm/elbow protectors usually cost around $40 to $60.

LEVEL 2: SHORT SWORD DEFENSE 69

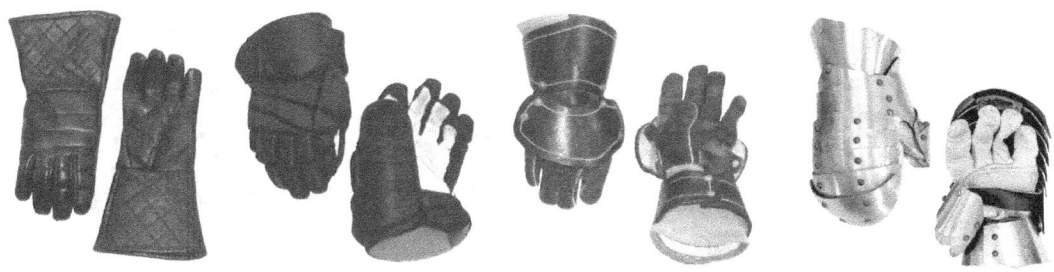

Hand Gear (L to R): Leather fencing gloves, hockey gloves, welder's gloves with leather half-gauntlets, and full steel clamshell gauntlets.

Head Protection

Your head and neck are vulnerable targets that must be protected. Therefore, it is wise to invest in a good helmet.

Fencing masks seem like they would be perfect, since they are designed for sword fighting. However, the equipment used in modern-day fencing has changed quite a bit since fencing became a sport. The swords, which are generally intended for thrusting from a distance, have now become very light and flexible. Therefore, fencing masks, while they offer superior face protection, do not protect the sides of your neck or back of your head very well. For this reason, they are best suited for controlled drilling and careful sparring with lightweight swords. This, and the fact that they are relatively inexpensive, makes the fencing mask a good choice for the novice swordsman who is just starting out and not ready to make a substantial investment in equipment.

For medium contact, a HEMA mask offers more protection than a standard fencing mask. A HEMA mask is basically a sturdy fencing mask mounted inside of a padded hood designed to cover any exposed areas. If you want to start small and upgrade later, you can begin by buying a plain fencing mask, then purchase the padded hood separately at a later time. Heavier versions of these hoods offer rigid plates in addition to the padding. A HEMA mask is a good choice for all-around sword fighting that will cost between $150 and $200.

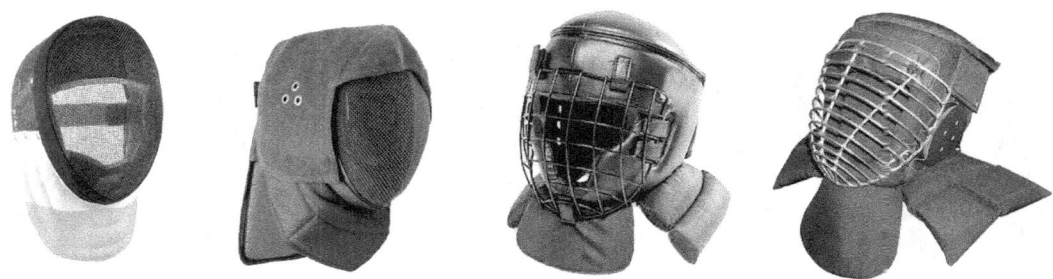

Head Gear (L to R): Fencing mask, HEMA mask, padded weapons helmet, eskrima helmet.

Heavier contact sword fighting, such as that seen in the SCA and Armored Combat League, requires substantially greater protection. Steel helmets designed for this type of combat easily cost upward of $500.

It is essential that the swords you are using do not fit through any gaps in the face mask. While eskrima headgear is well padded all the way around and has a large bib to protect your neck, the bars on the face cage are usually too wide for sword fighting. They are intended to stop a stick, not a sword, since most swords, even training swords, can easily slip between the bars on an eskrima helmet, making it unsuitable for sword fighting. An exception would be if you were using wood, rattan, or split bamboo training swords, such as a shinai. They have a sufficient diameter to prevent them from entering the bars.

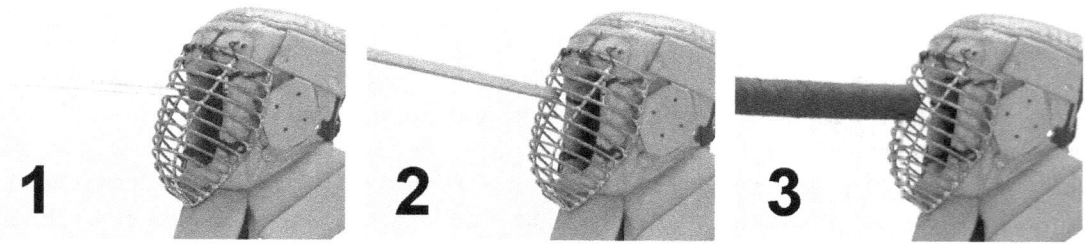

Check Your Face Cage: (1) This helmet is not suitable for use with a blunt steel sword, as it slips easily through the bars. (2) This wooden sword does not fit through the bars; however, it almost does, and, since a wooden blade does not flex, this helmet should only be used for light sparring with wooden blades. (3) This padded sword does not fit through the bars at all, and since its blade flexes easily, it is safe to use in full contact sparring.

Like your face, your neck is also a vulnerable target, which is why most helmets have a padded bib that covers your neck and throat. To increase this basic level of protection, it is a good idea to wear a separate piece of neck protection called a gorget (pronounced gore-jay). A light gorget, suitable for medium contact, is usually constructed using cloth padding that is sealed around plastic inserts, while a heavy-duty gorget, designed to stand up to the rigors of full-contact combat, is constructed of leather and steel.

Full HEMA Kits

Rather than piecemeal your equipment, you might choose to purchase a starter or full HEMA kit. When you buy all of your sword fighting equipment all at once, the price can be much less than if you purchase each piece of equipment separately.

An example of a HEMA starter kit including mask, gloves, synthetic short sword, fencing jacket, gorget (neck/throat protection), and knee/shin protectors.

Do Your Research

As I mentioned, new products become available, and old ones go out of production. So, it is important for you to do research. You can start by using keywords, such as HEMA gloves, HEMA mask, HEMA equipment, or HEMA full kit. You will find that there are many options available. I also include a list of reputable suppliers in Appendix 1 at the end of this book. To help you make a final decision, I recommend reading product reviews to learn about other people's experiences with the products that interest you. There are also many product reviews posted on websites, such as YouTube, that you may find helpful.

Now, let's get back to sword fighting!

Attack Zones

The initial stage of any attack is called *the acceleration zone*. This is when the strike is still building speed and momentum and has not yet reached its full power. The intended area of attack is called *the strike zone,* and it is where the opponent's attack will be at full speed and power. Moving away from an attack past your opponent's intended point of contact puts you in the *deceleration zone*. It is the part of the swing where the sword is no longer gaining speed but is actually slowing down and losing power.

A swordsman is most vulnerable during the acceleration and deceleration zones, when the sword does not pose an immediate threat. Moving into one of these zones can allow you to land a successful counterattack either at the beginning or end of his strike. Circling is one method of removing your body from your opponent's strike zone and moving into either the acceleration zone or deceleration zone. As you circle into these zones, maintain control of the line of combat by turning your body to keep the opponent centered in your own strike zone.

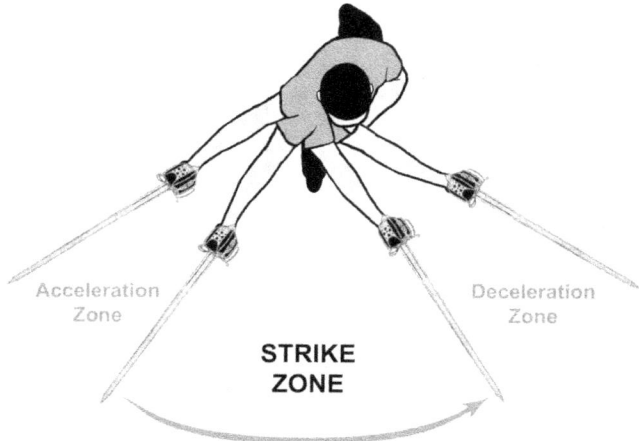

Analysis of a Strike: The attack begins in the acceleration zone where it gains speed, then moves through the strike zone, the strongest, most focused part of the strike, finally ending with the deceleration zone, where the attack loses significant speed and power.

Keep in mind that these same mechanics apply to each of your strikes as well, meaning your opponent can use these same strategies that we just mentioned against you. This is why you must strive to minimize both your backswing and follow through, either of which could momentarily expose you to a well-timed counter.

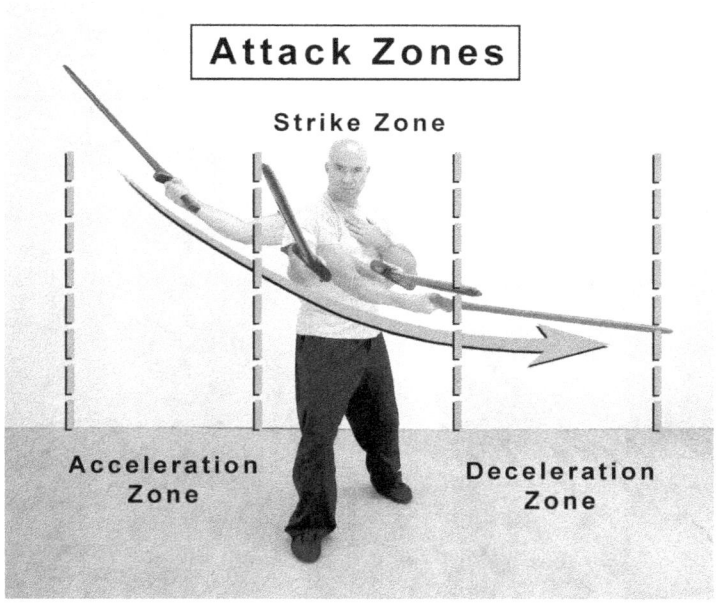

The Line of Combat

The line of combat is an imaginary line that extends from your centerline to your opponent's center. As you just learned, your strikes will be most powerful when you are aligned with the line of combat, when your opponent is right in front of you, instead of standing off to either side. Only then can you maximize the use of proper body mechanics to generate maximum force. Therefore, keep your weapon centered on your opponent.

If you want your opponent directly in front of you in order to maximize your striking power, it is also logical to assume that your opponent is seeking the same objective. Therefore, you must balance moving off of the opponent's line of combat in order to reduce his ability to strike you with his maximum power while at the same time remembering to keep centered on your opponent as much as possible to maximize your own striking potential. Circling is an effective method of achieving this goal.

Evasion

There are three basic ways of defending against an incoming attack: you can choose to block, parry, or evade. Your decision will often be dictated by the circumstances of the situation; however, understanding the differences between them is the first step to employing these different strategies effectively.

Fade: In this exchange, you can see how I faded my body back to evade my opponent's thrust, while still remaining in range, to simultaneously counterattack with a cut to his extended sword arm. (Photo taken at the 2015 Taiji Fencing Championships, Chinatown, Philadelphia.)

When you *evade,* you duck, lean (also called fade), or use footwork to move out of the path of an attack. The simplest form of evasion is to move backward out of range of the opponent's sword. If you back up too far, though, you will also be out of range to counterattack. *Fading*, however, allows you to withdraw the target from your opponent while remaining in range to counter. *Ducking* removes you from the path of your opponent's weapon and leaves you in a good position to counterattack. However, *ducking* is an advanced skill that relies on the ability to read your opponent's intentions *and* to respond with split-second timing. Should you misjudge in any way while ducking, you will have no back-up move and will get hit. For the most part, however, if you are successful in evading your opponent's attack no matter which method you use to accomplish it, you usually end up in a better position to counter.

LEVEL 2: SHORT SWORD DEFENSE 75

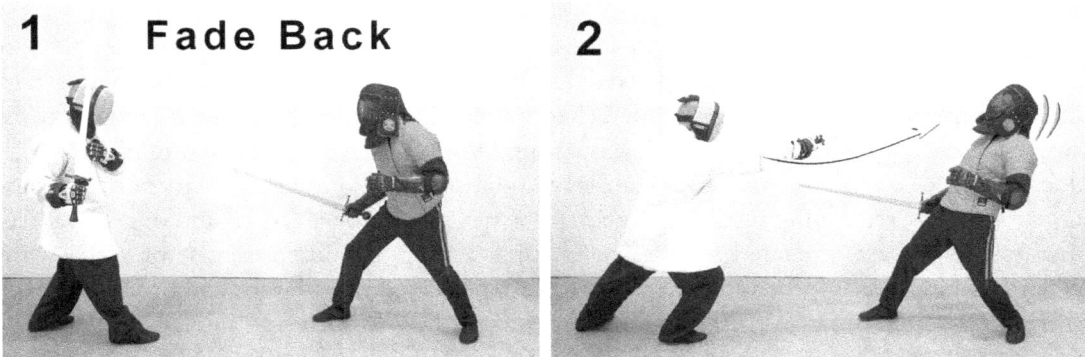

Fade Back: Hover just at the edge of your opponent's Circle of Death (1). When the opponent swings at your head, evade his strike by leaning back out of range. An unanticipated miss can momentarily throw your opponent off-balance and leave him exposed. As soon as his attack passes by, immediately lean back into range and counterattack to an exposed target (2).

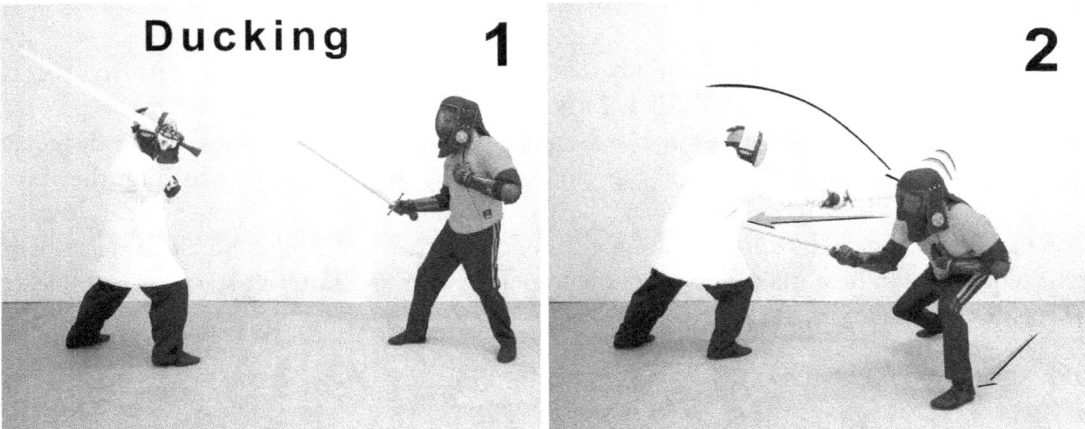

Ducking: Hover just at the edge of your opponent's Circle of Death (1). When the opponent swings at your head, evade his strike by ducking under his sword as you step to your left with your left foot. As you duck and step, simultaneously counterattack with a horizontal cut to his exposed abdomen (2).

Blocking and Parrying

If you do not see an incoming attack in time to use evasion, you will need to block it instead. *Blocking* is a defensive maneuver that impedes and momentarily stops the forward momentum of your opponent's sword. When a block is executed properly, it actually takes very little energy to block or deflect even strong blows. The physical structure of the block does most of the work for you, since it absorbs and disperses most of the energy of the incoming attack. Any remaining incoming force can be neutralized by an equal and opposite force. This energy is best generated and delivered using a short but intense pulse of your sword when you block, as opposed to generating force by just making a large swing to block. Furthermore, you can reduce the amount of energy required to successfully block your opponent's attack by catching it in the acceleration or deceleration zone. Blocking the opponent's sword when you are in his strike zone requires the greatest amount of strength.

While blocking neutralizes an opponent's attack by bringing his sword to a stop, parrying allows you to defend while keeping the opponent's sword moving. *Parrying* is the action of redirecting the momentum of the opponent's sword in such a way that it does not hit you while it remains in motion. It takes considerably more force to block and bring an opponent's sword to a complete stop than it does to deflect an opponent's sword and shift its course from its intended target.

The best defense is usually a combination of evading, blocking, and parrying. In order to learn and build these three skills, it is important to use a systematic, methodical process. You'll start by developing your static blocking in a partner exercise that uses stationary blocks and little or no footwork. Once you can block statically, you'll learn how to enter the acceleration zone and how to jam an attack. Learning to move into the opponent's deceleration zone and how to use dynamic blocking will follow next. Mastering these blocking skills in this sequence will help make learning how to parry easier and faster to learn. You will learn more about parrying in Level 3.

Static Blocking

When someone swings a sword at you, your body's natural reaction is to move quickly to defend yourself. The ability to stay calm while defending yourself begins with learning to control your reactions and training this instinctual flinch response so that you can use it to your advantage. Practicing your blocks in isolation, without regard to footwork, improves your blocks overall and teaches you how to stand your ground and "take the shot," an important ability in a fight. While moving with your block into the acceleration or deceleration zone is usually preferable in a sword fight, practicing how to block statically helps you become so confident in your blocking that you no longer panic and flinch when an opponent swings a sword at you. The ability to stay relaxed and control your reactions also gives you the calmness of mind to read the opponent's intentions and to respond appropriately throughout the fight.

Practice static blocking until you can observe your opponent calmly while he is swinging at you. Watch for telegraphing movements that tell you what side he will be striking from and at what level. If your opponent starts from a closed position, you know he is chambered for a backhand strike, whereas if his arm is held so that his body is open you know he is in a position to deliver a forehand strike. Other clues, such as the level of the weapon and where the opponent's eyes are directed, can tell you what level he is intending to attack. Use all this information to set up a block before he can get to the target.

The Six Basic Blocking Positions: (1) high outside (window), (2) high inside (roof), (3) middle outside, (4) middle inside, (5) low outside, (6) low inside.

You will use your blocks to defend three levels: high, middle, and low. Each level has an inside and an outside version of the block. Inside blocks cross your centerline, and, for a right-handed fighter, are used to defend against attacks on your left. Outside blocks are used to defend against attacks on your right. High blocks defend against downward attacks. Middle blocks are used to defend against horizontal attacks aimed above your waist and can be performed tip up or tip pointing down. Low blocks are used to defend against horizontal attacks aimed at the legs and are performed with the tip down. Remember that strikes aimed below the knee are best evaded by moving your foot back out of range rather than attempting to block the strike with the weak part of your blade.

High blocks are performed by lifting your sword over your head, with the tip of your sword pointing up or down. When the hilt is held higher than the tip, the inside high block is called a roof block, for its sloping structure. The outside high block with the tip down is referred to as a window block, due to the space created between your sword and your arm. In the roof block, your sword is the only thing crossing your centerline; however, in the window block, your sword arm crosses your center. Make sure you can see through your "window" and that your arm is not blocking your view of the opponent. In both the roof and window blocks, your sword arm is bent, not straight or locked.

The high inside block (roof block) and high outside block (window block) performed with the tip pointing down.

Just as high blocks are equated to roofs and windows, middle and low blocks can be thought of as walls. Middle blocks offer protection against strikes aimed above the waist, and they can be performed with the tip pointing up or the tip pointing down. Where you block usually depends on the orientation of your sword immediately preceding the blocking action. For example, if you initiate the block from a middle guard, you would block with the tip pointing up. Dropping the tip not only takes time, but momentarily leaves you open and vulnerable. Conversely, if you initiate the block from a hanging guard position, you would perform your middle block with the tip pointed down.

The middle inside block and middle outside block performed with the tip pointing down.

In the low block, the tip of your sword must necessarily point down to cover your legs. To perform this action quickly from a middle guard, pivot at the wrist and let the tip drop directly into the blocking position. This motion is naturally stronger when performed to the outside. When blocking to the inside, the elbow of your blocking hand is either raised up or tucked in. Though both blocks are effective, blocking with the elbow raised is more conducive to a speedy counterattack, as we will learn in a drill called tres-tres, presented later in this chapter. It is important to note that low blocks are really only effective to about knee level. Below knee level, you are forced to block with the weak part of your blade, so a stout swing has a good chance of simply blowing right through both sword and lower leg. Instead, strikes aimed below the knee are usually best evaded by quickly pulling your foot back out of range.

Practice your blocks solo in front of a mirror first to observe your movements better and perfect your positioning, location, and angle. Start from a guard position, then visualize your opponent attacking you with a strong cut and move to block it. Freeze and observe your final blocking position. If you see any part of your body exposed on the other side of your sword, you know that you would be vulnerable to being cut there and now need to train the appropriate adjustments to avoid this vulnerability in a real fight. Practice until you feel confident blocking high, middle, and low on both your left and right sides.

Next, practice with a partner to learn how to block an opponent's strikes. As always, begin this practice slowly with an introspective focus. Move smartly into position to stop the opponent's blade. Block just far enough so that the target is fully covered, taking care not to overextend. Blocking on a perpendicular angle will help bring the opponent's sword to a complete stop and prevent it from skittering up or down your blade. Intercept the weak part of your opponent's blade with the strong part of yours, about a third of the way up the blade, to keep your hand safely out of the strike zone. Meet each incoming strike with enough energy to kill the momentum of the incoming blow and prevent it from blowing through your block.

The Six Basic Blocks: The high and middle blocks are shown here with the tip pointing up, but can also be performed with the tip pointing down. Low blocks are almost always performed with the tip pointing down. Blocking low with the tip pointing up can be done but requires that you squat low enough and quickly enough to get the handle of your sword close to the floor.

After you block, you can add a counterattack, called a riposte, but always make sure that the blocking maneuver takes priority. For training purposes, once your block is complete, your partner should momentarily hold their position while you riposte to an open target. While having your partner freeze in this manner is an artificial construction and would not happen in a "real" fight, when training, it gives you the time you need to process the situation and make educated decisions to improve your execution. In a competitive sword match you need only to shorten the timing of your riposte to a half beat, so that your counter lands before the opponent can defend against it. However, for the sake of training, use a predictable, steady tempo in order to concentrate on making clean strikes and blocks in order to burn in the motions. This exercise leads naturally into the blocking/riposte drills.

Blocking/Riposte Drills

A good way to develop your blocking skills is to alternate blocking and striking with a partner in a prearranged pattern. Begin with high strikes and high blocks. One partner strikes first while the other blocks and then ripostes, striking back at the same level, allowing both partners to attack and defend. The proper evolution of the exercise is to start by blocking and striking to only one side of the body at a time. Limiting to only one side at first allows you to focus on building a strong, reliable block without the additional cognitive task of having to detect what side the attack is coming from. Next, block and strike to both sides in a prearranged pattern, so you can learn to see what the attack looks like when it is delivered from both the left and from the right. In the final stage of the drill, you employ this skill to defend to either side at random. Remember, this is a drill not a fight, so the emphasis is on perfecting your technique, not scoring on your training partner. Focus instead on developing good form and training to read the strikes. Return your sword to a solid guard position after each block and strike. This is a good habit to get into as it leaves you in a good defensive position.

Block and riposte against a high inside attack (top) and high outside attack (bottom), both performed with the tip of your sword facing up.

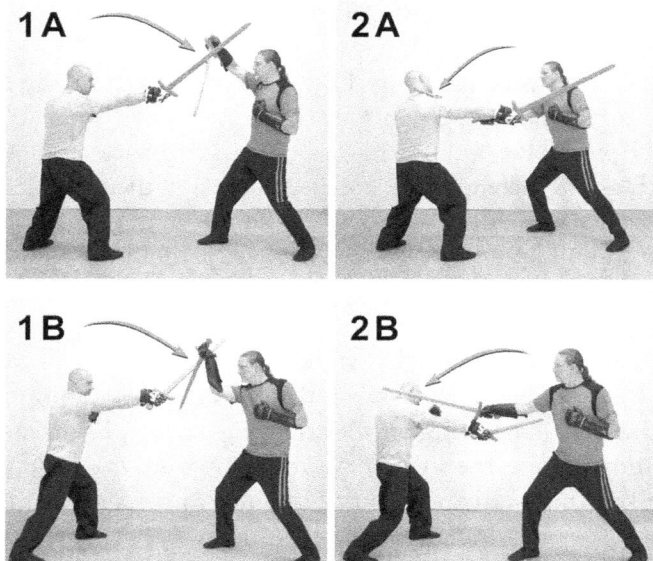

Block and riposte against a high inside attack (top) and high outside attack (bottom), both performed with the tip of your sword facing down.

Next, repeat the drill using mid-level horizontal cuts and middle blocks. Keep your blocking movements as economical as possible, meaning that if the tip of your sword is facing up when the opponent strikes, keep it up as you block, and vice-versa. Attempting to switch from a tip-up to a tip-down position mid-block leaves you momentarily exposed and unable to block at all.

Block and riposte against a middle-level inside attack (top) and middle outside attack (bottom).

Then, perform the drill using only low strikes and low blocks. Start striking and blocking on only one side. This is a drill, not a fight, so the emphasis is on perfecting your technique, not scoring on your training partner. Concentrate on good form and returning your sword to a solid guard position between each strike and block. Once you feel comfortable on one side, drill the low block and strike on the opposite side. When this pattern is easy on both sides, alternate the strikes in a prearranged fashion and then functionalize the low block by defending against low strikes delivered to either side at random.

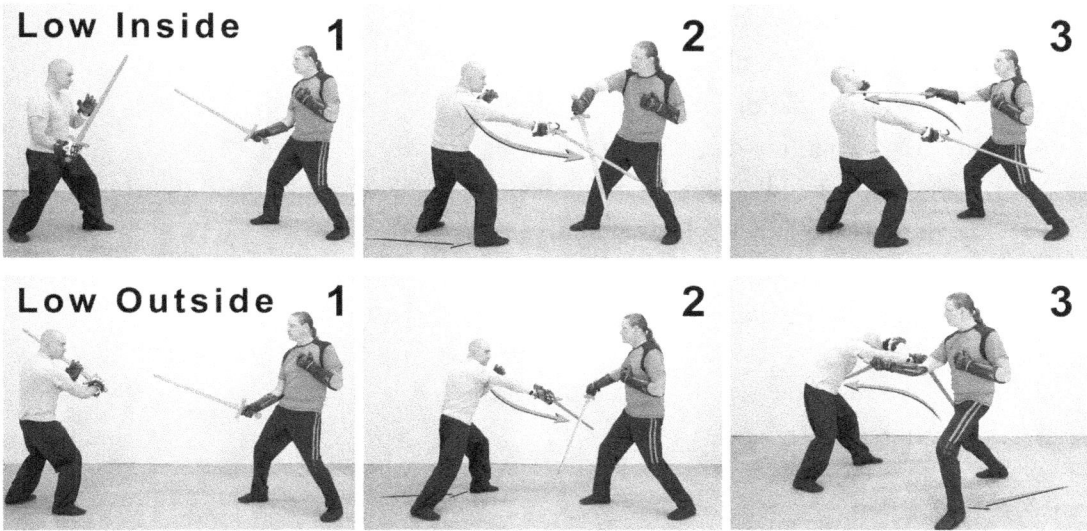

Block and riposte against a low inside attack (top) and low outside attack (bottom).

Once you have developed your blocks at a single level, you'll want to learn to defend against attacks directed at two different levels, such as high/middle or middle/low. Have your opponent attack to either of these levels, first only on one side of the body, then on the other. Next, alternate strikes to either side before moving on to stage four of the drill, striking at random.

Combine all three drills by alternating cuts and blocks with a partner to any level. Again, repeat the pattern of training on one side, then the other, before trying both. Start from the top, high/middle/low. Then reverse and practice blocking strikes aimed low/middle/high. Try different variations on this drill by changing the order of the blocks. Again, train one side, then the other, before alternating sides in a prearranged pattern. Freestyle practice should occur only as a final, culminating activity.

When blocking, be sure to intercept the opponent's sword with the middle of your sword on a perpendicular angle in order to absorb the energy of his strike and bring his sword to a complete stop. This action also acts to maximize your blocking surface, giving you a higher percentage of success blocking his attack. Blocking closer to the hilt may be stronger, but it also brings your hand closer to the opponent's blade.

Practice the basic blocking drill until you can calmly observe the opponent's movements and quickly identify from which side he will be striking and at what level. When you can stand your ground comfortably and not flinch when your partner swings at you, you will begin moving with more strength and confidence. You will also be ready to add in footwork, first by stepping into and out of range and later by stepping around in a circular pattern, as you strike and block. Then, learning jamming and dynamic blocking come next.

To summarize, the different versions of the blocking drills are:
1. Downward strike/roof block
2. Horizontal strike/wall block (tip up or down)
3. Leg strike/low block (tip down)
4. Double level (high/middle, middle/low, or high/low)
5. Triple level (low/middle/high, high/middle/low, middle/low/high, or middle/high/low)
6. Freestyle blocking (any level at random)

In two-man drills, the four exercises to develop your blocks are:
1. On one side
2. On the opposite side
3. Alternating / prearranged
4. Either side at random

In practice, for optimal learning, your partner should swing at a speed that allows you to achieve an 80-percent success rate. When you succeed consistently less than 80 percent, you can get discouraged and slow down your learning. If you succeed more than that, you are not being adequately challenged and you won't learn as much. Put differently your partner should strive to attack at a rate in which you get hit about one time out of five. Sometimes, it will be more, and sometimes it will be less; however, overall this ratio would help encourage personal growth. Of course, you and your partner should use enough control so that, when you do land a hit, it causes no injury.

Block with the Edge or the Flat?

Within the world of sword fighting, there has been much debate about whether to block with the edge or the flat of the blade. Some maintain that you must block with the flat of your blade because blocking with the edge can damage your sword. It is argued, also, that blocking with the flat of the blade distributes the force of the blow more evenly and reduces the risk of damage to your sword. Furthermore, many historical resources suggest blocking with the flat of the blade. However, those arguing that blocking with the edge is better cite many historical records as well, arguing that their sources instruct using the edge to block because the mechanics of the hand and arm are much stronger when blocking with the edge than with the flat. To further substantiate that edge-on-edge contact is the proper way to block, proponents claim that one needs only to examine the construction of the crossguard. Crossguards are aligned with the edge of the blade. If you were to block with the flat and your opponent's sword ran up your blade, there is nothing to prevent it from cutting your hand. It is important to note that, to address this weakness, side rings were sometimes added to the simple crossguard. In the end, perhaps knowing how to block with both is best, and here's why.

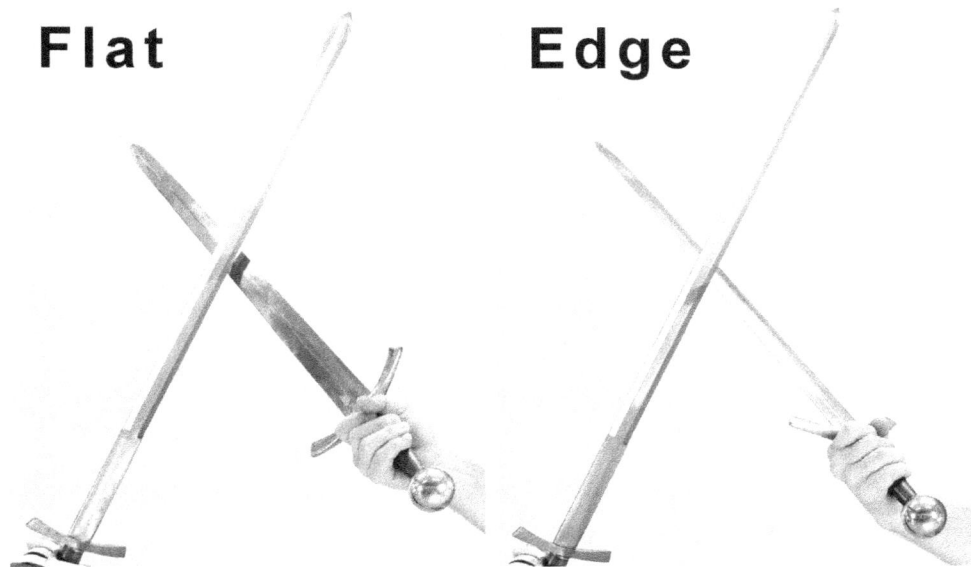

The argument that you should not block with the edge of your blade for fear of damaging it is unrealistic. You cannot fight if you are worried about protecting your sword. Your sword is there to protect you, not the other way around. In a swordfight, the reality is that you need to attack, and, when you do, your opponent is going to block. Seeing your opponent making his move, you should not give up proper edge alignment in a misguided attempt at preserving your blade edge. Accept the fact that, not only is your sword going to collide with your opponent's blade, it is also going to hit his armor. Any metal-on-metal contact is likely to damage the edge. In the end, a sword is just a tool, and while it is an important tool, it should be considered a consumable. In the course of a fight, it should be expected that your sword will get notched, bent, or even broken. Should these things happen, the fight is not lost if a swordsman can think quickly and switch his tactics, perhaps resorting to a secondary weapon.

Jamming Blocks

Jamming blocks allow you to take the initiative away from your opponent. To jam your opponent's block, you move into his attack and catch it in its acceleration zone. You must be able to read your opponent's intentions and know when and how to move into the strike quickly, without hesitation. Jamming blocks are unexpected bold moves that can disorient your opponent.

If the attacker chambers for a forehand strike, circle in to his right side with your left foot. If the opponent is chambered for a backhand strike, angle into his left with your right foot. In both scenarios, keep your centerline aligned with the line of combat. Know that the act of jamming the opponent's strike often carries you into close range. Therefore, you will need to use your sword to block and your free hand to trap the opponent's weapon hand.

You can practice how to jam using all the different blocking drills listed and detailed earlier in the Blocking/Riposte Drills section. Instead of merely blocking as you did before in these drills, move into the attack to jam it before it can gain any significant forward momentum.

Dynamic Blocking

Dynamic blocking uses circling footwork to help you avoid as much of the opponent's striking power as possible, by moving you into the deceleration zone where his strike has begun to slow down. Your sword neutralizes the incoming attack with a short but powerful "pulse strike."

Dynamic blocking is much like parrying. The difference is that when blocking, your sword is directly between you and your opponent's sword, whereas when parrying, your sword redirects the opponent's sword from the side or back.

The overhead block is actually somewhere between a block and a parry. Sometimes, the opponent's weapon impacts nearly perpendicular to your sword. In such a case, the incoming force is brought almost to a complete stop. If the opponent's sword impacts your sword on a greater angle, it tends to glance off and be safely redirected to the side. Because the opponent's weapon keeps moving, the technique is a parry, not a textbook example of a block.

Middle Inside Jamming Block

Low Inside Jamming Block

Middle Outside Jamming Block

Low Outside Jamming Block

High Inside Dynamic Block:
  1) Your opponent is chambered for a high inside strike.
  2) Use circling footwork, stepping offline with your right foot, to your right, into your opponent's deceleration zone.
  3) Perform a high inside block with the tip pointing down.
  4) Counterattack with a high horizontal cut to the neck.

High Outside Dynamic Block:
  1) Your opponent is chambered for a high outside strike.
  2) Step offline with your left foot, to your left, into your opponent's deceleration zone. Perform a high outside block with the tip pointing down.
  3) Counterattack with a high riposte.

Middle Inside Dynamic Block

Middle Inside Dynamic Block:
1) Your opponent is chambered for a middle-level inside strike.
2) Step offline with your right foot, to your right, into your opponent's deceleration zone. Perform a middle-level inside block with the tip pointing up.
3) Counterattack with a high riposte.

Middle Outside Dynamic Block

Middle Outside Dynamic Block:
1) Your opponent is chambered for a middle-level outside strike.
2) Step offline with your left foot, to your left, into your opponent's deceleration zone. Perform a middle outside block with the tip pointing up.
3) Counterattack with a middle-level riposte to the opponent's abdomen.

Low Dynamic Inside Block

Low Inside Dynamic Block:
1) Your opponent is chambered for a low-level inside strike.
2) Step offline with your right foot, to your right, into your opponent's deceleration zone. Perform a low-level inside block with the tip pointing down.
3) Counterattack with a high riposte.

Low Outside Dynamic Block

Low Outside Dynamic Block:
1) Your opponent is chambered for a low-level outside strike.
2) Step offline with your left foot, to your left, into your opponent's deceleration zone. Perform a low outside block with the tip pointing down.
4) Counterattack with a middle-level riposte to the opponent's abdomen.

Tres-Tres Drill

Originally a Spanish sword fighting exercise, tres-tres is a blocking and striking flow drill that, as its name suggests, consists or two sets of three moves that are performed on each side. The drill teaches three effective blocks followed by three very effective counterattacks. Tres-tres helps you develop effective distancing, footwork, and body movement.

To perform tres-tres, start by standing at maximum fighting range, just outside of your opponent's Circle of Death. When attacking, close the range on your opponent by lunging forward. When defending, evade your opponent's attack, by contracting your adductors (inner thigh muscles) to pull your front foot back into a stable cat stance. Always push off with the ball of the front foot, not your heel, regardless of if you are moving in or retreating. Work with a partner, alternating each move—meaning each attack and block, and flowing smoothly from one into the other. With practice your speed, timing, accuracy, and execution of the moves will improve, and they will be more effective in a fight.

LEVEL 2: SHORT SWORD DEFENSE 91

Tres Tres

Solo Practice:
1) Start from a middle guard position. Defend by dropping the tip of your sword and performing a right to left low block as you retreat your front foot into a cat stance. In the final position, your sword is held vertically with your thumb down and palm facing outward (toward the opponent), as though you were blocking a strike targeting the inside of your right leg.

2) Counterattack by stepping forward into a right lunge stance as you rotate your weapon hand in a clockwise circle, striking to the opponent's lead shoulder. It is important to move from the wrist and not from the elbow.

3) Withdraw your right foot into a right cat stance as you perform a high roof block with your sword held over your head, the tip angled downward slightly.

4) Step forward into a right lunge stance with a low cut from right to left aiming for the opponent's lead knee. However, do not strike through the target. Rather, stop as soon as you sense that your opponent has successfully blocked your strike.

5) Push off with the ball of your front foot and contract your adductors to withdraw your right foot into a right cat stance as you perform a middle-level window block (sometimes called a wing block) with your sword held over your right (lead) shoulder, the tip angled slightly downward.

6) Step forward into a right lunge stance with a vertical downward strike to the opponent's head. You have now completed one revolution of the drill. Start over again and repeat.

The pattern repeats low, middle, high and attack, defend, attack. Practicing the drill over and over again allows you to do massive repetitions of the strikes and blocks, as well as drill quick lunging and retreating footwork. As your skill level increases, vary the footwork, such as practicing circling, and experiment with changing the range, flowing from long through middle to close range and back again. Your ultimate goal is to be able to apply these blocks and counters in a free fighting situation. Lots of time practicing these drills will help.

When at long range, keep your free hand out of range by holding it against your chest. This keeps your hand in a ready position to check and control your partner's weapon hand should the fight suddenly move to close range. If you were to use your checking hand on any of your blocks to hook, grab, trap, or otherwise impede your partner's blocking motion for even a split second, he will be unable to defend against your counterattack.

When practicing tres-tres, be on the lookout for "footwork creep." The tendency is to start the drill at proper measure, but after a few iterations, inadvertently begin to close distance. While changing range is an acceptable and encouraged part of the drill, it should only be done intentionally and with purpose.

Tres-Tres with a Partner (opposite page):
1) A (left): Attack with a low downward diagonal strike to the inside of B's lead knee.
    B (right): Defend low with a right to left inverted block, leading with the knuckles.
2) B: Attack middle with a vertical downward half strike to the right shoulder.
    A: Defend by withdrawing to an inverted block over your right shoulder, commonly called a wing block.
3) A: Attack high with a vertical downward strike to B's head.
    B: Defend high with a roof block, tip over your left shoulder.

Reverse roles and repeat.

4) B: Attack low with a downward diagonal strike to the inside of A's lead knee.
    A: Defend low with a right to left inverted block, palm facing out.
5) A: Attack middle with a vertical downward half strike to the right shoulder.
    B: Defend middle by withdrawing to a right wing block.
6) B: Attack high with a #7 vertical downward strike to A's head.
    A: Defend high with a roof block, tip over your left shoulder.

   1) Start the sequence over again, beginning with move #1.

LEVEL 2: SHORT SWORD DEFENSE

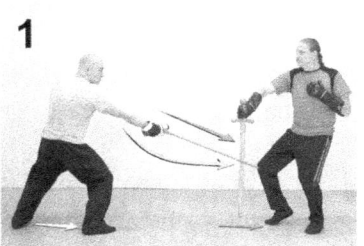

Training Equipment: The Pell

> A stake was planted in the ground by each recruit in such a manner that it projected six feet in height and could not sway. Against this stake the recruit practiced with his wickerwork shield and wooden stick just as if he were fighting a real enemy. Sometimes he aimed against the head or the face, sometimes he threatened from the flanks, sometimes he endeavored to strike down the knees and the legs. He gave ground, he attacked, he assaulted, and he assailed the stake with all the skill and energy required in actual fighting…
> —Roman General Flavius Renatus, circa AD 400

The pell (from the Latin word *palus*, meaning a pole or stake) is an ancient martial arts training tool shaped roughly in the form of a man that is used for practicing hard strikes. As its name implies, the traditional pell was usually a wooden post set in the ground. Modern variations on this training tool include all manner of free standing and hanging heavy objects that offer a wide variety of different sword training opportunities.

The pell provides the same advantage to a sword fighter that a punching bag gives a boxer: it provides a target for developing aim, distance, focus, and power. Pell training can also improve proper striking technique because it provides immediate feedback on each strike.

Your first reaction to having a target to hit may be to see how hard and fast you can strike. Although you should focus on power and speed eventually, not striking hard and fast at first allows you to work on accuracy, proper body mechanics, and footwork. Develop control of your sword by practicing how to stop all of your attacks just short of striking the target. When you feel comfortable with this skill, begin striking the dummy softly with each technique until you know you are making contact correctly. Then, gradually add speed and power to your strikes. Slow down whenever you feel clumsy or inaccurate in your strikes, and take the time to analyze what you are doing and to figure out how to resolve the issues. This way of training can actually lead to faster progress and, ultimately, a deeper understanding of the alignment and structure behind all your sword techniques.

For maximum power transfer, your blade must be aligned with the arc of your strike. Otherwise, your cut is likely to glance off the target. Strive to strike deceptively without telegraphing your intent while at the same time focusing on concentrating all the energy of the strike into the point of contact. In order to strike with focused force, your entire body needs to move in concert. It is very important that you accelerate the sword through your target and not just at the target's surface. Just be careful not to hurt your wrist or break your sword. Heavy strikes are hard on wrists and can quickly and irreversibly damage most training swords. The most durable alternatives are polypropylene swords or even a rattan stick. If you use a rattan stick, you can build up the grip with tape to give it a "handle" and mark the "blade edge" with a strip of tape so that you can maintain edge alignment as you practice.

The secret to success in anything is consistency, so be sure to practice regularly. The pell should be used daily to help improve your physical conditioning and swordsmanship skills. Vary your attacks, practicing all techniques from all angles and to all levels. Spend time training on the bag or dummy wearing some or all of the equipment you expect to wear while fighting, including a helmet and gloves.

Constructing a Pell

Keep in mind that you may not need to construct anything. Your training equipment does not have to be fancy or complex. In fact, sometimes the best solutions are the simplest. A dead tree, post, or pole are good substitutes for a stationary pell. If these are not available, a durable yet inexpensive pell can be made from an eight-foot log or similar length wooden post. For stability, your post should be at least 4" × 4" (100mm × 100mm). You can screw two 2 × 4's together to make the 4 × 4, if necessary. Dig a hole about two feet deep and toss a few inches of gravel to the bottom of the hole for drainage. Stand the post upright in the center of the hole and secure it in place with quick drying concrete or a two-component polyurethane resin fence post mix (A).

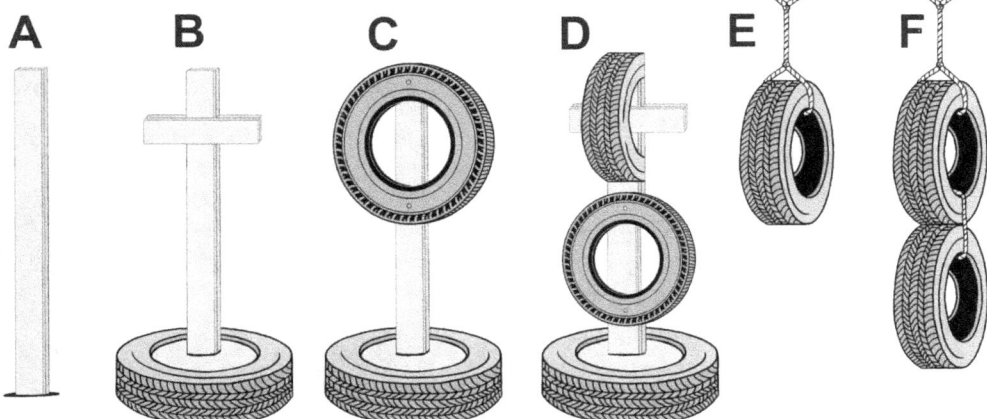

A freestanding dummy may be more desirable since it can be moved. An outdoor version can be made cheaply using a concrete-filled tire to secure the striking post. Before filling the tire base, duct tape a plastic bag onto the inside of the bottom of it to keep the concrete from leaking out when you pour it. Screw a cross bar to the bottom of your post for additional support before setting it into the concrete (B). Keep in mind that there is more than one way to make a pell. Therefore feel free to get creative with your designs (C and D). For a more mobile setup, mount your post on a wheeled base. Cut a 2' × 2' base out of 3/4" plywood and screw heavy duty swivel wheels in the corners. Mount the post from below using lag bolts, then reinforce from above with diagonal supports on each side.

Repeatedly hitting any solid wooden post can be hard on your sword as well as on your body, so you may consider adding some padding to your pell. Not only will your sword last longer, but it will reduce the impact your strikes have on your joints. You can use anything from pieces of carpeting to old towels as padding. Simply strap them on with duct tape, being sure to replace them when they wear out. Wrapping the pell with rope not only provides some padding but also gives it a sleek, finished look.

Another simple but highly effective striking target can be made by hanging an old tire (E). Used rubber tires are inexpensive, easily obtainable, durable, weather resistant, available in a variety of sizes, and made to have some "give" when hit. You can even combine two tires to practice striking at multiple angles at multiple levels. Simply tie another tire to the bottom of the first one to practice your low line attacks (F). These types of tire dummies require no cutting, drilling, or special tools to make, and you can spend more time training, not building. Just hang it up and start thumping!

Using a Hanging Pell to Train Footwork

The footwork needed to fight effectively can be developed by moving around the pell, dodging and traversing with combinations of feints and strikes. A hanging bag has an advantage over a stationary pell because it moves more realistically when struck, like an opponent might in a real fight. To get more swing, simply hang your target higher, from a longer rope or chain. You can set the tire or bag swinging with your hand and begin hitting it as it moves. Or you can begin hitting the target when hanging still and continue to hit as it swings in reaction to your strikes. The target will even charge and run away at times, all on its own, in response to your strikes. Having a moving target is the best way to train for a moving opponent when you have no training partner.

Even if your pell is stationary, you can still improve your footwork and movement by changing your angle of attack, moving in and out of range, and cutting and thrusting from opening to opening (high/low, left/right). In fact, strive to practice every technique you know on the pell. Practice the accuracy of your thrusts intermingled with your cuts and feints. Develop combinations, building from simple, direct strikes into longer, logical sequence of techniques. Take the time to properly develop each combination of techniques until they become reflexive actions, the result of muscle memory gained through countless repetitions.

Arming Your Dummy

You can "arm" your training dummy with its own weapons by attaching a long stick or staff with bungie cords or duct tape. If you are using a tire dummy, you can drill a hole in the wall of the tire using a paddle bit and then drive a stick or staff through the hole. For a tight fit, make the hole slightly smaller than the diameter of the stick you want to use. A weapon attached to your tire dummy allows you to practice techniques that involve blocking or otherwise manipulating an opponent's sword as you enter.

Modifying your training and equipment often will help avoid the monotony and plateaus that can test the resolve of even the most dedicated athletes. Personally, I suggest starting with simple training equipment and working your way up to more sophisticated tools as your skills and understandings evolve. You want to spend your time practicing, not making the equipment. (Although that can be fun, too!) The good news is that tire dummies are relatively cheap and easy to make. So try new designs and uses that will keep your workouts fresh and exciting.

Level 2 Workout

This 60-to-90-minute workout is designed to improve your swordsmanship by combining a strong defense with an effective offensive flow.

1. Warm-Up: 15–20 minutes. Start with five minutes of light stretching for your upper and lower body. Follow this with three to five minutes of cardio work, such as jumping rope, jogging in place, or doing jumping jacks until you feel tired, and your heartrate is elevated. Then do five more minutes of light stretching until your heart rate returns back to normal. Next, grab your sword and do five minutes of basic footwork while practicing your blocks, parries, cuts, and thrusts. Start slowly and gradually speed up.

2. Targeting/Distancing/Control: 30–45 minutes. Spend a few minutes practicing each of the six different versions of the blocking drill with a partner.

1. Downward strike/roof block
2. Horizontal strike/wall block (tip up or down)
3. Leg strike/low block (tip down)
4. Double level (high/middle, middle/low, or high/low)
5. Triple level (low/middle/high, high/middle/low, middle/low/high, or middle/high/low)
6. Freestyle blocking drill (any level at random)

Utilize these four stages of development to methodically train each version with a partner:
1. Practice only on one side, throwing a single strike and performing a single block.
2. Next, practice only on the opposite side, using the same techniques as in #1.
3. When you and a partner are comfortable with #1 and #2, begin alternating sides, in a prearranged pattern
4. Finally, strike and block to either side at random.

Solo practice is also important. On days when you do not have a training partner, use a pell to practice your offense, developing combinations that incorporate all of the above blocks.

3. Footwork and Flow: 10–15 minutes. Practice the tres-tres fencing drill with a partner. Remember to stand outside of your opponent's circle of death and to use proper footwork to control the distance, lunging into range to attack and retreating out of range into a cat stance as you defend. If you do not have a partner, practice performing your side of the drill, visualizing an opponent attacking and defending you as you execute the moves.

4. Cool Down: 5–10 minutes. Take a few minutes to take your body from being in "Fight or Flight" mode into "Rest and Digest" mode. Then, use static stretching to increase your flexibility and break up the lactic acid that has accumulated in your muscles.

5. Follow-Up: When you are done working out, record each of your workouts in a training log. Include how long you trained and a short synopsis of the material you covered in the session. Set a goal for yourself, such as performing the above workout ten times before moving on to Level 3. Be consistent, and work hard. Stay motivated. Literally, tell yourself that you are doing great. Remind yourself, also, that every completed practice improves your skills and deepens your understanding of sword fighting!

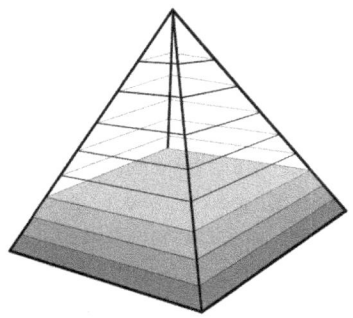

LEVEL 3:
Short Sword Fencing

In Level 1, the focus was on solo work and mastering the basics. In Level 2, you practiced with a partner to develop a strong defense and to apply your offensive skills against a live opponent. However, the tactics were simple and incorporated what is commonly referred to as a "hack and slash" approach to sword fighting. While a necessary stage of training and effective method of fighting, it is rudimentary. In Level 3, our focus will shift to more sophisticated strategies and tactics that focus on controlling the centerline. However, you should consider getting some body protection first. You'll be glad you did.

Training Equipment: Body Armor

You should already have a pair of gloves and a fencing mask to protect your hands and head. It is also important to protect your body and arms during training and competition. A fencing jacket and a gambeson are both types of protective clothing; however, they are designed for different purposes and, therefore, have unique features to meet the specific needs of their intended use.

Fencing jackets are designed for use in modern sport fencing and offer protection against light swords. They are typically lightweight and flexible, made from heavy cotton or synthetic materials, and padded in key areas to provide protection against the force of a sport fencing sword. Compared to the gambeson, fencing jackets have a more streamlined, functional design that is specifically optimized for the sport of modern fencing.

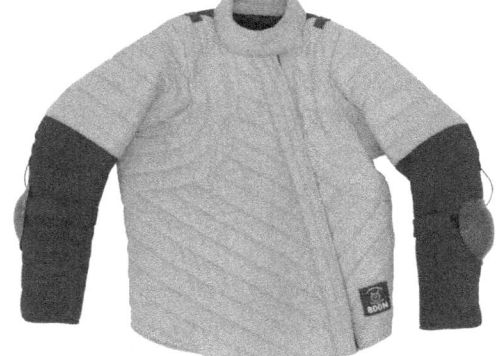

The jacket I wear in this book is Superior Fencing's Thermo Ventilation HEMA Jacket (800n).

Some jackets have a special lining that prevents a blade from puncturing the fabric. N-ratings are the system used to classify the level of protection provided by a piece of fencing equipment, such as a fencing jacket or mask. The ratings are determined based on the amount of force that a piece of equipment can withstand before it fails or allows a penetration.

Light jackets are typically lightweight and flexible, making them comfortable to wear and easy to move in. While suitable for drills and controlled sparring, a light jacket may not provide sufficient protection for more intense or competitive sword fighting.

Medium weight jackets (350n) typically offer a good balance of flexibility, mobility, protection, without a lot of weight, making them a popular choice. The gambeson, a popular medium weight padded jacket, originated in Medieval times. Worn either as a stand-alone armor or as a padded layer under chain mail or plate armor, gambesons are typically much thicker and heavier than modern fencing jackets, and so they offer more comprehensive protection against a wider range of attacks. A medium weight jacket's protection could be increased by wearing an impact vest underneath it for tournament play or fighting with heavy swords.

Heavy duty jackets (800n) provide the most protection, often including rigid plastic or even steel plates. They are typically worn by fencers that engage in high-intensity bouts and those who fight with heavy swords. Additionally, fencers that have had previous injuries or who are particularly concerned about the risk of injury may choose to wear a heavy jacket for added peace of mind. While heavy jackets offer the highest level of protection, they are less flexible than lower-rated jackets, which could affect your mobility and comfort during training or competition. While warm, a heavy jacket with rigid elbow protection is suitable for most fighting.

Rigid chest protection, in the form of a breastplate or plastron, is available and can be worn under a fencing jacket or padded gambeson to offer additional protection, especially against thrusting attacks. It is important to restate the point that your training weapons need to flex if you are going to thrust with anything other than the utmost control, and any kind of real fighting requires that the blades give for safe thrusting.

When choosing a fencing jacket, consider your individual needs, preferences, and level of experience, as well as consult the specific rules and regulations of any particular sport fencing in which you might want to participate. It's always best to do your own research by reading reviews and talking to other sword fighters to find a jacket or gambeson that meets your specific needs and preferences. Whichever type of protection you choose, the fit should be snug enough to prevent it from moving around while fencing, but not so tight that it restricts your breathing or movement.

Neck Protection

In sword fighting, the neck is often a target area for your opponent because it is a relatively exposed target compared to other parts of the body. Unfortunately, a strike to the neck, even with a wooden sword, could cause severe injury or even death. Your neck contains vital structures such as the windpipe (trachea) and the esophagus. Damage to these structures can impair breathing or result in difficulty swallowing. Furthermore, the neck also houses the upper portion of the spinal cord, which is responsible for transmitting signals between your brain and the rest of your body. An injury to your neck can potentially damage your spinal cord, leading to paralysis or loss of motor function.

To mitigate these risks, sword fighters often wear protective gear called a gorget. The gorget is a collar-like piece of armor that covers your throat and neck, providing protection against attacks aimed at these vulnerable areas. The potential dangers of a strike to your unprotected throat makes a gorget an essential piece of protective gear, which is why it is required to fence at most venues.

This thrust to the throat, from the 2004 LSFA Championships, is a perfect example of 1) how a straight thrust can be faster than a wide, arcing strike, and 2) why you should always wear a gorget when sparring. Luckily, I had good control, and my friend, Joe McLaughlin, was not injured.

Fencing versus Hack and Slash

"Hack and slash" is a term used to describe a style of fighting that incorporates pronounced strikes delivered at long range. Picture two armored combatants with heavy swords taking big swings at each other and protecting themselves with strong blocks. All the drills and principles presented to you in Levels 1 and 2 have been focused on this style of fighting to develop the foundational skills you need to prepare you for more sophisticated methods of sword fighting. The moves used when fencing tend to be smaller and more subtle compared to the hack and slash style. When at long range, fighting is performed in absence of the blade, meaning that the swords only momentarily touch at the moment of impact during a block or parry, then immediately disengage again. Once you are operating at middle range, close enough that you are able to easily touch your opponent with your sword, your opponent is also in range to attack you, therefore it is essential that you engage his sword in order to control it. This type of sword fighting is commonly referred to as classical fencing. Picture two unarmored musketeers dueling with light, fast rapiers. While fencing techniques can be performed with any single-handed sword, the style was developed for and lends itself best to long slender swords such as these.

Center, Centerline, and the Line of Combat

In order to grasp the subtle dynamics of fencing, it is necessary to understand the concepts of center, centerline, and the line of combat. For the sake of this discussion, let's consider the spine as the body's *center*. Your *centerline* is an imaginary line that runs bilaterally straight down the center of your body and extends in a vertical plane in front of you. The *line of combat* is an imaginary line that connects your center with your opponent's center. It represents the most direct path of attack (A). It is usually best to keep your centerline turned toward your opponent. This is because, with your opponent right in front of you, you can make optimal use of both your weapon and your free hand. If you and your opponent are both standing directly in front of each other, however, then neither of you holds a tactical advantage (B). Therefore, your job is to stay off of your opponent's centerline, while keeping your centerline on him. A quick shuffle step to the opponent's left (your right) places you in his deceleration zone, taking away his ability to strike you with maximum force while allowing you to attack him with maximum force. Remember to immediately realign your centerline to the line of combat after your attack to replace and keep your opponent in the middle of your strike zone (C).

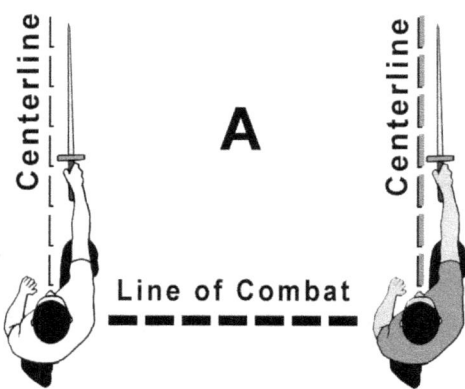

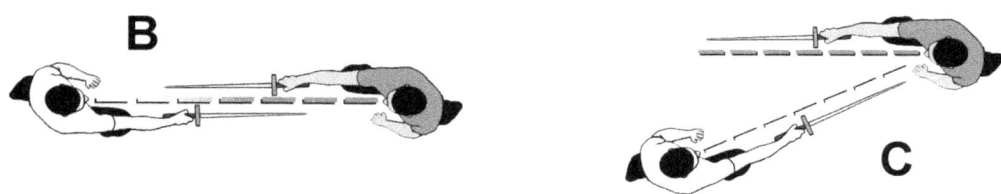

Knowing how to control the line of combat puts you in a strong defensive position while putting your opponent under imminent threat. Keeping your sword aimed at your opponent's throat or face, two targets that are on your opponent's centerline, puts him on the defensive and prevents him from entering striking range without having to first either move or get around your weapon. If your opponent gives up the center to deliver an arcing strike, he opens a line of attack between the tip of your sword and his face or body. Thrust forward quickly into the gap and your straight-line technique should land first.

Engagement and the Bind

If your opponent chooses to fight in absence of the blade, that is, without any sword-to-sword contact, it will be very difficult to control his weapon. To persuade him to engage your sword, assume a true guard, pointing the tip of your sword directly at his face, forcing your opponent to contend with this immediate threat.

It is difficult to find the opponent's blade if your swords are being held parallel to each other. Therefore, angle your sword to cross your opponent's blade at a steeper angle. Once you have found the opponent's blade, your swords are engaged in a bind. Engagement may be very brief, but it is still considerably longer than the momentary contact that results from blocking.

The term *engagement* describes prolonged contact between swords, while the bind describes the particular type of contact being made. When the weak part of your sword is crossing the weak part of your opponent's blade (foible), you are in a light bind (A). When the strong part of your sword contacts the weak part of your opponent's, you have more leverage, allowing you to control the flow of the action. This is called "gaining the blade." (B). When the strong parts of your blades cross, you are in a heavy bind, where you can each exert equal force upon the other's sword (C).

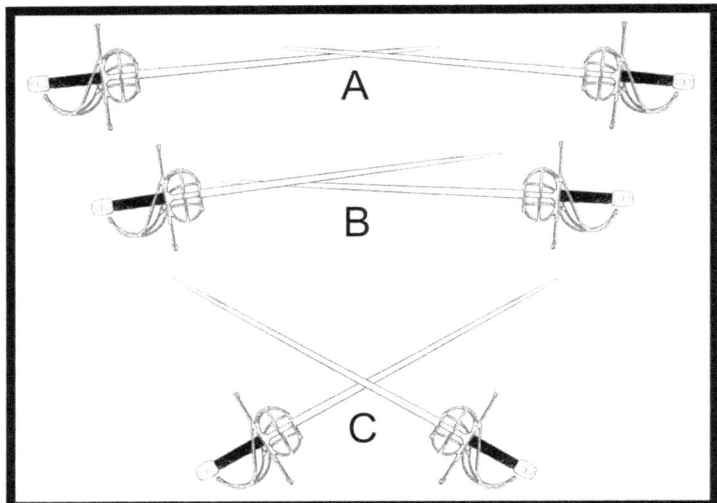

Using heavy pressure from your sword is generally discouraged, as it can easily be turned against you. Whereas light pressure, also described as "soft" or "sticky" energy, allows you to sense any pressure your opponent may exert upon your blade. These subtle, tactile clues from your opponent's blade can reveal your opponent's intentions before you can visually perceive any physical motion. When you are within striking range, you must not leave any open lines that would allow your opponent to land a simple quick cut or thrust. If your opponent's sword is on the left side of your blade, close his primary lines of attack by positioning your blade slightly to the left, aiming your tip at his left shoulder, to create a wall on your left side with your sword. Likewise, if your opponent's blade is on the right side of yours, move your sword slightly to the right to create a defensive wall on your right side, aiming your tip at his right shoulder. Your goal is to simultaneously limit your opponent's ability to attack or defend, while creating an open line of attack for you to strike or thrust with your sword.

Gaining the Opponent's Blade

Gaining control over your opponent's sword literally means that you have control of his weapon. Controlling his weapon begins with the proper positioning of your blade in relation to that of your opponent's. Gaining control usually occurs when your swords are engaged, or crossed. However, it can be advantageous to avoid touching blades too early because any contact with your opponent's blade can alert him as to your next move. If possible, simply float your blade over your opponent's, without touching it, until you are positioned and ready to launch your attack. You want to position your sword so that more of your blade is over less of your opponent's blade. This position puts the strong part of your sword against the weaker part of his, which gives you a mechanical advantage. Positioning your blade over your opponent's blade also allows you to utilize the force of gravity to your benefit. When engaged with your opponent, remember to keep your point on target, both to provide you with immediate threat protection and to set you up for a thrusting attack. When it comes time to engage the opponent's sword, press with your true edge against the flat of his blade. This press not only maximizes your power, it puts your crossguard in position to catch your opponent's blade.

Gaining the Opponent's Blade: Begin at long distance, in absence of the blade (1). To engage with your opponent, extend your sword arm as you shuffle forward to cross swords with your opponent, intentionally placing more of your blade over less of his, while also turning your true edge to the flat of his blade to maximize your mechanical advantage (2).

Glide

There is a saying in sword fighting, "If you are looking down your opponent's blade, you are already dead." Likewise, if your opponent is looking directly down your blade, your sword has an open line of attack. Knowing how to *glide* will help you take advantage of and be in control of this open line of attack. Once you have gained your opponent's blade, quickly thrust straight forward into the gap, without pulling back or losing cohesion with his sword. When performed with proper timing, your sword will *glide* along the opponent's blade, checking it without displacing it, driving the tip of your sword into the target with little or no opposition.

The Glide: You have gained the opponent's blade (1). Subtly maneuver your blade so that the tip of your sword is pointed directly at your opponent. As soon as you are in proper alignment, straighten your arm, your lead foot following close behind as you do, and slide along the opponent's sword without moving it significantly. As you then thrust forward, turn your sword slightly so the opponent's blade is caught by your crossguard. (2)

The Cone of Defense

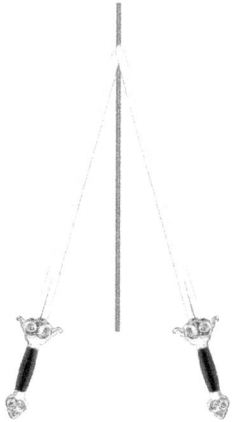

Your opponent will naturally attempt to get around your defense. When he does, you must reposition your sword to check his blade, while keeping your tip pointed toward him to maintain a constant threat. This dual movement can be accomplished using the four hand positions that form the Cone of Defense.

If you imagine looking at a clockface, when you are in middle guard with your sword held on your centerline, your sword hand is at 6 o'clock. Position 1 is the high outside position, with your hand at about 2 o'clock. Move your hand down to about 4 o'clock, and you are in position 2. Likewise, if you block to the inside, moving your hand to the left to about 8 o'clock, you are in position 3. Continue to rotate your hand to about 10 o'clock to cover your left highline, and you are in position 4.

These four positions are merely reference points. In reality, each position defends a broader area. For example, while in position 1, your hand is held at about 2 o'clock, but it can move to cover anywhere from 12 to 3 o'clock. It follows then that position 2 covers the inside midline from 3 to 6 o'clock, position 3 covers the right outside midline, from 6 to 9 o'clock, and position 4 covers your outside highline, from 9 to 12 o'clock.

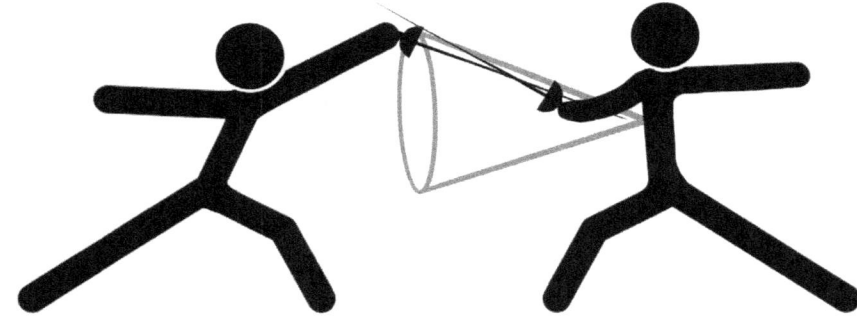

The four positions that comprise the Cone of Defense: Position 1 blocks the high outside quadrant, anywhere from 12 to 3 o'clock. Position 2 covers your low outside line, from 3 to 6 'clock. Position 3 defends your low inside quadrant, from 6 to 9 o'clock. Position 4 defends your high inside quadrant, from 9 to 12 o'clock

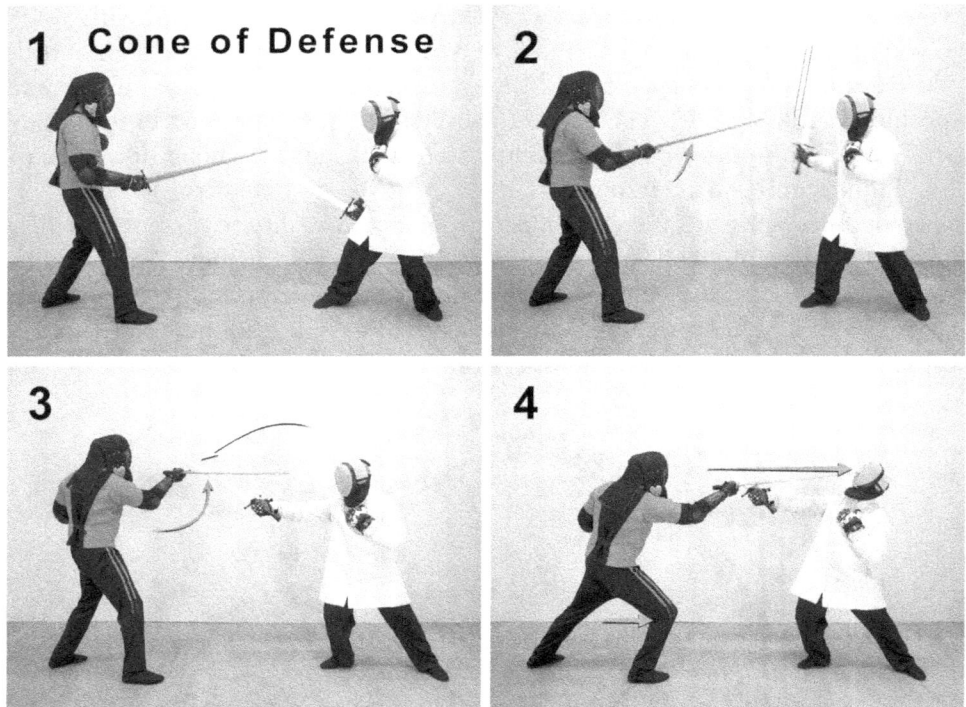

Cone of Defense against a Forehand Strike: Face off against your opponent, watching for any movements that telegraph his intentions (1). When the opponent withdraws his sword, giving away his intention to strike, turn and move the hilt of your sword to follow his blade (2). As the opponent strikes, block his attack using the Cone of Defense position #4 (3). Immediately thrust forward into the opponent's open high line (4).

Cone of Defense against a Backhand Strike: Block using Cone of Defense position 1, keeping the tip of your sword aimed at the opponent (1). Maintain checking the opponent's blade as you thrust forward with your sword and shift simultaneously into a forward stance (2).

LEVEL 3: SHORT SWORD FENCING   109

Cone of Defense against a Low Backhand Strike: Face off against your opponent, watching for any movements that telegraph his intentions (1). The opponent withdraws his sword, giving away his intention to strike. Move the hilt of your sword to follow his blade (2). As the opponent strikes, block his attack using Cone of Defense position #2 (3). Immediately thrust forward into the opponent's open high line (4).

Press

When you apply pressure to displace your opponent's blade while maintaining cohesion in order to control it, it is called a *press*. From an engaged position, extend your sword arm to intercept the weak part of your opponent's blade with the middle part of yours. This positioning gives you a mechanical advantage in leverage that allows you to press, or push, the opponent's sword sideways as you thrust into the resulting opening.

When you press the opponent's blade, it is common for him to press back in return. If you are expecting this, you can use his own energy against him. For example, you press the opponent's sword, and he presses back to reclaim the line. When he does, you circle under his sword and pop up on its opposite side, thereby making a change of engagement (techniques which you will be learning in the next few pages) before gliding forward with a thrust, driving the tip of your sword into the target.

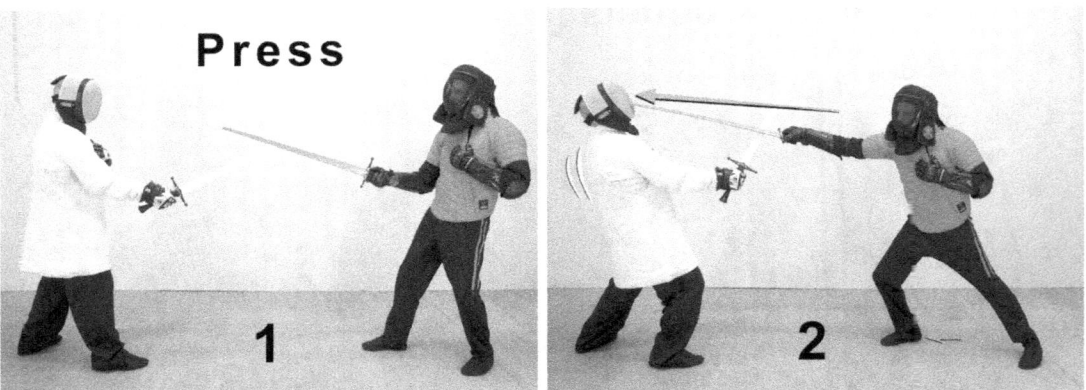

Press: You have gained the opponent's blade, but he is maintaining his centerline (1). Keeping the tip of your sword pointing at his face, turn your true edge against the flat of your opponent's blade and press his blade off the line, as you extend your arm and lunge forward (2).

Beat

Beating entails striking the opponent's sword in order to disrupt his defenses and open up a viable line of attack. To beat the opponent's sword, hit it with a quick, sharp half strike. For maximum effect, strike to the weakest part of the opponent's sword, hitting as close to the end of his sword as possible. Hitting near the hands doesn't work as well because the sword is stronger structurally there, so the strike results in less movement of the opponent's sword. Don't overcommit when executing a beat, since you will have but an instant to take advantage of the opening you created. Optimally, after a beat, your sword will still be on the Line of Combat, pointed at your opponent and in position to thrust forward into the target.

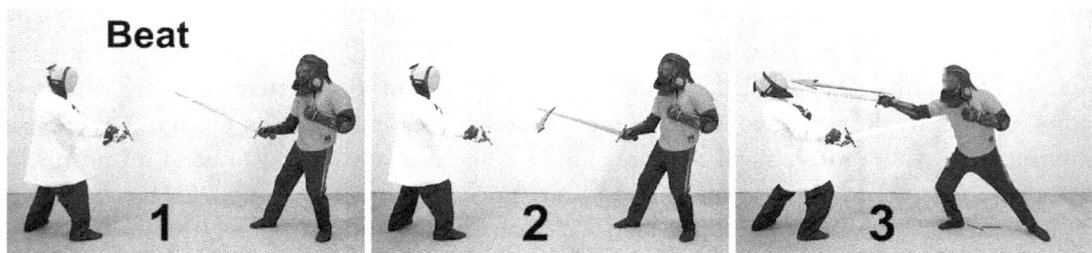

Beat: Your blades are engaged, and your opponent is holding center (1). Using as small a motion as possible, knock the opponent's blade to the side, without following it to hold center (2). Immediately thrust forward before the opponent can reengage (3).

Change of Engagement

The change of engagement, also called a cut under, is useful in maintaining control over your opponent's sword. The change entails separating ever so slightly from, and circling around, your opponent's sword in order to create an open line of attack. It is used when your sword makes contact with your opponent's sword and he pushes laterally against your sword in an effort to control it.

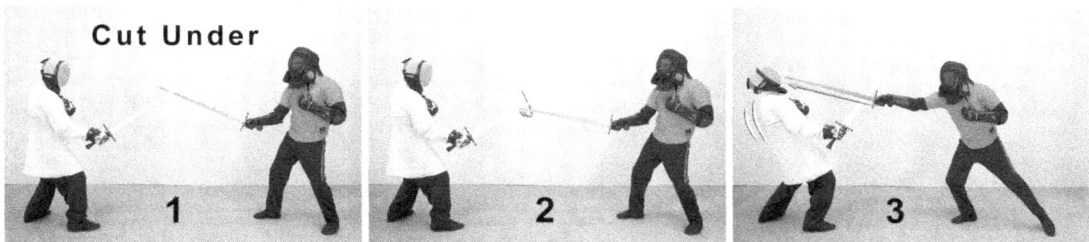

Change of Engagement: To execute a change of engagement, you must be sensitive to changes in pressure on your sword (1). As soon as you feel your opponent's sword pressing on yours, relax, sneak the tip of your sword under your opponent's blade in a tight circular motion (2). You must execute a strike or thrust immediately after suddenly and unexpectedly appearing on the other side, before your opponent can react with a block or attempt to reclaim the center (3).

Double Change

The double change consists of a combination of two consecutive changes of engagement performed in quick succession. Your first change is actually a feint. It causes the opponent to over-block in an attempt to protect his threatened line. When he does, you perform a second change, returning to your original line of attack. When done properly, your sword hand hardly moves. Don't worry about making contact with the opponent's sword between changes. If you counter quickly with a thrust or strike, your opponent will have trouble blocking or reclaiming the center.

Double Change: Press on your opponent's blade, causing him to press back in an attempt to hold the center (1). Make a change of engagement (2). When the opponent moves his sword to find your blade, cut under his blade again (3). Lunge forward with a thrust before your opponent can recover (4).

Cut Over

The cut over is similar to the change of engagement except that, instead of passing under your opponent's blade, you go over its tip. This technique is used whenever the tip of your opponent's sword is close to your blade, making it more economical to pass over his tip with your blade than passing under his blade with your tip. You must move quickly, raising your sword only enough to clear the tip of his sword, immediately delivering a strike or thrust along the open line before your opponent can parry your attack. It helps to think of this as a scissoring motion, pulling up only to quickly cut down along the same line.

LEVEL 3: SHORT SWORD FENCING 113

Cut Over: You find yourself engaged with more of your blade over your opponent's blade, making it faster to cut over than to cut under (1). Raise the tip of your sword to lift your blade over your opponent's, straightening your arm as you clear his blade (2). As you complete your thrust, turn your sword to check his blade with your crossguard (3).

Parry

A parry redirects the opponent's weapon without stopping it, making it an exceptionally useful defense against thrusting attacks. The parry intercepts the opponent's sword and moves it off its intended line of attack. Blocking stops the opponent's sword; however, parrying uses the momentum of the opponent's attack against him. While it is possible to parry after a block, once you have stopped the opponent's sword, it takes time and energy to get your sword moving again. Therefore, it is better to deflect his sword while it is still in motion, without blocking it. A good parry can add unexpected force to the opponent's strike, carrying his sword further than intended. So, once you have parried the opponent's sword, you must quickly strike to an open target before he can regain his guard.

There are three types of parry: the small parry, which moves horizontally, from side-to-side; the semi-circular parry, which changes levels from highline to lowline; and the full circular parry, which starts at the highline, then moves through the lowline, only to return to the highline.

Since the human body is taller than it is wide, it is easiest to use the small parry because it allows you to redirect the strike clear of your body with a small motion, since your body is thinner than it is tall. Against a right-handed opponent, it is generally safer to parry your opponent's sword to your right because it places you behind him. Parry with the middle of your blade and avoid parrying with the flat. By parrying with the edge, you minimize the contact between the blades, thus maximizing the amount of pressure you can exert on your opponent's sword. This blade alignment is accomplished through proper hand positioning. Only parry as far as needed to expose an open line of attack. Over parrying can leave you exposed and out of position to quickly riposte.

Semi-Circular Parry: A semi-circular parry moves the opponent's blade from the middle line to the low line, or vise-versa. For example, you have gained the opponent's blade in a middle inside guard (1). Parry the opponent's blade in a counterclockwise circle, downward to his outside, pressing forward to cut his exposed lead leg.

Circular Parry: A circular parry redirects your opponent's sword in a complete circle, returning to the original line without ever losing cohesion. Begin by gaining the opponent's blade (1). Use your mechanical advantage to push the opponent's sword down in a counterclockwise circle (2). Continue the circular motion, advancing your sword as you do so (3). By the time your sword returns to the original line, you should be in position to land an attack (4).

Optimal Learning Zone

You want to train as realistically as possible, yet at a rate that is conducive to optimal learning. As a training partner, you do not want to resist so much that your partner cannot successfully apply a technique, or he can't learn. However, if you do not resist enough and just let him score easily, he will never learn how to properly apply the technique. So how hard should you fight with your partner during practice? The answer is that you want to train as realistically as possible, yet at a rate that is conducive to learning. To maximize your growth, studies have shown that you want to train at a pace where you are successful between 50 and 80 percent of the time. This is called the Goldilocks Rule, because it is "just right." Any easier, and you are not being adequately challenged. Any harder, and you get discouraged. As frustration begins to set in, your growth is hindered.

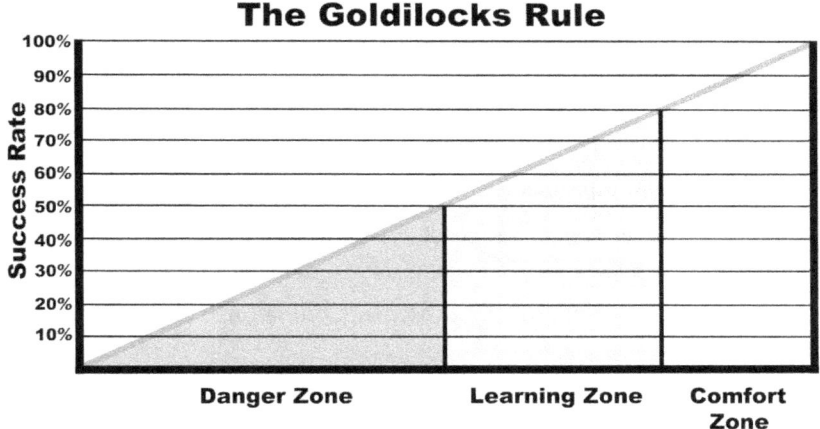

The Goldilocks Rule: The Comfort Zone (too easy) has an 80–100 percent success rate. The Learning Zone (just right) has a 50–80 percent success rate. The Danger Zone (too hard) has a less than 50 percent success rate.

A Sample Bout

Fencing is not unlike a game of physical chess. By examining a match, you can learn a great deal about the strategy and tactics of the game. Like chess, there are practically infinite possible combinations that could play out, too many to include here. The following example, however, will provide you with a good sampling of a skilled exchange. Work through it with a partner, taking turns playing the different roles, just as chess students replay old games between grandmasters to learn their strategies and tactics.

1) Swordsman A faces off against Swordsman B, beginning well out of range.

2) As the fighters approach the edge of the Circle of Death, Swordsman A assumes a middle guard, pointing the tip of his sword at B's face. Swordsman B responds by assuming middle guard as well.

3) As the fighters cross into range, the weak parts of their swords engage in an outside position. Swordsman A extends his arm to gain control of B's blade by crossing more of his blade over B's blade than B has over A's blade, giving Swordsman A the mechanical advantage which he uses to press B's sword to the outside.

4) Swordsman B counters A's gain with a change of engagement, passing her tip under A's blade to reengage it on the opposite side. The fighter's swords are now crossed on the inside.

5) Swordsman A moves into Cone of Defense position 4 and uses his edge to press B's blade to the left, in an attempt to claim the inside line.

6) Swordsman B responds by flowing into a double change of engagement, dipping the tip of her sword under A's blade again and moving the swords back into an outside position.

7) Swordsman A responds by moving back to middle guard, closing B's line of attack. This is immediately followed by a lunge forward with a pressing thrust to B's chest.

8) Swordsman B moves out of range of A's thrust by retreating into a cat stance and, having gained A's blade, uses a small parry to deflect it to her right.

9) Swordsman B then counters with a thrusting cut along the open high line, attacking A's head.

10) Caught out of position and unable to defend, Swordsman A suffers a blow to the head. Swordsman B immediately retreats, covering her retreat with her sword as she moves safely out of range.

Level 3 Workout

This 60-to-90-minute workout is designed to develop your fencing skills with a single-handed sword.

1. Warm-Up: 15–20 minutes. Start with five minutes of light stretching for your upper and lower body. Follow this with five minutes of cardio work, such as jumping rope, jogging in place, or doing jumping jacks. Strive to maintain a high activity level until you feel tired and your heartrate becomes elevated. Then, do five more minutes of light stretching until your heart rate returns to normal. Next, grab your sword and work through some basic footwork as you practice your blocks, parries, cuts, and thrusts at the same time, first slowly then gradually speeding up.

2. The Cone of Defense: 10–15 minutes.
Drill 1: Practice all four hand positions.
Drill 2: Lunge forward moving from position 2 to position 3.
Drill 3: Clear a stationary sword while lunging, moving from 2 to 3.
Drill 4: Clear a thrust while lunging, moving from 2 to 3.
Drill 5: Same drill, but clear the thrust and stab your partner at the same time.

Begin moving slowly in Drills 1 to 5, until you have the mechanics of the techniques correct, then gradually add speed and power to each drill. While you might be tempted to train without full gear, especially when you are going slowly, it is recommended that you suit up for safety.

3. Fencing Drills: 20–25 minutes. Work through the various techniques presented in Level 3 with a partner. Start by practicing engaging your partner's blade. Once engaged, play gently for control of the center line using the glide and press. At first, you get to play the part of the aggressor, thrusting forward when you see an opening, while your training partner moves to defend the open line. Then, switch roles. Remember, the goal is to drill and develop good habits, not score points on your partner. Sometimes your thrust will land, sometimes it won't. Shoot for the Goldilocks zone of a 70–80 percent success rate. Missing one in four or five actually promotes learning and makes you better. Start moving slowly, gradually increasing the speed and intensity. Work together to maximize your mutual learning experiences. Switch roles and repeat.

Next, take turns practicing the change of engagement. Such practice could consist of a cut over or a cut under the opponent's blade, depending on the positioning of the swords. Then, practice the double change while your partner defends. Your partner should retreat as you advance to maintain correct fencing distance. Reverse roles and repeat the drill. Then, practice using the beat to open a line of attack, while your partner attempts to defend.

Finally, put all the techniques together as you practice with your partner, using each to their best effect as a situation arises requiring them. Remember, these are drills, not sparring. Keep the focus on developing your execution of the techniques and strategies. The idea is to practice many repetitions with the focus on developing optimal technique. If you are worried about scoring and being scored upon, you cannot focus on learning and performing the techniques to the best of your ability.

4. Sparring: 10–15 minutes. The only way to know what techniques work best under what conditions is to test them out against a non-compliant opponent. Maintain a strong defense at all times, then focus on analyzing your opponent's defense and exploiting his weaknesses to land specific moves. Even though you should be wearing full safety equipment when you spar, you should still control the strength of your strikes and take care not to injure your training partner. A good guideline is to not hit your partner any harder than you want to be hit.

5. Cool Down: 5–10 minutes. Take a few minutes to take your body from "Fight or Flight" into "Rest and Digest." Stretch to increase your flexibility and break up the lactic acid that has accumulated in your muscles. This will help you recover faster and feel better for your next workout!

6. Follow-Up: When you are done, record each of your workouts in a training log. Include how long you trained and a short synopsis of the material you covered in the session. Set a goal for yourself, such as performing the above workout ten times before moving on to Level 4. You've come a long way already. Stay motivated, remain disciplined, be consistent, and work hard. Level 4 is where you get to apply and hone all of your sword fighting skills.

By now, you hopefully have a copy of *The Art and Science of Sword Fighting* companion video series. As you read the book, you should be watching the video lessons and doing the homework assignments provided at the end of each lesson.

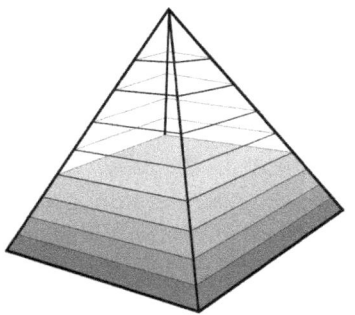

LEVEL 4:
Advanced Short Sword

Training Equipment: Lower Body Protection

By this time in your training, your upper body should be well protected. You should have gloves to protect your hands, a mask to protect your head, and a jacket to protect your torso and arms. However, your legs are targets as well. Therefore, it is recommended that you protect your lower body also, specifically by using protective gear for your hips, legs, and groin.

While a long gambeson or fencing jacket can offer some protection for your hips and thighs, you may benefit from additional protective gear specially made to protect your lower body. Hockey pants are a common solution, as are padded breeches specifically designed for HEMA. Both have built-in padding or additional layers of protective fabric in vulnerable areas like the hips, thighs, and knees. However, these short knicker-like pants usually do not protect your lower legs. Therefore, leg guards, also called greaves, are needed to protect your shins and ankles. Leg guards are made from plastic, leather, or metal.

Another lower body protection option is the *tare*, a skirt-like hip protector common to Japanese kendo. The tare is worn around your waist like a belt and has protective flaps that protect your groin and upper thighs.

While the groin is not a legal target in competition, the unfortunate truth is that accidents happen, and the groin gets hit. A direct strike or impact to the groin can cause intense pain and potentially serious injury for both men and women. Therefore, groin protection in the form of an athletic cup should be an essential part of your sword fighting gear. Athletic cups are designed to absorb and redistribute the force of impacts, greatly reducing your risk of injury.

The Outside Game

This offensive long-range strategy is simple: attack by striking the closest available target at your longest range, while maintaining maximum distance between you and your opponent. The first targets to cross into your Circle of Death are usually your opponent's lead arm and leg.

When targeting the leg, aim for the lead knee. Be ready to attack as soon as your opponent moves into your circle. To prevent your opponent from simply stepping back out of range, try to anticipate his advance. If you can catch him mid-stride as he enters, it will be difficult for him to withdraw his leg before your strike lands. Remember that attacking your opponent's low line leaves your high line open and your head exposed. Therefore, it is essential that you strike from your maximum hitting range to avoid any counter cut. As always, be prepared to capitalize on the success or failure of your initial strike. If your strike misses, be prepared to maintain the initiative by flowing directly into a second attack. If your attack is successful, quickly move back out of range to avoid your opponent's counterattack.

When targeting the hand, full strikes can leave you exposed should your attack fail. Therefore, use half strikes when attacking the hand. Returning quickly to your original guarded position in between your half strikes minimizes the amount of time you are exposed.

A good strategy for a hand-snipe is to aim for the forearm because, if you're slightly off target or the opponent withdraws, your strike will still land. In addition, if your first cut misses, you can use a double strike to make a second, unexpected attack to the same target. If your opponent avoided your strike by pulling his hands back and out of range, compensate by leaning in slightly farther with your second strike.

Keep in mind that merely striking the opponent's weapon hand may not be enough to end the confrontation. Be prepared to either continue striking or quickly move safely out of range.

Outside Game: You and your opponent are facing off just out of range. Your opponent notices that your lead leg is extended and exposed (1). As he attacks, pull your lead foot back, out of range of his attack, simultaneously striking his weapon hand (2). This is also a good example of baiting and drawing

Baiting and Drawing

A cautious opponent will not simply enter into your Circle of Death in an attempt to strike you; he must be enticed into making a rash move. Baiting and drawing are strategies in which you purposely leave an opening in an attempt to get your opponent to attack you. While this may seem counterintuitive, it can be useful to create an opening for you to counterattack, and, since you are expecting the attack, you will be prepared to evade or defend.

Control the fight by subtly setting up your opponent. A setup can be done by *drawing an attack*. Begin by readying your mind to set the trap. You must be prepared to retract the bait before you even put it out. Next, leave an opening your opponent can exploit and will find hard to resist. As soon as the opponent makes his attack, retract the bait and hit him where you know he is vulnerable.

For example, since a right-to-left downward diagonal strike is the habitual method of attack, there is a very good chance that you can draw a right high strike from your opponent by leaving your head slightly exposed. Lure your opponent into striking your head using this habitual method of attack by gradually relaxing your guard. If this posture draws no response, try extending your empty hand a little or leaning your head forward slightly. This setup is an easier sell if you can do it while moving. Be careful not to be too obvious, though, as the opponent must believe your deception if you are to successfully draw him into taking the bait and attacking you. Make your motions *look* as though you are being careless and relaxing your guard, when in actuality it is only an act. Know that you are psychologically manipulating your opponent into making the strike that *you* want him to make, allowing you to predict where his hand will be at a particular moment in time before he even launches his attack.

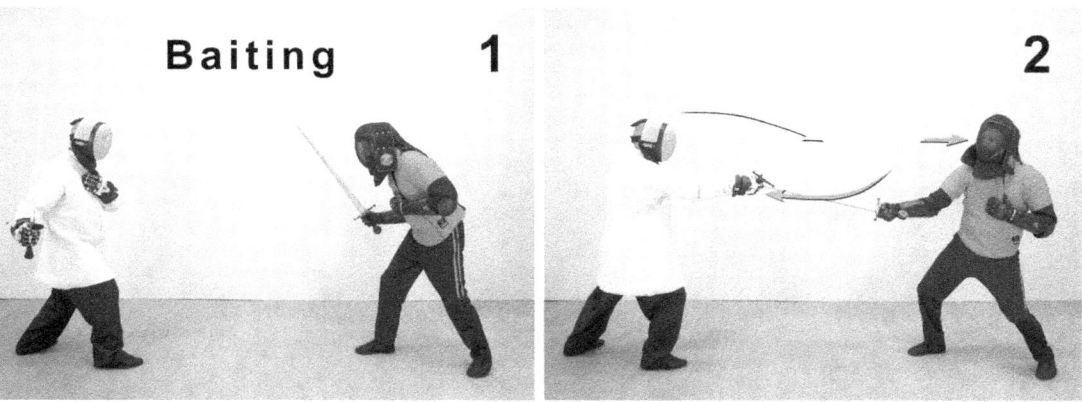

Baiting: Lure your opponent into striking by leaning your head forward slightly (1). As soon as he takes the bait, lean back out of range to avoid his strike, simultaneously striking his hand (2).

Never forget that when you attempt to draw an attack you are placing yourself in a perilous position. If the opponent takes the bait, he will strike fast and hard, and he may do so the instant you offer it. You must be fully prepared to react to your opponent *before* setting the trap, being ready to block or evade the instant he strikes.

> Hold out baits to entice the enemy. Feign disorder, and then crush him. Pretend inferiority and encourage his arrogance.
> —Sun Tzu, *The Art of War*

Feinting

A feint is a fake attack. Feinting is an excellent way to create an open line of attack. It begins with an attack that seems to the opponent like a committed one, causing him to react. As he does, cut your first technique short and launch a second attack from a different direction, while the opponent is still committed to the defense of the first. If your opponent does not defend against your initial feint, then it simply becomes a strike, which is why your first strike must be a real attack. In order for your feint to be successful, your opponent must perceive and be threatened by your initial attack. If your opponent does not understand that your action is threatening him, you will not get the reaction you are looking for.

When feinting, stay committed to your initial attack until you see that the opponent is sufficiently committed to his block and that it will be difficult for him to quickly change his initiated plan of action. Then, quickly and smoothly change your strike to a second target area. If timed properly, your second strike will come in on the half-beat, meaning between the count of one for your first strike and the expected count of two for a typically timed second strike, giving your opponent no time to react.

LEVEL 4: ADVANCED SHORT SWORD

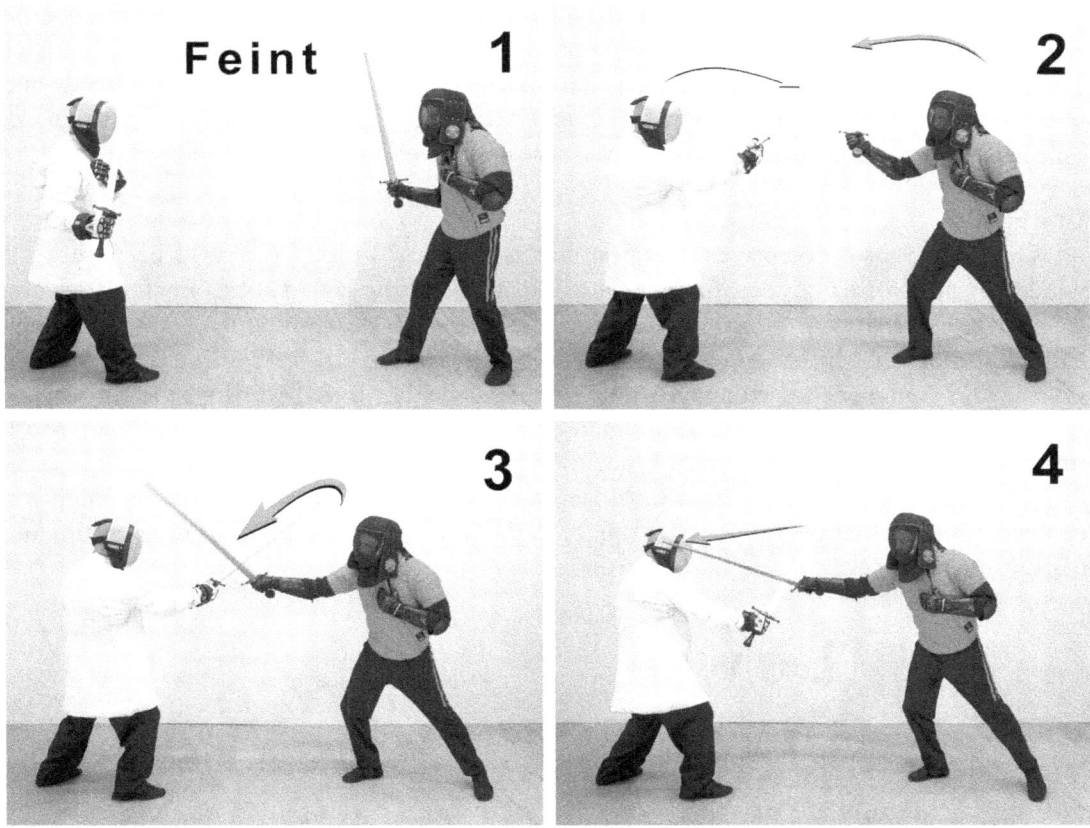

Feint: You begin facing off against your opponent, each of you in a loaded guard (1). Initiate an attack to the opponent's undefended left highline. He moves to close the line with a high block, as you expected and wanted him to do (2). As soon as you are sure that he is committed to his block, cut around his blade with a flick of your wrist (3). Complete your attack, striking along his now open right high line (4).

Trick Guards

Up until now, we have worked mainly from the two true guards (middle and hanging) and the six loaded guards (inside/outside, high/middle/low). While these guards are essential standard guards and should be mastered, they are not the only ones available to you. Trick guards are not designed to protect you. Instead, they are traps that deceive your opponent into brashly attacking you, hence the name *trick* guards. Trick guards are also a type of psychological control. You are the one making your opponent attack where and when you want, predicting his movements, and fully expecting him to strike, all the while being ready with your response.

Assuming a trick guard at the beginning of a fight, before your swords engage, makes your intentions obvious. Instead of starting from a trick guard, allowing your opponent to study your position and potentially figure out your plan, it is more effective to adopt a trick guard suddenly, in the midst of combat. Your opponent is far more likely to get greedy and take the bait in the heat of the moment. Even experienced fighters can fall for a trick guard, especially when it is suddenly and unexpectedly interjected into the thick of the fight.

Low Guard

One of the most deceptive ready positions is the fool's guard, so named because while you leave your entire body seemingly exposed to attack, as the saying goes, only fools rush in. In the fool's guard, your sword is held at middle level with the tip pointing down. Strategically, lowering the tip of your sword opens a potential and irresistible line of attack that invites your opponent to strike your now undefended high line. In reality, the tip of your sword is close to your opponent and a mere flex of your wrist can lift the tip of your sword into his path as he moves to attack. Once the opponent begins stepping forward, he is committed to moving in that direction until he can replant his foot. If your timing is good, you can catch him midstride, hitting him square in the face or chest, killing his momentum and disrupting his attack.

Low Guard Practice: Begin standing out of range. Drop your sword to bait your opponent into attacking (1). As soon as the opponent moves to attack, lunge forward as you raise the tip of your sword (2).

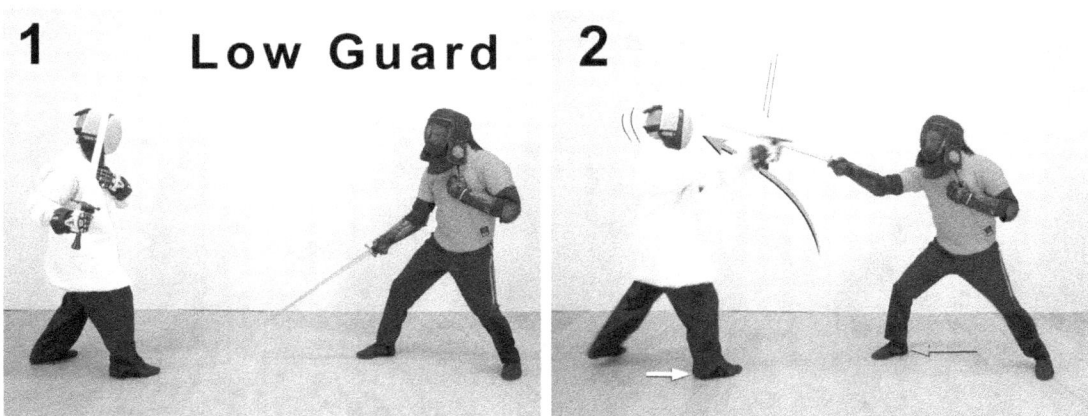

Low Guard Application: Begin standing out of range. Drop your sword to bait your opponent into attacking. This move is most effective when quickly inserted between other techniques (1). As soon as the opponent moves to attack, lunge forward as you raise the tip of your sword (2). When performed with good timing, the opponent impales himself upon your sword.

Rear High Guard

The rear guard was the signature defensive stance of the 19th century French stick fighter, Pierre Vigny and was described in "L'art de la Canne," an article first published in 1912.

The Vigny guard position is, in essence, a combat guard. The left arm is held in front as if bearing a shield; the right arm is raised at the rear, with the weapon held above the head, in a perpetual "spring hold."

"When you are being attacked, quickly retreat with a swift guard change and bring your cane down powerfully upon the opponent's arm or hand. In doing this, you can be mathematically certain of reaching and damaging your target."

Standing and holding your sword up in the air with your rear hand, on purpose, leaves you exposed to an attack, and leading with your empty hand limits your range and offers your opponent another tempting target. When he takes you up on one of these perfect invitations and attacks you, you can either step forward with your rear foot to suddenly and unexpectedly close the gap or step back with your front foot to maintain proper distancing, in case your opponent rushes you. Switching guards so that your sword is now in your front hand and loaded to attack is another maneuver that places you in a strong position. As with all tricks, you must take care not to overuse your ploy, or your opponent will catch on to your trickeries.

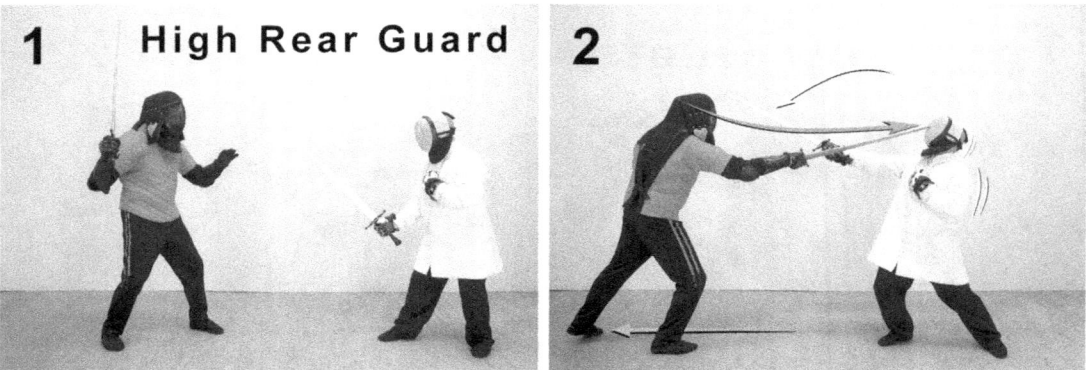

High Rear Guard: Set yourself up by leading with your off-side foot. If you are careful, you can use your off hand as bait (1). As the opponent attacks, step your front foot back as you swing your sword for his lead hand or head… or both (2)!

Low Rear Guard

You can also adopt a low rear guard defense, commonly referred to as a tail guard. The tail guard works in the same way as the high rear guard, but, since the tip of your sword is low, you seem even more vulnerable and defenseless to your opponent. When your opponent moves to attack, make a full passing step forward with your rear foot, or backward with your front foot, to switch your guard and go suddenly on the attack, the most economical of which would be a diagonal upward strike with your sword.

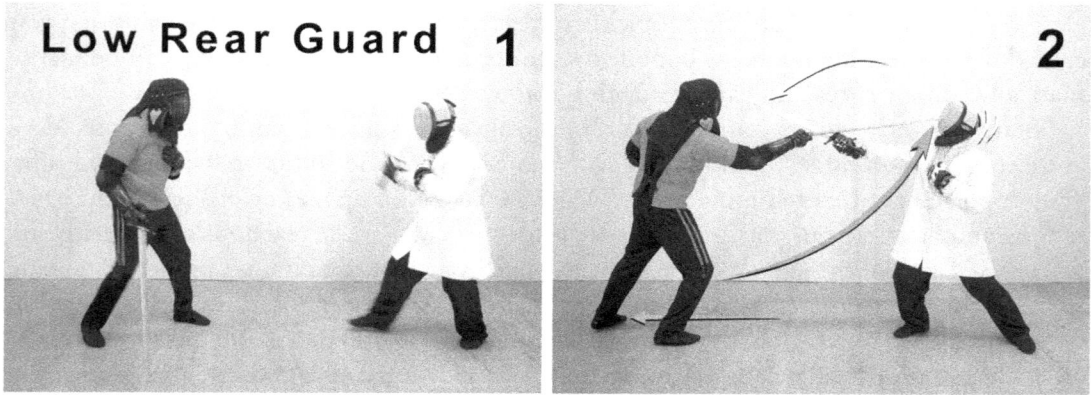

Low Rear Guard: Set yourself up by leading with your off-side foot. Drop your sword tip and let it drift off to the side, leaving your high left line open to attack. This baiting technique is most effective when suddenly inserted between other moves (1). As the opponent takes the bait, step your front foot back and raise your sword to strike him in the head (2).

Fancy Footwork

Outmaneuvering your opponent is a critical element of successful sword fighting. You have already learned the basic stances and movement patterns, but if your opponent is using similar footwork, he may be able to counter your attempts to close the range to attack him. Therefore, it helps to have some unexpected tricks up your sleeve. Here are a few ways to cross the gap and land an attack before your opponent can move out of range.

Revisiting the Lunge

You already learned the lunge back in Level 1; however, lunging is so important when fencing that it is worth revisiting to examine some of its finer points. As you know, lunging is primarily used offensively because it allows you to maximize your range to deliver a fast and powerful thrust. A well-executed lunge allows you to suddenly close the distance between you and your opponent with a single quick step, hopefully catching your opponent off guard and making it difficult for him to parry or counterattack.

When performed correctly, the lunge also adds a significant amount of power to your attack. This power can increase your chances of penetrating your opponent's defense. However, keep in mind that you need to recover quickly after a lunge to defend against possible counterattacks. To recover quickly you must push backward off the ball of your front foot, as you contract your adductors strongly, to pull your front leg back. If your opponent retreats out of range of your initial lunge, you can recover your ground by stepping your back foot forward, which also chambers you to lunge with your front foot and thrust again.

Training and practice are essential for developing a quick, effective lunge. Practice slowly at first, lunging well short of your maximum range. As you warm up and your muscles are able to stretch more, lunge deeper and reach farther with your sword tip. At maximum extension, your rear leg should be straight with your lead knee bent deeply at about a 90-degree angle but not extended past the toes of your front foot.

Incorporating lunges into your repertoire can vary your attack patterns enough to keep your opponent guessing, making it harder for him to anticipate and defend against your attacks. This confusion that *you* create can give you a strategic advantage because it disrupts your opponent's rhythm and forces him to adjust his defensive tactics.

Hop-Lunge

The hop-lunge, also known as a ballestra, is an aggressive advancing technique used to surprise and overwhelm your opponent. It requires precise timing, coordination, and a good sense of distance.

Hop-Lunge Practice: Starting from outside of the Circle of Death (1), hop your rear foot forward, replacing your front foot (2). At the same time, unweight your front foot (3) so that you can immediately lunge forward and thrust into the target (4).

Hop-Lunge Application: Begin outside of range, causing your opponent to temporarily relax his guard (1). Quickly hop into range, skipping your rear foot forward to replace your front foot (2). Press off your rear foot, lunging forward with a straight thrust, striking before your opponent can defend himself (3).

Master Cuts and Thrusts

A master cut in sword fighting is a highly skilled, precise technique used to counter an opponent's attack and defeat them in the same motion. Master cuts combine two concepts that you've already learned: jamming blocks from Level 2 and the Cone of Defense from Level 3. Jamming blocks and the Cone of Defense each take two moves to defend and counterattack, while master cuts are performed in one, swift movement that exploits a weakness in an opponent's defenses by using it to simultaneously check the opponent's weapon and deliver a powerful and decisive blow. Master cuts typically involve a combination of precise footwork, impeccable timing, and a deep understanding of the mechanics of sword fighting. When performed correctly, master cuts and thrusts are both unexpected and difficult to counter. However, as the name implies, master cuts can require years of training and practice to perfect, or master, as do thrusts.

Whether delivered high, middle, or low to the inside or to the outside, master cuts must accomplish two things at the same time: defending and attacking. First, you must defend yourself by checking the opponent's sword. This check is done with the forte, or the strong part of the sword, closer to the hilt. Second, your sword must simultaneously strike a vulnerable target area on the opponent using the foible or distal end of your blade. Striking with the end of the sword closer to the tip allows you to utilize the full range of your sword and maximizes the length of the lever, both of which together allow you to strike the target with maximum force.

Just as there are master cuts, there are master thrusts, too. The basic idea of a simultaneous attack and defense is the same in a master thrust, only now your attack is more linear since it is a stab with the tip rather than cut with the edge of the blade.

High Inside Master Cut: Face off against your opponent, watching for any movements that telegraph your opponent's intentions to deliver a high forehand strike (1). Your opponent withdraws his sword, giving away his intention to strike. Move the hilt of your sword to follow his blade (2). As the opponent strikes, block his attack using the Cone of Defense position 4, as you simultaneously thrust forward into the opponent's open high line (3).

High Master Cut

High Outside Master Cut: Face off against your opponent, watching for any movements that telegraph his intentions to deliver a high backhand strike (1). Your opponent withdraws his sword, giving away his intention to strike (2). As the opponent strikes, simultaneously block his strike and cut across his face using the Cone of Defense position 1 (3).

Low Master Thrust

Low Outside Master Thrust: Face off against your opponent, watching for any movements that telegraph his intentions to deliver a low backhand strike (1). Your opponent withdraws his sword, giving away his intention to strike. Move the hilt of your sword to follow his blade (2). As the opponent strikes, block his attack using the Cone of Defense position 2 as you simultaneously thrust forward into the open high line (3).

In-Fighting

You are in close range when you can touch any part of your opponent's body with your free hand. This close-range position opens up new avenues of attack, including immobilizing and disarming the opponent's sword; however, first you need to learn how to work the bind.

The Heavy Bind

As we mentioned in Level 3, a heavy bind is created when the strong parts of your blades cross, locking together close to the hilt, allowing you each to exert equal force upon the other's sword. Unlike the unrealistic binds you see in the movies, when the combatants have a conversation while their blades are locked between them, a bind only lasts an instant in reality. No matter how long it occurs, there are several techniques that can *only* be performed in that instance, including striking with the pommel of your sword, striking with your free hand, grabbing, disarming, kicking, and foot sweeping. Hence the reason why you need to know how to bind, how to use a bind, and how to get out of a bind.

Binding: You stand across from your opponent, your swords engaged (1). Make a full step forward with your rear foot, quickly closing the gap between you and your opponent (2). Your swords will run along each other until they stop at the crossguards. You are now in a high heavy bind (3).

Pommel Strike

Pommel strikes can be effective in close combat situations where there isn't enough room to use the full range of your sword's blade effectively. A sudden strike with the pommel can surprise and stun your opponent, making him more vulnerable to follow-up attacks. While executing the pommel strike, it is important to check your opponent's sword first, which can be done either by using your free hand to grab and control his weapon hand or by maintaining cohesion between your blades and checking the opponent's sword throughout your attack.

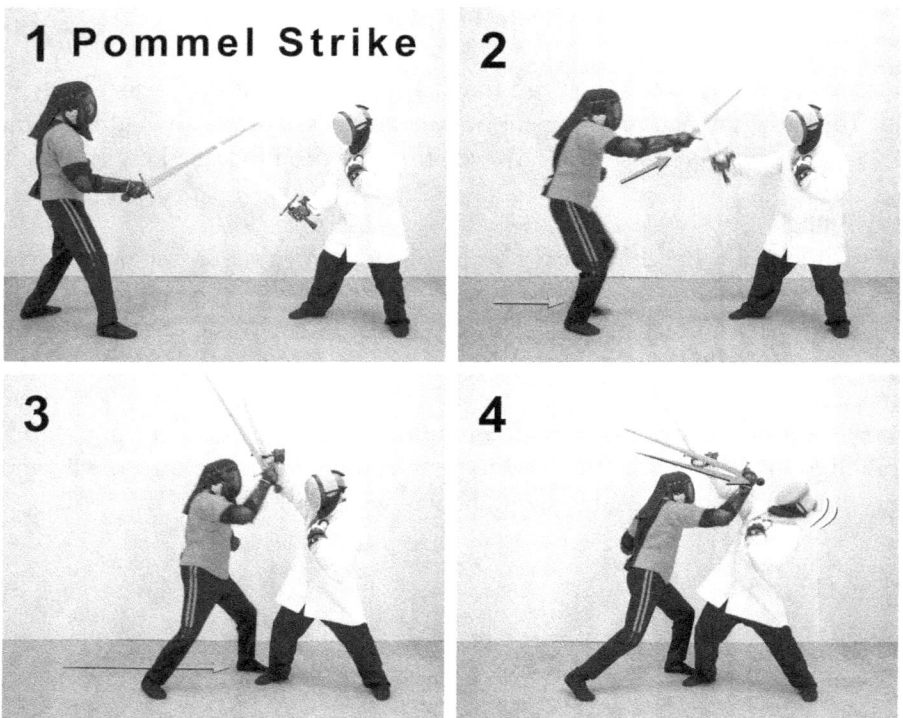

Pommel Strike: Begin with your swords engaged at middle distance (1). Step forward as you slide your sword up his blade, resulting in a heavy bind (2). Check his blade with your own as you continue driving the handle forward (3). Maintain your check on your opponent's sword as you strike him in the face with the pommel of your sword (4).

Striking with Your Free Hand

When in close range, your free hand can be used to suddenly and unexpectedly strike your opponent. You will probably only get one shot, so you'll need to make it count. Therefore, you not only need to know how to hit, but precisely where to hit for maximum effect.

A strike can take on many forms, such as a slap, punch, or chop. However, a *tiger claw* strike is usually the most dependable and effective. The tiger claw strike is a hand technique formed by tensing, curving, and spreading your fingers outward, not unlike when palming a basketball. Striking straight to the eyes with a tiger claw, using the tips of your fingers, can be more effective than punching because, with minimal effort, it yields maximum results against your attacker and at the same time poses less chance of injury to you. It can even temporarily blind any attacker regardless of size or strength, a very important effect because the average person receives up to 80 percent of all external stimuli by means of their sight. A tiger claw to the eyes also has a particularly high percentage of effectiveness because the eyes are very sensitive to contact of any sort and are susceptible to attack from virtually any angle. As if these multiple effects listed above weren't enough, your five fingers multiplied by your opponent's two eyes gives you ten opportunities for landing a successful strike.

Striking the eyes with sufficient force will make your opponent turn away, breaking his structure and allowing you to land a finishing blow with your sword. Of course, you should never actually poke your training partner in the eye. It is only safe to practice landing the strike when you and your partner are wearing masks to protect your faces. When practicing tiger claw or any other techniques near the eyes, you must always remember that, just like a cut or thrust to the face, a successful eye poke would be a fight ender. When practicing the tiger claw against an opponent wearing a mask, yell "Eyes!" to let them know the intended target of your strike was their eyes. In this way, wearing a mask does not foster a false sense of protection.

Eye Strike: You have the opponent's sword momentarily checked in a bind (1). Since the swords are tied up, use your free hand to suddenly and unexpectedly strike the opponent in the eyes with your fingertips using a tiger claw (2).

A man can't see, he can't fight.
—Terry Silver, *The Karate Kid III*

Grabbing

You can also use your free hand to grab your opponent. Grabbing is a very helpful technique since it can be used for multiple reasons, the following four being most important. First, it allows you to momentarily immobilize the opponent's weapon hand. Second, grabbing gives you a point of contact on your opponent's body that allows you to push and pull him in order to disrupt his balance and control his actions. Third, a grab can be particularly effective when combined with a foot sweep or attack with your sword. Fourth, grabbing to anchor the opponent's weapon arm can allow you to use blade-to-blade pressure to manipulate his weapon, either pressing it toward the opponent or stripping it from his grip. So, don't forget to use your hands!

High Grab: Begin from the high heavy bind (1). With your free hand, grab the opponent's wrist and disengage your sword (2). Immediately and quickly strike your opponent in the face with the pommel of your sword (3).

Low Grab: Begin from an engaged position (1). Check your opponent's blade as you take a full step forward, and, as soon as you are in range, use your free hand to grab the opponent's wrist (2). Thrust your opponent in the face with the tip of your sword (3).

Disarming

Taking an opponent's sword in combat is a difficult task that requires skill and timing. Use a heavy bind to control your opponent's sword while disarming him. This disarm can be accomplished by reaching out and grabbing the opponent's sword by the hilt, below the opponent's hand on the pommel end of the grip. This grab is easiest when blocking to the outside of your body. When blocking to the inside, cross over your blocking arm, reaching either under your sword in the case of a high block, or over your sword when blocking low. In any case, once you have a hold on your opponent's sword, pull it toward you and lever it out of his hand. You can cut him with your sword as you use your blade-on-blade pressure to assist you in completing the disarm. The specific technique you employ will depend on the type of sword your opponent is using and the situational circumstances.

LEVEL 4: ADVANCED SHORT SWORD 135

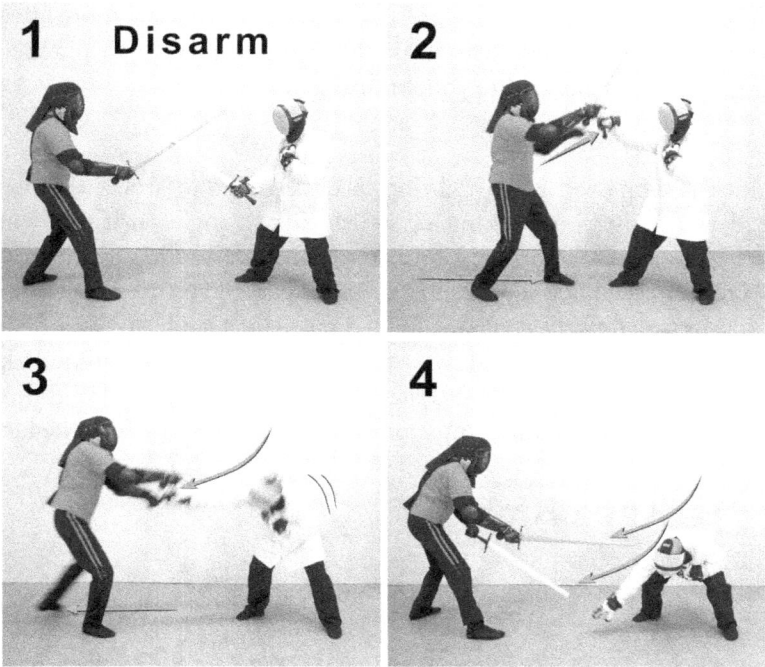

Disarm: Begin across from your opponent, your swords engaged (1). Take a full step forward, running your swords together into a heavy bind. As you do, use your free hand to grab the pommel of the opponent's sword (2). The moment you have a hold of his handle, step back again, pulling his pommel toward you. His hand acts as a fulcrum, levering his sword back toward him (3). As you finish your retreat, cut the opponent with one or even both swords (4).

Kicking

Kicking in a swordfight is generally not recommended when fighting at long or even middle range because your leg and foot would be vulnerable to being cut. That said, there are situations where kicking is useful in sword fighting, especially when your opponent is close and your swords are in a heavy bind. Since your opponent's attention will usually be focused on the action occurring between the swords, using your lower body to suddenly attack can catch your opponent by surprise. Even faking a kick can cause your opponent to flinch in response, which breaks his structure, takes his mind off his sword and opens him up to attack.

To prevent telegraphing, keep your hips and shoulders the same height throughout the kick. Move smoothly and quickly, using your whole body (especially your hips) to generate power. Remain relaxed until the precise moment of impact. Keep your supporting leg bent slightly, with your foot flat on the floor and your eyes on your opponent at all times. Always pull back your kicks as fast as you can and regain a stable, balanced stance as quickly as possible.

While a kick is seldom a fight ender, it is often enough to break your opponent's focus, disrupt their structure, or break the bind, setting you up to deliver a more effective follow-up attack with your sword. Of course, you must use good control when practicing these techniques, taking great care to not injure your training partner.

Knee Kick

The knee kick is employed when fighting in close range to attack the opponent's thigh, groin, or solar plexus. Raise your kicking leg swiftly and strongly, thrusting your knee up and forward into the target. Use the spring of your supporting leg and hip to add power to the technique. For balance, shift your body's center of gravity slightly and rest it directly above the center of your supporting foot. Keep your supporting leg bent slightly to maintain your balance and absorb the shock of the impact with your target. As with other techniques, keep your body straight and upright, exhale when you execute the kick, and remain relaxed until the moment of impact, at which point you should tense your body to add energy into the kick.

Knee Kick: Starting from a middle guard (1), take a full step forward as you run your sword up the opponent's blade, coming to rest in a high bind, at which point you grab the opponent's wrist with your free hand (2). Your opponent responds by grasping the wrist of your sword arm with his free hand. The high line is momentarily frozen. The first person to use his legs will have a big advantage (3). If the opponent is very close, you can strike him with your knee (4).

Front Kick

The front kick is a powerful, natural motion that a can be used to attack the groin. To execute a front kick, shift your body's center of gravity directly over your supporting foot and raise your kicking knee at the same time and on a line between your hip and your intended target. Flow smoothly through this position and straighten your leg with a strong snapping motion. Thrust your hips forward slightly as you straighten your leg to add range and power to your kick. Keep your ankle straight and fully extended, point your toes, and strike with the instep (top of your foot) and shin. Your opponent's thighs will naturally funnel your kick into his groin.

Front Kick: You are locked in a high bind with your opponent grasping your wrist (1). While his attention is focused on the high line, target his groin, point your toes and strike with the top of your foot (2). Alternately, you could target the opponent's solar plexus and strike with the ball of your foot (3) or kick his lower abdomen using a stomping motion, striking with the heel of your foot (4).

Stamping Kick

Stamping kicks are typically used to attack your opponent's knees to disable his locomotor system. To chamber for a stamping kick, raise your knee with your foot fully flexed, ankle bent, with your toes pulled back toward your shin. The kick can be performed at any angle: to the front, sides, or behind you. While you can strike with your heel, turning your foot and striking with the outer edge of your foot provides a broader striking surface, making it easier to strike the knee, shin, or instep of your attacker. After striking the target, you should either withdraw your knee quickly or continue through your target, hyperextending his knee or, if his knee remains strongly bent, scraping your foot down his shin to stomp powerfully on his foot.

Stamping Kick: You find yourself in a high bind, with both you and your opponent grasping each other's wrists to control your opponent's weapon (1). While your opponent's attention is on the high line, suddenly lift your rear knee into a high chambered position (2). Forcefully stamp on your opponent's knee, straightening and hyperextending the joint (3).

Foot Sweeps

An unexpected foot sweep can suddenly sway the odds in your favor. Foot sweeps create openings through disrupting your opponent's balance by attacking their stance. You can use your front or rear leg to attack your opponent's lead foot, sweeping with the arch, instep, or heel of your foot. Swing your leg in a shallow arc, skimming the ground lightly with your foot, to intercept your opponent's foot just below the ankle. To effectively set up and sweep an opponent, you must unbalance your opponent first and be prepared to quickly follow up with the sweep during this momentary loss of balance. For safety, only sweep to the back of your opponent's leg, never to the front. Be certain your partner knows how and is prepared to fall before sweeping him. Do not practice sweeps that are above your partner's falling capabilities.

LEVEL 4: ADVANCED SHORT SWORD 139

Instep or Arch Sweep: Begin with you and your opponent facing each other in right stances, your swords locked in a heavy outside bind (1). Bring your left (rear) foot forward in a shallow arc. Lightly skim the ground with your foot and intercept your opponent's right (lead) foot from the outside and behind with the instep (top) or arch (bottom) of your left foot. Contact the base of your opponent's right foot sharply, sweeping it up and across your opponent's body while pulling your opponent in the opposite direction of the sweep. Use this opportunity to win the bind (2).

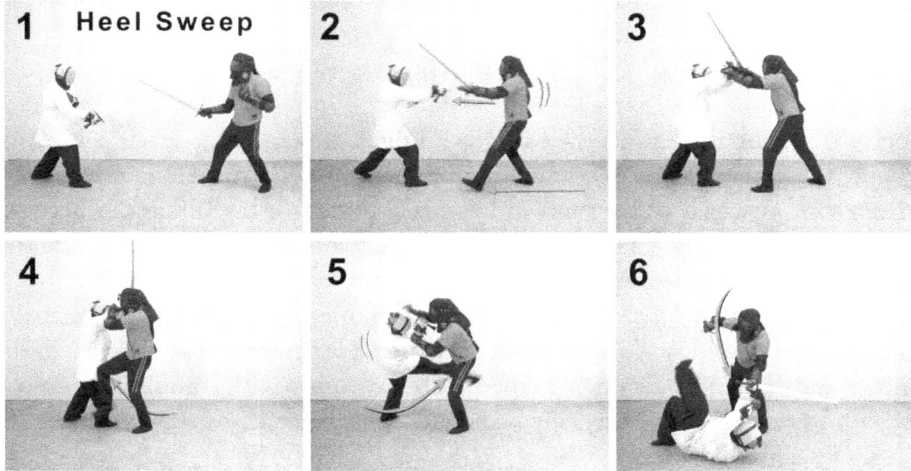

Heel Sweep: You and your opponent are facing each other in right stances, your swords in middle guard (1). Take a full step forward, running up his sword with yours, and reach forward to grab the opponent's wrist (2). Your opponent grabs your wrist as well, locking you in a high bind (3). Shifting all your weight to your left foot, quickly sweep your right foot in a shallow arc outside and behind your opponent's right (front) foot (4). Bring the backs of your calves together, contacting the base of your opponent's right (lead) foot with your heel, and sweep his leg out from under him. Note that your sweeping leg and your opponent's swept leg should be nearly parallel for maximum power (5). Immediately follow up with a thrust to the opponent's throat (6). All these steps need to be performed in a single, fluid motion.

Foot Pin

While not technically a sweep, the foot pin is a subtle trick you can use to momentarily disrupt your opponent's footwork. The idea is to step forward naturally, inconspicuously placing your lead foot on top of your opponent's. This move is not a stomping motion. It's just a subtle little toe cover that throws off his next step. When he tries to step, his foot won't move, throwing him off balance and opening him up to a quick attack.

Foot Pin: Begin at medium range with your swords engaged. Open your front foot to facilitate a quick step forward (1). Take a full step forward as you grab the opponent's wrist with your free hand and raise the hilt of your sword to line up for a thrust (2). Pin the opponent's lead foot with your foot, preventing him from stepping backward as you thrust to the opponent's throat (3).

Sparring

If you've trained hard and learned the techniques presented in Levels 1 to 4, then it is time to apply them against a non-compliant opponent in a sparring match. It is not unusual for sparring with a sword to feel awkward at first. There is a big difference between doing drills with a partner and the chaos of combat between you and an opponent, one that is trying his best to hit you while not getting hit himself. Stick with it. Your techniques may not work well at first, and you *will* get hit, and often. Sometimes, it will even hurt. Don't get angry, though, and never lose your composure. Instead, learn from that moment and upgrade your abilities and strategies. Be open to the thrill that comes with training in combat sports, the satisfaction of overcoming hardships, and the confidence that grows with knowing that your techniques actually work.

Since the moves in a fight are not pre-arranged, you must use and rely on keen observational skills to predict and determine your opponent's moves, especially the very next one. Watch for telegraphing, or signaling a move, such as pulling back to chamber a technique before throwing it, then quickly block or beat your opponent to the cut. It is imperative that you remain relaxed, alert, and ready for anything. Stay on your toes and use your footwork and body mobility to both evade incoming attacks and put yourself in advantageous positions to attack and to defend. Be confident and aggressive but not overly so. Test and analyze your opponent's defense, and then attack with strategic combinations. Fight your fight, taking maximum advantage of your strong points and your opponent's weak points. At the same time, remember to employ a variety of techniques and avoid falling into a set pattern or rhythm that your opponent can use against you.

Developing good habits and effective techniques takes a great deal of time and practice. It is very important to do a variety of drills to develop specific skills for free sparring. Train diligently and often with a partner, taking turns attacking and defending, to develop attributes such as strength, flexibility, agility, and endurance. Work on techniques such as evading, circling to the weak side, blocking, and countering. And, for safety, always wear *all* of your protective gear when sparring.

Salute

When sword fighting, it is customary etiquette to salute your opponent prior to a match. Since a match is not a life-or-death duel, there are rules to keep the participants safe. When saluting, you are consenting to the unwritten contract of sword fighting, saying silently that you will abide by the agreed-upon rules and not intentionally injure your opponent. There is no set method of salutation and therefore this sign of respect can take on many forms, often according to style.

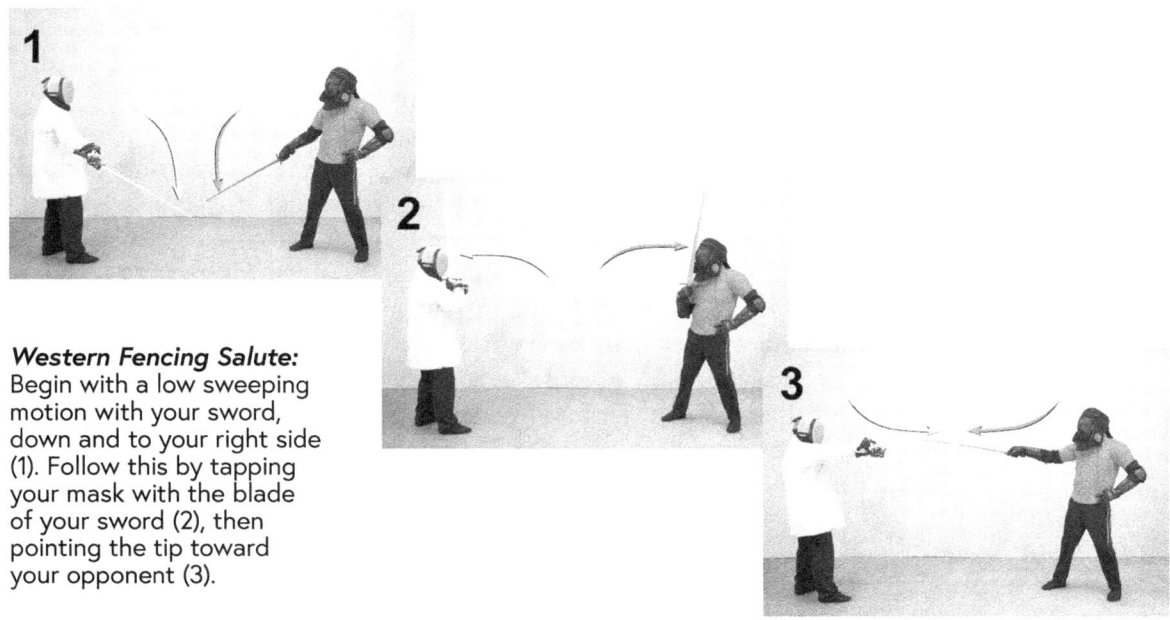

Western Fencing Salute: Begin with a low sweeping motion with your sword, down and to your right side (1). Follow this by tapping your mask with the blade of your sword (2), then pointing the tip toward your opponent (3).

En Garde!

Remember that sparring is just mock combat and that no amount of protective gear can make up for a good temperament, good technique, and good control. The fact is that injuries can occur whenever you are engaging in activities that involve physical contact, and even more so when fighting with weapons. Remember that you are not out to actually hurt your partner. Discuss how hard of a hit you are each comfortable with, as well as other rules, such as no punching or kicking, stop if the fight ties up or goes to the ground, or only controlled takedowns.

Prior to engaging your opponent, take a moment to mentally, physically, and spiritually prepare yourself for the encounter. If things get heated, keep your cool and do not overreact. Anticipate your opponent's next move by carefully observing and quickly evaluating his intentions. Be prepared to respond without hesitation.

Start out fighting slowly and with little power but remain fully engaged and ready for action. Light sparring is a good way to mentally and physically warm up, as well as an opportunity to feel out your opponent. After a few moments, begin gradually stepping it up until you are fighting at an intensity level that is agreeable to you and your opponent. Always keep your head together and never lose your cool, even when things get hectic. Take your weapons and the fight seriously, keeping in mind that, if these were real swords, even a single blow, especially a shot to the hand, could decide everything. Training with such a mindset will improve your weapons skills much more quickly than a "hit them more than they hit me" attitude. Remember that good defense is essential. Try to anticipate where your opponent will strike you and then block or move out of range; however, remember that defense alone will not win a fight. As for specific fighting tactics, remember to stay flexible and to adapt continually to the ever-changing circumstances of the fight.

Sparring does not always mean free fighting at full speed and power. While intense sparring is a good test of your skills, fighting slowly at less than top speed gives you time to think, learn, try new techniques, and improve. Before each practice session, answer questions such as these: what are my goals for this sparring session? Am I sparring to develop a specific skill or skill set, such as defending the low line or defending then counterattacking? What level of intensity do I want or am I comfortable with? With your sparring partner, agree in advance of sparring upon a set of rules to maintain safety and promote effective training. You might limit attacks to specific target areas (e.g., only leg attacks or only strikes to the body will score). Decide ahead of time if foot sweeps and takedowns will be allowed. These rules can be changed between rounds to add variety to your sparring, making it more helpful to your progress and more fun.

Types of Matches

When you finally square off with your partner, you should each have a good idea of what the rules are for your sparring match. The rules often depend on what type of match you are fighting.

Point Fighting

In a fight, the first hit can have a great impact on how the rest of the fight progresses. That is why, in point matches, the first contestant to score a solid blow is awarded a point. Sometimes different points are awarded for different targets according to their difficulty. For example, a hand or arm shot may be worth one point, while a body shot is scored as two points, and a headshot gets you three points. These matches usually take place at long range, only occasionally going to middle range. They can be held with judges and referees to call the points, but this is not always feasible or desirable. It is usually simple and preferable for you and your partner to call your own points. Double hits, where you each score at nearly the same time, should not count for either fighter since you both took potential damage. If there is a dispute as to whether a point was scored, let it go and move on. The point is to fight, not to argue.

Continuous Fighting

Inspired by Western boxing, continuous fighting is just that, a fight in which the participants do not stop fighting until the round ends. In such matches, you can use boxing's standard 10-Point Must System for scoring, in which judges score using a 10-point scale. Most rounds will end 10–9, with the more dominant fighter receiving 10 points, the other receiving 9. If an opponent is disarmed, the referee deducts an additional point from that fighter's score before the fighters are rearmed and the fight continues. Of course, you could just fight and not worry about who won and who lost, engaging in the match for the exercise, practice, and thrill of the fight.

House Rules

While it is possible that a fight could be ended with a single, well-placed strike to a vulnerable target, the truth is that the human body is very resilient and fights are rarely ended by the first shot. For a more realistic fighting/sparring experience, let each exchange run its course, then break and reset. At some point, you may decide that a strike was enough to stop the fight and reset the match, or you may judge that a strike did not have sufficient stopping power and let the fighting continue, usually until one participant gives in and admits defeat. This is my preferred format, as it is perhaps the most realistic method of testing your sword fighting skills. Our house rules are most often, "No harm, no foul" and "It's not over until it's over." Otherwise, just about anything goes. As long as you have sufficient skill and use good control, you can kick, punch, pommel strike, takedown, and even grapple with the sword for as long as you like. Disarmed? No problem; just keep fighting until you feel you can no longer reasonably go on.

Understanding Timing

When it comes to sparring, timing is a very important concept to study and understand in order to be successful. There are three types of timing in sparring: before, during, and after. These different types of timing are useful to us in understanding how to control and win a fight.

After Timing is the most basic timing. It means to counterattack after your response to the initial attack. For example, your opponent swings at you, and, in response, you block or do some other technique, such as evade, and then strike back. First, there was the attack, followed by your response an instant later. There was a small delay between the two. This simple timing is the one most commonly employed by beginning students of sword fighting.

During Timing is an intermediate timing method and indicates a simultaneous response to an incoming attack. In other words, when you are attacked, you counter at the same time. There is no gap, no delay between techniques.

Before Timing refers to a preemptive movement or technique. Your opponent intends to launch an attack, but you prevent it before it can even take form. Before timing is the most advanced form of timing, representing the highest state of awareness and control, because it is the act of reading the opponent's intentions and knowing what they are going to do, almost before they do. It is a level of competency and understanding that only comes with years of diligent training.

Examples of Types of Timing in Sparring

So, say your opponent somehow gets the jump on you and swings their sword downward, intending to crack your skull. You barely have time to throw up a roof block to stop his attack before counterattacking with a cut of your own. This exchange is a good example of attacking *after* the attack. Next, the opponent pulls back to strike at you again. You are not surprised to see he has unconsciously chosen the most common habitual method of attack, a downward diagonal strike aimed at your head, so you instantly plot the trajectory of his attack and initiate your own attack, intercepting the opponent's front hand mid-swing. This exchange is a good example of attacking *during* the attack. Finally, your frustrated opponent moves to make a third swing, but before he can even initiate his attack, you attack his front thigh with a quick thrust. Your thrust straightens his front knee, killing his momentum by preventing him from shifting his weight into the attack, and stopping his strike before he could execute it. This exchange is an example of attacking *before* the attack.

Strategy and Tactics

A fight can be likened to a game of chess, the basic moves of chess representing the various movements of the combatants. When playing chess, it is one thing to know how the pieces move and another to be familiar with the strategies and tactics of the game. If you lack a coherent strategy, you will find yourself, at best, at a tremendous disadvantage and, at worst, uselessly flailing around the board. With many variables to consider, the chessboard, like a fight, can be very confusing, making you easy prey for a more experienced opponent.

First and foremost, a chess player must realize that the objective of the game is to capture the opponent's king. Many novice players make the mistake of concentrating instead on capturing as many of the opponent's pieces as possible. While this approach might eventually win you the game, an experienced player can usually read the situation and take advantage of your two-dimensional strategy to defeat you. In the same way, a novice swordsman is easily baited, attacking any seemingly open target, while a more experienced fencer quickly observes the situation, develops a strategy to outwit or out skill their opponent, and employs tactics to end the fight in as safe and reliable a manner as possible.

The chess expert sees things differently than the beginner. He knows how and when to apply certain moves, but, more importantly, how to "see ahead" several moves. It's not that they actually see the future, mind you, but rather they see the possible outcomes of a given situation and prepares for them, essentially taking control of the game. A skilled swordsman works in much the same way. Through diligent training, he or she learns specific common reference positions. Reference positions are recognizable positions in which you and your opponent find yourselves, from which there are effective ways to proceed if you train them.

As a swordsman, you must learn how to quickly read a situation, find a reference point, and successfully execute a logical flow of techniques to its final conclusion. For example, if an opponent attempts to strike you in the head with a downward diagonal strike, and if the angle 1 loaded position that precedes the strike has become a reference point for you, you will quickly and *intuitively* recognize the attack and know how to counter it effectively. Learning what the possible outcomes are for any particular reference point allows you, in effect, to see ahead and prepare your next move or series of moves. Thinking in this manner gives you the initiative and lets you take control of the situation, just like the chess master.

In chess, you often hear of masters planning several moves ahead of actual play in order to set an opponent up for a finishing move. This tactic applies to sword fighting as well. But how do you think three or four moves ahead in-fighting with swords? After all, you can't always predict how your opponent will react. What you need is a strategy that will allow you to predict what your opponent is likely to do next and to react effectively when he does. A strategy is your overall battle plan. The specific moves you decide on to implement your plan are called tactics. So, now, let's work on this ability to sword fight like a chess player using strategies and tactics smartly.

In this book, you have learned many techniques and concepts that apply to fighting with a sword that could be employed in your battle plan, including:
- **The Outside Game**: Using footwork and evasion skills to stay out of the opponent's effective striking range, while sniping at the edges, targeting his hand or the nearest target.
- **Drawing**: Making an attack or other movement designed to elicit a particular response, such as a block.
- **Baiting**: Intentionally leaving a target open in order to get your opponent to attack.
- **Feinting**: Attacking a primary target, only to change to a secondary target once the opponent is committed to defending the first.
- **Programming**: Attacking a specific target repeatedly until the opponent begins to expect that attack, then feinting to get a reaction before striking him where you know he will be exposed.

While sound, these strategies are just general concepts. To actually employ them, they must be further developed and refined. For example, here is a simple yet effective three-step strategy built around the concepts of feinting and programming:

1) Attack: Look for an open target on your opponent, then attack it. If your strike lands, be sure to follow up and quickly finish your opponent. If your opponent blocks, quickly return to your defensive guard.

2) Feint/Attack: As soon as possible, attack the same target again. If your strike lands, be sure to follow up and quickly finish your opponent. If you can see that your strike is going to be blocked, turn the initial strike into a feint and instead attack to a vulnerable target on the opposite side of the body. If the opponent successfully blocks both attacks, quickly recover to your defensive guard.

3) Double Feint/Attack: Should your opponent block both attacks, double up the feint. Feint to your first target, only to feint to the secondary target as well, finally committing all of your resources to the success of a third attack.

While this basic strategy is shaping up, it is still not complete. It remains to be fleshed out with the specific tactics and techniques you will use to enact the strategy. The examples provided in this chapter will provide you with some good options, but they represent only a small sampling of the total possibilities. Your personal arsenal of techniques can only be acquired through careful study and practice; however, it is a worthwhile investment in time and energy that is sure to pay off for you later. By developing strategies and tactics beforehand, you will be better equipped to deal with your opponent because you have a battle plan. Your moves are no longer random techniques thrown haphazardly in an attempt to score but are instead part of a systematic, logical plan to control and overcome your opponent, just like the chess master. Be forewarned, though, that since all opponents are different and no two situations are exactly alike, you will need to be flexible and able to adapt the tactics you use so that your strategies will still be effective in any given situation.

Victorious warriors win first and then go to war, while defeated warriors go to war first and then seek to win.
—Sun Tzu, *The Art of War*

The Seven Principal Rules

The Schoole of the Noble and Worthy Science of Defence was written by English fencing master Joseph Swetnam in 1617. In it, he lays out his "seven principal rules where on true defence is grounded." Even in modern times, these rules still make up the foundation swordsmanship. You would do well to learn them. I have listed them below for you in an abridged form, as they appeared in Swetnam's book.

1. **A Good Guard:** ...when thou hast thy guard it is not enough to know it, but to keep it so long as thou art within reach or danger of thy enemie.

2. **True Observing of Distance:** ...thou shouldest stand so far off from thine enemy, as thou canst, but reach him when thou dost step forth with thy blow or thrust...

3. **To Know the Place:** ...thou must marke which is the nearest part of thine enemie toward thee, and which lieth most unregarded, whether it be his ... hand, his knee, or his leg, or where thous maist best hurt him at a large distance without danger to thy selfe.

4. **To Take Time:** ...when opportunity is proffered thee ... then make a quicke answer ... quicker than I can speake it...

5. **To Keep Space:** ...if thou charge thy enemy... recover thy weapons into their place, and draw thy selfe into thy guard againe, and so preparing thy selfe for to defend, and likewise to make a fresh assault with discretion...

6. **Patience:** ...is one of the greatest virtues that can be in a man: the Wise man saith, he is a foole which cannot governe himself...

7. **Often Practice:** ...without practice the Proverbe says, a man may forget his Pater noster*... For skill to everie reasonable man is a friend ... by which meanes such have great advantage of the ignorant and unskillful...

*Pater noster is Latin for "Our Father," a prayer so prevalent in Swetnam's society that it was unthinkable that anyone could ever forget it.

Level 4 Workout

This 60-to-90-minute workout is designed to round out your swordsmanship skills with a single-handed sword.

1. Warm-Up: 15–20 minutes. Start with five minutes of light stretching for your upper and lower body. Follow this with five minutes of cardio work such as jumping rope, jogging in place, doing jumping jacks, etc. Go until you feel tired and your heartrate is elevated, then five more minutes of light stretching until your heart rate returns to normal. Next, grab your sword and work through some basic footwork while you practice your blocks, parries, cuts, and thrusts, first slowly then gradually speeding up.

2. Long Range: 10–15 minutes. Take turns playing the outside game with your partner, using various long-range techniques to target each other's lead hand and leg. Begin moving slowly until you have the mechanics of the technique correct, then gradually add speed, remembering to control your power so as not to injure your training partner. While you might be tempted to train without full gear, especially when you are going slowly, it is recommended that you still wear your gloves and mask for safety.

3. Middle Range: 10–15 minutes. Move slightly closer and practice baiting and drawing using the trick guards, feinting, and applying fancy footwork. At first, practice structured drills concentrating on a single technique, alternating the roles of attacker and defender in a prearranged pattern. Later, once you have a firm grasp of the techniques in isolation, you can practice them in unscripted combinations; however, it must be remembered that this free form drill is *not* sparring. Don't worry if your opponent's techniques score. In fact, his techniques *should* score about four out of five times in order for him to train in his optimal learning zone. The same goes for you. If you are scoring less, your partner is defending too strongly, and you are not in your optimal learning zone. If this scenario happens, simply tell your partner so that you can both make the appropriate adjustments and continue training.

4. Close Range: 10–15 minutes. Work through all close range techniques presented in Level 4 with your training partner. Practice the pommel strike, striking with your free hand, grabbing, disarming, kicking, and foot sweeps. As always, begin practicing a single technique slowly until you have the mechanics correct, then gradually add speed and power, taking care not to injure your partner. Once you can perform the techniques well by themselves, start linking them together into logical and effective combinations. Again, don't worry if your opponent's techniques score; his techniques *should* score, and so should yours.

5. Sparring: 10–15 minutes. The only way to know what techniques work best under what conditions is to test them out against a non-compliant opponent. Maintain a strong defense at all times, then focus on analyzing your opponent's defense and exploiting his weaknesses to land specific moves. Even though you should be wearing full safety equipment when you spar, you should still control the strength of your strikes and take care not to injure your training partner. Now is a good time to pull out your boffer swords (see Appendix 4 at the end of this book). Whatever weapons you are using, it is always a good guideline to not hit your partner any harder than you want to be hit.

6. Cool Down: 5–10 minutes. Take a few minutes to take your body's autonomic nervous system from "Fight or Flight" into "Rest and Digest." Now is the time to use static stretching to increase your flexibility and break up the lactic acid that has accumulated in your muscles.

7. Follow-Up: When you are done, record each of your workouts in a training log. Include how long you trained and a short synopsis of the material you covered in the session. Set a goal for yourself, such as performing the above workout ten times before moving on to Level 5 and Part 2, Long Sword. You've come a long way already. Stay motivated, remain disciplined, be consistent, and work hard to hone your sword fighting skills.

Part 2: Long Sword

In Part 1, you developed the basic skills required to wield the short sword effectively. In Part 2, you will build upon these skills as you learn how to use a long sword. If some of the material seems familiar, that is because we are using the same framework that you already followed when training the short sword to expediate and inform your training with the long sword.

In Level 5, Long Sword Offense, you will learn the different stances, guards, and strikes used when wielding a sword in two hands. In Level 6, Long Sword Defense, the focus will be on not getting cut or stabbed. Level 7, Long Sword Fencing, will teach you how to play for and control the centerline with the long sword, while in Level 8, Advanced Long Sword, you will learn master cuts, trick guards, in-fighting, disarms, and takedowns with the two-handed sword. Finally, in Level 9, Great Sword, you will apply what you have learned to wield a sword as big as you are... or bigger!

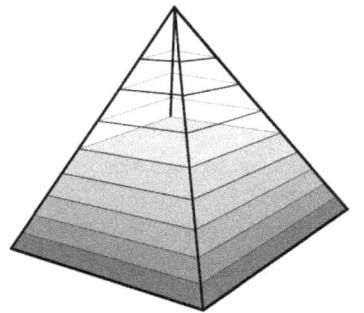

LEVEL 5:
Long Sword Offense

A Closer Look at Two-Handed Swords

At the beginning of Part 1, we examined some of the advantages that a short sword has over a long sword, namely accessibility and maneuverability. Likewise, to wield your long sword to its best effect, you'll need to first be familiar with this weapon's advantages and disadvantages, in comparison to the short sword. Before we start, however, let's reiterate that the term "short sword" refers to the length of a sword's handle, not the length of its blade, thereby making the following discussion one of generalities. It needs to be understood that there are always going to be some rare exceptions.

The most obvious advantage of a long sword is usually its greater reach. The longer blade of a two-handed sword allows you to strike from a greater distance than a single-handed sword (keeping in mind that we said this is not always the case). This ability of a long sword has the dual effect of making it easier to attack your opponent from a distance while helping to keep you safely out of his effective striking range. However, having both hands on the handle of your long sword actually restricts the range of your forward thrust to the full extension of your back arm. You can actually thrust farther with a sword held in just one hand because you can twist your torso as you lunge and automatically extend your arm farther. While you may get away with wielding your long sword with just one hand to momentarily get more reach, this can leave you in a structurally weak position should the opponent counter your attack.

A sharp long sword cuts with surprising ease. The greater length and mass of the blade makes the long sword capable of striking harder and more easily than short swords because having both hands on the hilt allows you to generate more power and momentum in a cut than a single-handed sword. This is why you never see a baseball player batting with one hand. In addition to greater power and momentum, this two-handed lever action allows you to maneuver your long sword quickly, despite its greater mass.

Not only are long swords longer and heavier, making them less convenient to carry around and therefore generally less accessible than short swords, the heavier the sword, the more training and physical strength are required to wield it effectively. Even though the long sword can hit fast and hard at a distance and change angles quickly when in the hands of a skilled swordsman, at close range or in confined spaces, a two-handed sword may still not be as versatile and would therefore be less effective. Since shorter blades are more maneuverable at close range, the general rule is, the shorter the blade, the more treacherous the grapple.

Training Equipment: Choosing a Sword

Before you can start training, you are going to need a two-handed sword. There are many available on the market, and choosing the right one for you is not merely a matter of personal preference. It is important you know how to choose a sword that fits your body size and feels good in your hand. It must also be of appropriate construction for the type of training you will be engaging in.

Materials

When it comes to buying your first long sword, the first consideration is probably the type of material used to construct the training sword. The fact is that you usually get what you pay for, so let's start with the least expensive alternatives and move up in quality and price from there.

Shinai are a type of bamboo sword commonly used in the Japanese art of kendo. Comprised of split bamboo, the blade of the shinai is circular. While roughly the size and shape of a long sword, shinai usually lack a crossguard. Shinai do bend a little when cutting; however, they do not flex in the thrust. At only $30 to $40, shinai are an inexpensive option for a long sword trainer.

Like the shinai, polypropylene long sword trainers are relatively inexpensive, costing around $40 to $50. They come in many styles and are extremely durable, making them perfect for pell work. Like the shinai, most have little or no flex, and can, in fact, be heavier than a steel sword, which means that they hit very hard. This is not to say that all polypropylene trainers are bad. Some do have lighter, more realistic blades.

Wooden long swords cost about the same as polypropylene trainers and share many of the same traits. Wooden swords, or wasters, are relatively heavy and do not flex, so they, too, can hit hard. Wooden wasters are also durable enough to withstand the wear and tear of hard training, so they do not need to be replaced very often, although they do have to be checked regularly for cracks and splinters. Minor damage to a wooden sword is easily fixed with sandpaper, and small cracks can sometimes be mended with high-quality wood glue and clamps. However, a large crack is a clear sign that it is time to retire that waster. If historical accuracy in a sword is important to you, this is a great option.

Plastic and low-end synthetic trainers tend to have more flex and a more realistic weight than polypropylene swords. Plastic long swords tend to cost more than polypropylene, coming in at about $80 to $100. The downside of plastic swords is that the inexpensive, low-end ones usually either flex too much or are so heavy that they hit harder than a blunt steel sword. On the other hand, high quality synthetic long swords are different than plastic trainers.

Costing around $150 to $200, they handle well and are as good a substitute for a sharp steel sword as you can get without having a metal blade.

Aluminum swords can provide a more realistic feel than a wooden or synthetic trainer, both in handling as well as in the bind. Since aluminum is lighter than steel, swords can be made with thicker blades that have safer edges while still retaining a realistic weight. Though some low-end aluminum swords are less expensive, a good quality aluminum sword can cost almost as much as a steel sword.

Training with blunt steel blades is very exciting and most closely replicates using a live blade. Made of metal, they handle very similarly to a sharp long sword. The prices for blunts start at around $250 and go up to about $600. When purchasing a steel sword, one consideration should be the type of tip it has. A long sword should never have a rubber tip because the force generated by a thrust, coupled with the grip of the rubber, can "grab" the mesh of a sparring mask and violently move the head. A rounded tip is good for training or sparring. It is rounded to prevent injury and make it safer for practice. A rolled tip is even better as the very end of the blade is rolled or curled over, creating a rounded and smooth end to the blade. While a rolled tip is usually very good for preventing injury, they are known for "scooping" bits of flesh on glancing blows when the opponent has even a little exposed skin. So, be sure to wear proper protective gear when using a rolled tip. Nicks or bends in a blunt sword require maintenance and, even when fixed, can create weak spots where the blade may be subject to future breakage under stress.

Foam padded swords can be fun for light sparring with minimal protective gear. However, they generally lack the weight and heft of a real sword and therefore do not make very good trainers. Not only do they lack the feel of the genuine article, but padded swords designed for cosplay or LARP (live action role playing) are generally not designed to hold up in intensive training. Their weaker, often hollow plastic cores cannot stand up to hard collisions, especially against denser and heavier wooden or synthetic swords. However, foam swords can stick together in the bind like sharp blades would, making them good for developing certain skills.

Historical replicas, fantasy swords, and other swords created for display purposes lack the structural integrity required for safe training and likewise should not be used. And, let me say it one more time, just to be clear: DO NOT use a sharp sword, even for solo work. Sharps are dangerous, requiring the utmost attentiveness when wielding, and should only be used for test cutting under very controlled conditions.

Training Equipment: Protective Gear

Free sparring with long swords requires substantial protective equipment, even more so if you are sparring with steel trainers. We already covered the basics of protective equipment in Part 1, so you should already have a mask, gloves, and torso protection. If you are engaging in controlled drills and light sparring, you can get away with wearing lighter gear; however, free sparring with steel long swords requires heavier gear that offers maximum protection.

While a full suit of plate may be overkill, your mask, gloves, and jacket do need to be heavy enough to absorb strong blows. Hard shell protection for your hands, forearms, elbows, shoulders, groin, knees, and shins is highly recommended. You can also wear a chest plate under your jacket, called a plastron; it is often required in bouts, even if you have an 800n heavy jacket. Hard shell protection can be made of plastic, rigid leather, or metal. Padded underarm protection is highly recommended when wearing a medium jacket, although this is usually not required. Padded pants can be worn to protect your hips and thighs. One piece of equipment that should never be overlooked is a gorget to protect your neck and throat.

While pain is a great teacher, injuries can be expensive and prevent you from training. Therefore, buy the best equipment you can afford and wear it. While good sword fighting gear is admittedly costly to buy and bothersome to put on, it will always be cheaper and more convenient than a hospital visit.

Despite your best efforts to avoid an accident, sword fighting injuries can and do happen. Have a first aid kit on hand and know how to use it. Periodic CPR and first aid training courses can help you learn how handle accidents and injuries better, as well. Whenever you are sword fighting, it is advisable to have a third-party nearby to go for help if necessary. Preferably, you should have easy access to a land line or cell phone to call 911 if needed.

Gripping the Long Sword

Grasp the hilt of the sword with both hands. Your dominant hand should be on the top, just under the crossguard. Your other hand clasps the bottom of the handle, just above the pommel of the sword. Make sure your grip is firm, but not too tight, and that your wrists are relaxed. When blocking, you will want to use a hammer grip to assure a strong, rigid structure. When striking, however, a handshake grip can provide you with additional fluidity and range.

Practice your grips by starting in a middle guard with a firm hammer grip. Extend your arms out in front of you, keeping the sword parallel to the ground, and adjust your grip as necessary to find a comfortable and balanced position. Remember to keep your wrist as straight as possible and to avoid assuming a weak, hyperextended, "broken wrist" position. That said, your bottom hand needs to remain flexible enough so that it can move around the pommel freely.

Some cuts and guards may require you to loosen your grip on the hilt with your right hand, rotating the handle to avoid assuming a broken wrist position. This aligns the knuckles that usually align with the cutting edge with the flat of the blade. To make up for any loss of control, place your thumb on the flat of the blade, just above the crossguard, to allow you to use this thumb pressure to align and support the blade through the cut. This positioning of your thumb is referred to as a thumbs-up grip.

LEVEL 5: LONG SWORD OFFENSE

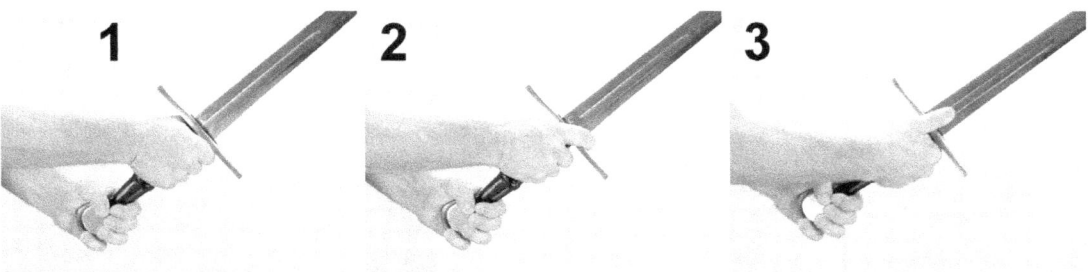

Long Sword Grips: Hammer grip (1), finger grip (2), thumbs-up grip (3).

Stances

The stances used with the long sword are the same as those you learned in Part 1 with the short sword, specifically: cat, back, neutral, forward, and lunge. Collectively, these different stances allow you to maintain a stable, balanced base and strong structure as you move while fighting, advancing and retreating in response to your opponent.

The progression of stances, from the shortest to longest.

The cat and back stance are generally defensive in nature, as they allow you to quickly retreat out of range. However, they are also loaded positions from which you can suddenly and unexpectedly spring forward. On the other hand, the forward and lunge stance are more offensive because they are usually used when attacking.

Cat - Back - Neutral

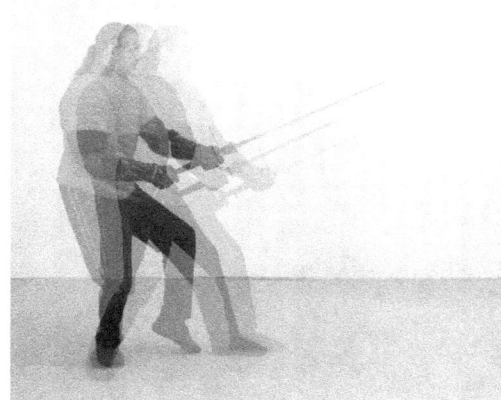

Neutral - Forward - Lunge

Defensive stances (left) as compared to more offensive stances (right).

Guards

There are a great many long sword guards, and each has its pros and cons. There is no one perfect guard that can protect your entire body and allow you to fight effectively at the same time. It is best to read your opponent and flow between guards as the situation changes.

As with the short sword, there are two true guards with the long sword, the middle guard and the hanging guard. These are the only guards where the blade of your sword is between you and your opponent, offering passive resistance by their mere presence occupying the center. While true guards offer maximum defense, offensively they limit your immediate attack options to thrusts.

Other positions, such as the high guard, are loaded guards. They offer no immediate resistance to your opponent's advance, but they put you in an excellent offensive position, with your sword coiled to strike.

The crown guard is an extreme version of the high guard, with your hands held high over your head, as a crown might be. The crown guard is a loaded trick guard. Your body is exposed to invite an attack, but your sword looms menacingly overhead, ready to strike. Low guards are also trick guards. In a low guard, you drop the tip of your sword in an attempt to deceive your opponent into thinking you are vulnerable to attack, which you are and aren't at the same time. You know that you dropped into a low guard intentionally to bait your opponent into striking, and you know exactly how you are going to attack, and when, from this guard. In a low guard, if the tip of the sword remains in front of your body, it is termed a fool's guard, while if the tip is pointed to the rear it is called a tail guard. We'll address each of these—crown, fool's, and tail guard—in greater detail in Level 8, Advanced Long Sword.

Middle Guard

To assume a middle guard, hold the long sword in front of you at your hip level with the tip pointing toward your opponent. This position is the most instinctive way to hold a sword. In HEMA, it is commonly referred to as the "plow." In the right middle guard, lead with your right foot, and, in the left middle guard, lead with your left foot.

A right middle guard from the side (left) and from the front (right).

Hanging Guard

To assume a hanging guard, historically referred to as the "ox," raise your hands to shoulder level while keeping the tip of the sword pointed at your opponent. The hanging guard can be performed with both right and left leads.

A right hanging guard from the side (left) and front (right).

High Guard

The high guard can look like you are just standing there with the sword resting on your shoulder. The appearance is one of being open and defenseless, and you are... as open and defenseless as a bear trap. Lead with your left foot as you stand just out of range of your opponent, holding your sword over your right shoulder. The idea is to look so relaxed that you invite an overt attack. The high guard is a common loaded position, with the tip pulled back and the sword ready to strike. It is very easy to switch between the middle guard, hanging guard, and high guard as a situation warrants. The high guard can also be assumed on either the left or right sides. When on the left side (for a right-handed swordsman), you can assume a thumbs up grip, with your thumb bracing the blade.

If the opponent approaches cautiously, you can advance on him by stepping forward with your rear foot to close the gap unexpectedly as you strike with your sword. Conversely, if the opponent rushes in to close the gap, retreat by stepping backward with your lead foot, giving just enough ground to maintain proper distancing for a focused strike with the end of your sword.

Two High Guards: A relaxed high guard can be used to bait your opponent or lull him into a false sense of security (1) compared to a more traditional, ready position (2).

Distancing and Footwork

Footwork is essential for maintaining balance and control while fighting with a long sword. You need to be able to move quickly and smoothly to maintain the right distance, dodge attacks, and strike your opponent. In general, the closer you are to your opponent, the more control you have over their sword; however, you are also more vulnerable to attacks. Since the maximum distance between you and your opponent is determined by the length of the sword, and the long sword usually has a greater range than the short sword, you will have more ground to cover when fighting with it. Therefore, footwork plays an even greater role in controlling that critical distance when fighting with a long sword.

You can use the same footwork patterns with the long sword that you learned with the short sword: advancing, retreating, shuffling, sidestepping, and circling. However, since you have more ground to cover, the most important footwork technique for long sword fighting is the full passing step, which allows you to cover a large amount of ground quickly. The full step can be used to advance, close the distance to strike, or retreat to escape from danger.

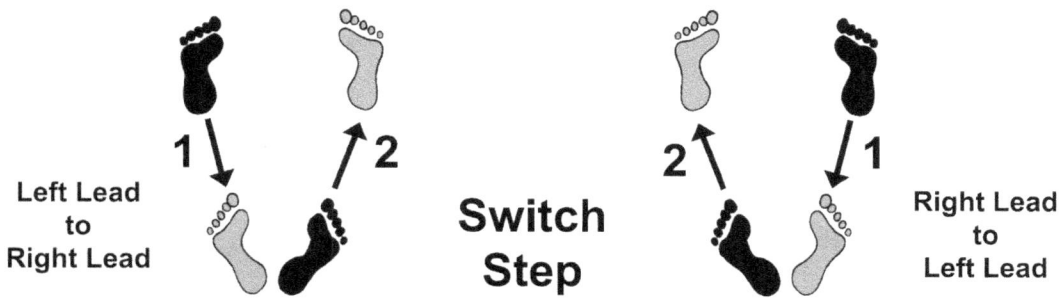

Switch Step

Another important footwork pattern, not often used when wielding a sword in one hand, is the switch step. This move allows you to quickly and safely change your stance from right leading to left leading or vise-versa, something you do often when fighting with the long sword. To perform a switch step, step back first with your lead foot, then step forward with what had just been your rear foot. You are now leading with the opposite side of our body. Retreating with your lead leg first keeps you out of range of your opponent while your feet are together and you are balanced on a small base of support. Again, the switch step is footwork that would not be used often with a single-handed sword, but very useful when wielding a long sword.

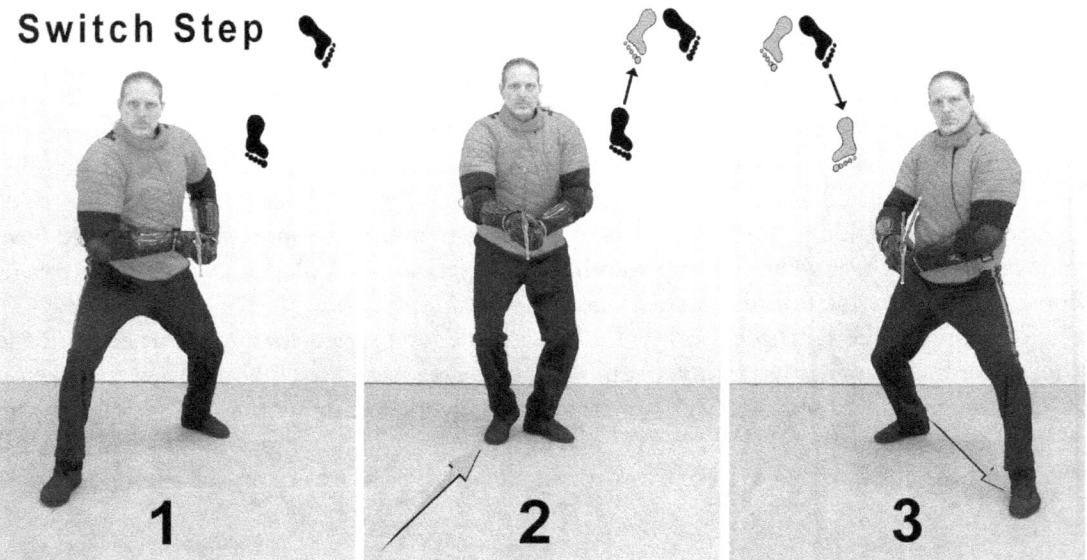

Switch Step: Starting from a right lead with the long sword loaded at your left hip (1), step your front foot back to your rear foot (2) before stepping your rear foot forward to assume a left lead with the sword chambered at your right hip (3).

Targeting

When it comes to understanding the long sword, it helps to review the history and evolution of the weapon. As we mentioned in the introduction, swords started out as one-handed weapons, often used in conjunction with a shield. Swords then developed into longer, two-handed weapons during the Middle Ages, when advances in metallurgy allowed for the creation of plate armor. This highly protective armor had to be tailor fitted, unlike chainmail, which hangs on you like a potato sack. Though tailor-made plate was expensive, it was worth the cost because of the great advantage it provided over less heavily armored opponents. These advances in metallurgy that led to the creation of metal armor also spurred the forging of longer, heavier swords that required two hands to wield.

Fighting a heavily armored opponent requires a different approach than fighting an unarmored opponent, even when using a large sword. Plate armor is strong and durable, so attacking it straight-on is futile. The solution is to target the joints and gaps between the armor's pieces, such as near the armpits, groin, or neck. These areas are vulnerable to thrusts or quick strikes, and a well-placed strike in these areas can incapacitate or even kill your opponent.

LEVEL 5: LONG SWORD OFFENSE

At closer range, combatants used *half-swording*, a technique in which you grip the blade of the sword with one hand and use it as a thrusting weapon. This technique allows you to penetrate more effectively through those gaps in the armor, including the visor of the helmet. You can also strike with the pommel or crossguard to incapacitate your opponent. Grappling and wrestling techniques were (and still are) other common ways to overcome a heavily armored opponent. Of course, fighting in close range also provides opportunities to use locks, foot sweeps, and throws.

Although most modern long sword matches are held in full protective gear with blunt swords, matches are usually scored as though the combatants were unarmored and the swords were sharp. Scoring systems often prioritize targets by awarding more points for more "critical" target areas, such as having the arms and legs worth one point, a successful strike or thrust to the body worth two points, and a solid strike to the head worth three points.

Even in extreme cases in which combatants are heavily armored in functional plate mail, and the combatants are going at it as hard as they can in continuous fighting with heavy rattan swords (such as you might see in the SCA) or, even more extreme, the blunt steel swords used in the Armored Combat Sports (search that on YouTube), matches are scored subjectively based on strikes to armored body parts. For safety's sake, the most effective moves must necessarily be banned, which is why it is always against the rules to purposely stab into a gap, which would injure your opponent.

Basic Strikes

While there are many basic striking patterns with the long sword, for efficiency and economy in training time, you can use the same set of basic strikes you used when learning the short sword.

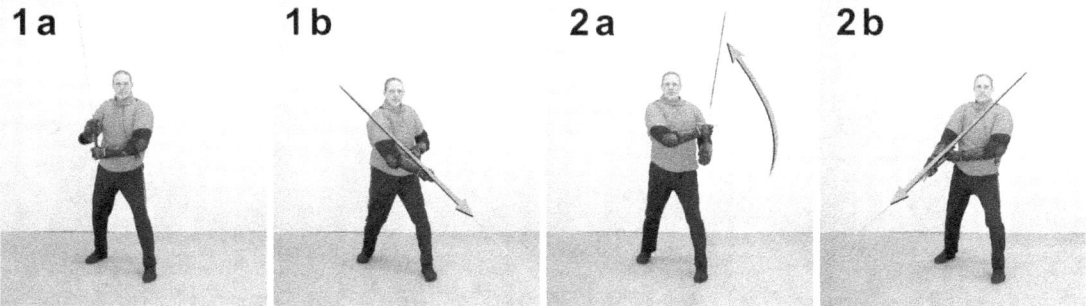

Strikes 1 and 2 are downward diagonal strikes. Your first strike starts from a right high guard (1a). Strike downward diagonally from right to left (1b). Let the momentum of your sword from your strike carry it up to a high loaded position on your left side (2a) to be ready for the second downward diagonal strike (2b). When thrown consecutively and repeatedly, these two downward strikes form a downward figure-eight pattern.

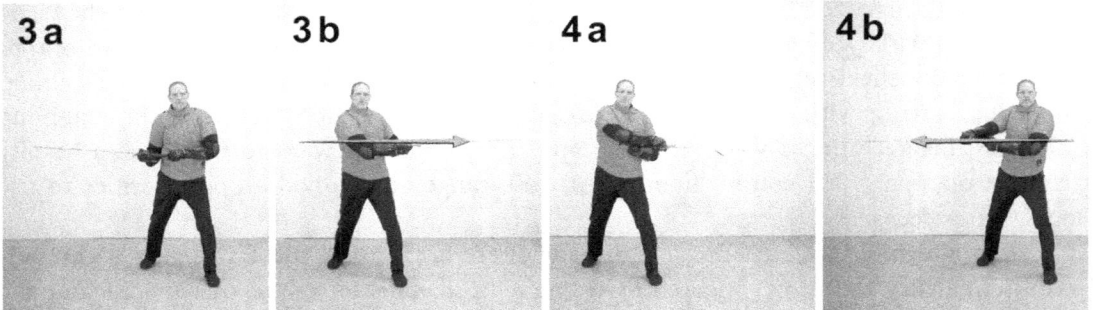

Strikes 3 and 4 and are horizontal cuts, striking first from right to left (3a) and (3b), then returning from left to right (4a) and (4b).

Strikes 5 and 6 are upward diagonal strikes. Lower the tip of your sword to your right side (5a), then cut diagonally upward from right to left (5b). Immediately drop the tip of the sword to your left side (6a) before cutting diagonally upward from left to right (6b). Like strikes 1 and 2, strikes 5 and 6 can be thrown consecutively and repeatedly to form an upward figure-eight pattern.

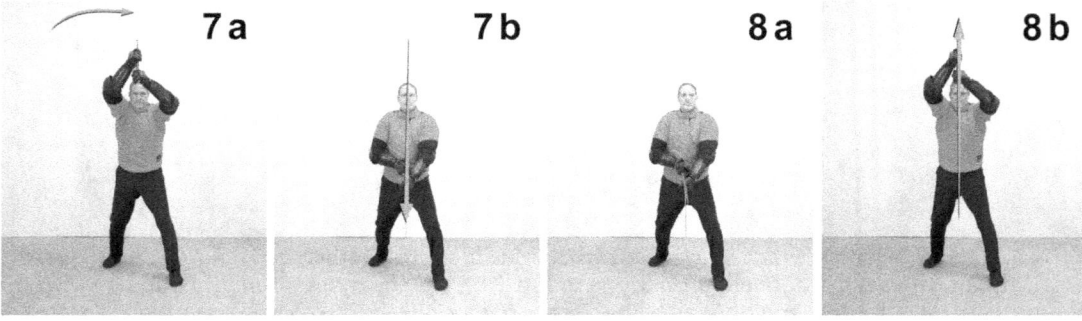

Strike 7 travels vertically downward through the centerline (7a and 7b), while strike 8 retraces that line with an upward vertical cut (8a and 8b).

LEVEL 5: LONG SWORD OFFENSE 163

9a **9b**

The ninth strike is a forward thrust to the center of the target with the tip of your sword. Begin by pulling the handle of your sword to your right hip as you align the tip with your target (9a), before thrusting forward (9b).

At first, practice these all strikes using the true edge of your sword. Then, practice a combination of true and false edge strikes, or even exclusively back/false edge cuts using the same pattern and footwork. We'll explore using both strikes more in the next section on edge alignment.

Practice the basic cuts in isolation at first, then in pairs, before linking three or more strikes together. Practice in the air, both in front of a target board to perfect your accuracy and distancing and in front of a mirror to check your form. It is also important that you take time to hit a solid target, such as a wooden pell or tire dummy. Of course, your ultimate goal should be to be able to deliver the strikes properly in any order as a particular fighting situation dictates.

Once you can perform the basic strikes with full cuts, try performing them with half strikes and double strikes.

Edge Alignment

As we mentioned, long swords often have two edges, a true edge that aligns with your knuckles and a back or false edge. Both edges are capable of cutting, with the true edge providing the greatest biomechanical advantage. Sometimes, when cutting with the back edge, it becomes necessary to assume a thumbs-up grip. Pressing your thumb against the flat of the blade gives you the grip flexibility necessary for a false edge cut while also providing you with additional blade control.

Practice each full cut, striking with the true edge and then striking with the false edge. Next, perform them as half strikes, using the true and false edges. Finally, when you double strike, you can practice several different variations:

1) Strike with true edge followed by the false.

2) Strike with the false edge followed by the true.

3) Strike with the true edge then turning over to cut back with the true edge again.

4) Strike with the false edge then turning over to cut back with the false edge again.

The Four Thrusts

When in a true guard, the tip of your sword is pointed at the opponent and chambered for a thrust. Since there are two true guards, middle and hanging, and each has a left and right variation, there are four basic positions from which to start your thrust. Practice thrusting from a left or right middle guard and from a left or right hanging guard. When thrusting as a follow-up after delivering another technique, you must first align the tip of your sword with the target, meaning you will have to flow through one of the four positions below to deliver the thrust. The level of your thrust could be high, middle, or low. Immediately draw back to a guarded position after thrusting and not necessarily back to the one your thrust came from. To develop accuracy, practice thrusting to a pell or another target.

The Four Thrusts: Whether you start from a right hanging guard (1), left hanging guard (2), right middle guard (3), or left middle guard (4), all lead into the same final thrusting position (5).

Patterns and Combinations

Your practice of the basic strikes should progress from performing single strikes to combining strikes into combinations of several basic moves performed consecutively. Repetitive practice of patterns and combinations creates new neural pathways in your brain, often referred to as muscle memory, that will allow you to perform the movements without thinking about the mechanics of the physical motion. Of course, the ultimate goal is to transcend patterns and be able to perform any motions with the long sword in any order, as quickly and effectively as needed. One of the best training tools to help achieve this goal you are (or should be) already very familiar with by now, the Meyer's Square.

Meyer's Square Training

Making the long sword feel and move like an extension of your body takes practice. Training your combinations on a Meyer's Square is the fastest way to perfect your angles, blade orientation, tip control, distancing, and footwork. At first, stand at your maximum striking range to the target so that a fully extended cut will come within one to three inches of the target. Initiate each cut by bringing the tip of your sword directly to the beginning of the line on your target that you intend to cut, striving for as straight an approach as possible to avoid telegraphing your intentions with a wide, arcing strike. Cut precisely along the entire length of the line. At the end of the line, when your cut is finished, you should immediately recover to a guarded position or rechamber your sword for the next cut.

Next, you need to practice from proper fencing range, meaning a range that includes a full passing step to make a proper cut. As always, move the tip of your sword first, in as direct a line as possible, to the start of your cut line. Straighten your arms before initiating the step. Trace the line of attack as closely as possible, paying particular attention to the orientation of your blade. Again, immediately recover to a guarded position stepping back to where you started or rechambering your sword for your next strike.

Start your distance training by stepping in with a single full cut, then retreating back out to a guarded position. Practice each cut in this manner before linking them. Next, step in with one cut, and immediately follow up with a second cut as you retreat back out of range. For example, you might close the gap with a number 1 strike, downward diagonally from right to left, only to follow-up with a left-to-right horizontal cut as you retreat.

Remember to push yourself to execute each strike using ideal form. Intentionally making yourself execute strikes with good form will aide in making these strikes second nature to you and make them feel as natural as possible. If you practice this way, in a real fight, your strikes will have a higher chance of being effective, even from all sorts of unusual positions, because they were ingrained properly and put into your body memory.

Full Strikes

Full cuts are the most basic type of cut. They make a complete arc, which allows you to maximize the power of your strike. A full cut starts from a loaded position (1), accelerates through the target (2), then decelerates as quickly as possible. To initiate the strike, your top, dominant hand acts as a fulcrum, pushing forward, while your bottom hand pulls back on the pommel to maximize your leverage on the sword. Likewise, use both hands to bring your strike to a quick stop.

A number 1 strike performed as a full overhand cut.

The Changer

The changer is a term used for a specific pattern that attacks on one line then quickly changes the line of attack for a second strike from a new and unexpected angle. The changer describes a path that resembles a remembrance ribbon. For example, if you were to open with a diagonal upward cut from right to left (1 and 2), your sword would loop around clockwise at the top (3) to make a second cut diagonally downward from right to left (4). The same motion can also be reversed (5 to 8). You could perform the changer opening with any of the basic strikes, switching on the top, bottom, left, or right. Switching on the sides results in a partial figure-eight, either upward or downward.

Half Strikes

Once you have established competency with full strikes, practice the basic strikes using half strikes and double strikes. Half strikes cut along the line to the center of the target, then usually reverse directions to cut back along the same line. In advanced half striking, you might attack along one line, but return along a different line, ending in a position other than the one you started in. This training will help you develop good tip control with your sword. When practicing half strikes on the Meyer's Square, since you only cut halfway through the target on any given cut, this drill is sometimes referred to as Meyer's Half Square.

Overhand Half Strike: Start in a high guard (1). Execute a downward diagonal strike, stopping just through the center of the target (2). Immediately snap back to a loaded position (3).

Double Strikes

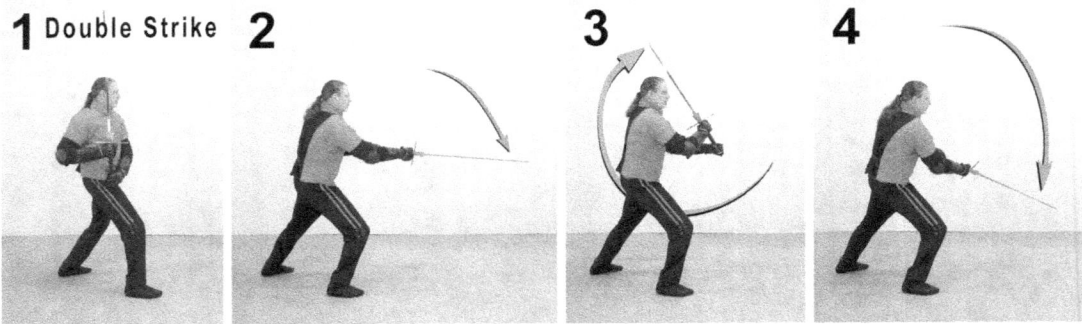

Double strikes cut twice on the same angle, striking once only to loop back to cut along the same line again. As with the other strikes, begin by practicing them while standing in range, gradually increasing the distance until you are a full step away from the target. Step into striking range with your rear foot as you perform a double cut, before retreating with a double cut on a different angle, finishing back out of range in a guarded position.

Combinations

Practicing combinations is important because in a fight, you are going to need them. Begin by practicing every strike delivered from every guard. Think of two cuts to combine together and practice just those two cuts on their own several times before then practicing them together in a combo. Then, follow up with another combination of two cuts and practice them the same way. Once you can perform any two cuts as a set by themselves in isolation, try practicing sets of two cuts together as a longer combination. You can then link multiple sets of two cuts together and practice those. When you think about the fact that there are nine angles of attack, three types of cuts (half, full, and double), and two edges to the blade to strike with (true and false), it becomes obvious that there is a plethora of possible combinations to practice. The secret is to view each repetition as another opportunity to perform the combination with even more skill and precision. Practicing like this will never get old, and you will get better and better at fighting with your longsword.

Freestyling

While practicing prearranged patterns and combinations is a very necessary step toward developing strong swordsmanship skills, you do not want them to constrain you. On the contrary, they should prepare you for the final stage of solo practice, free styling. Freestyling is like shadow boxing in that you combine your offense, defense, and footwork as you respond to an invisible opponent. Visualization is a key element of free style training. You must see your imaginary opponent in your mind's eye, responding to his movements as though it were an actual fight.

Start from a guard and imagine your opponent moving in to attack. Counter this imagined attack and then counterattack in full time. Quickly recover to a solid guard and repeat. The guarded positions act as rest stops, putting you in a strong position while you figure out your next moves. Beginners will naturally spend more time in between combinations, but as your stamina and skills in swordsmanship increase, you should find yourself more and more in constant motion with the sword.

The Pell Revisited

As we mentioned in Part 1, striking a target with your sword is an important activity that you will want to work into your training. Hitting a pell or tire dummy provides you with instantaneous feedback concerning everything from your blade orientation to your body alignment. If you haven't done so already, follow the plans shown in Level 2 to construct a striking target that is conducive to your training area.

Train your basic strikes, first in isolation, working up to progressively more complicated combinations. Begin standing in range of the target, striking with light force at first, then gradually increasing the power of your strikes as you become more comfortable managing the mechanics of the impact. Practice every strike by itself several times, striving to make each repetition better than the last.

Once you are comfortable striking the target when in range, step out of range, assuming a proper fencing distance. Then practice each strike again, this time lunging or stepping into striking range. Practice each strike to the pell or striking target, first in isolation, and then in increasingly more complex combinations.

Level 5 Workout

This 60–90-minute workout is designed to help you develop the strength, proper body mechanics, accurate targeting, distancing, footwork, and power needed to wield the two-handed sword effectively.

1. Warm-Up: 15–20 minutes. Start with some light stretching. Follow this with five to ten minutes of cardio work such as jumping rope. Go until you feel tired and your heartrate is elevated, then do some more light stretching until your heart rate returns to normal. Next, grab your long sword and work through some basic footwork (advancing, retreating, side-to-side, and circling). Use a footwork pattern while you practice your basic cuts (diagonal, horizontal, and vertical), first slowly then gradually speeding up. Remember to intersperse thrusts into your cuts. Cut, cut, thrust!

2. Targeting/Distancing/Control: 15–20 minutes. Perform the nine basic strikes to a Meyer's Square. Strike strong and quickly, but do not actually hit the target. Instead, strike just short of contacting the target, preferably one to three inches away. Practice each strike singly at first, then in combinations of two, building up to combinations of three to five techniques.

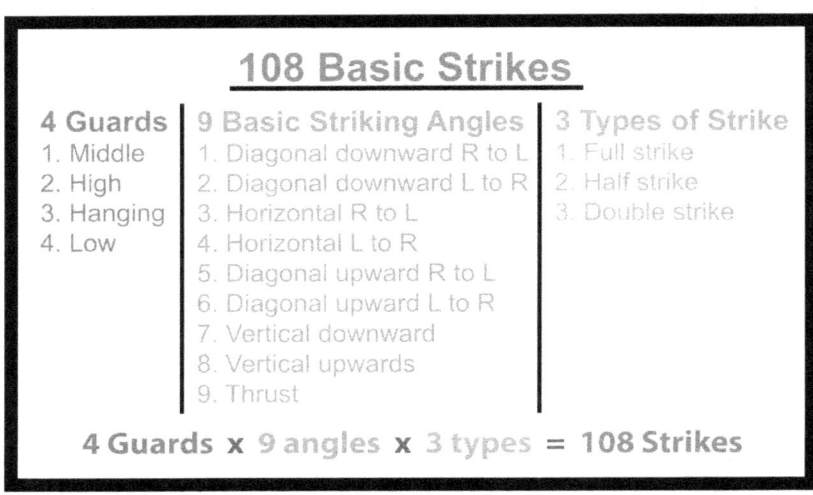

3. Variety: 15–20 minutes. Keep your workout fresh by switching things up. The nine basic strikes can be performed many different ways. Each of the nine strikes can be performed from any of four different guards (right and left hanging and right and left middle), and in three different ways (half, full, and double), making 108 different strikes. Additionally, each could also be aimed high, middle, or low. When you are ready, incorporate different types of footwork into the exercise.

4. Power Training: 10–20 minutes. Practice the nine basic strikes to a pell or tire dummy. Use a sturdy training sword and take care not to break it. At first, perform the strikes one at a time, then in combinations of two, building up to combinations of three to five techniques. Include footwork by starting at a distance, closing the gap, entering with feints and combinations, then exiting on a new angle.

5. Cool Down: 5–10 minutes. Take a few minutes to take your body's autonomic nervous system from "Fight or Flight" back to "Rest and Digest." Now is the time to use static stretching to increase your flexibility and break up the lactic acid that has accumulated in your muscles.

6. Follow-Up: When you are done, record each of your workouts in a training log. Include how long you trained and a short synopsis of the material you covered in the session. Set a goal for yourself, such as performing the above workout ten times before moving on to Level 6. Stay motivated, remain disciplined, be consistent, and work hard. With practice, you will continue to improve your skills and deepen your understanding of the long sword. You're just getting started!

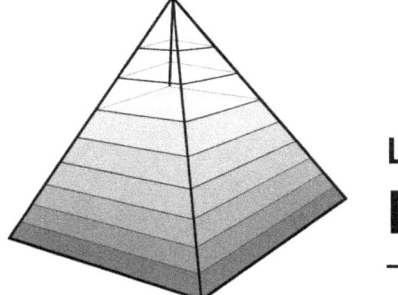

LEVEL 6:
Long Sword Defense

Building a Solid Defense

Level 6 is a reprise of Level 2: Building a Strong Defense, only this time with a long sword. If the material sounds familiar, that's because it is! Using the same formula for learning the long sword that we used when training the short sword, you'll soon realize that you aren't learning something new and are, instead, expanding on things you already know.

The primary goal in any fight should be self-preservation. By prioritizing defense, you minimize the risk of being hit, injured, or incapacitated by your opponent's attacks. A good defense begins with adopting a defensive mindset that is constantly aware of potential threats during a fight. Expect sudden attacks and changes in tactics on the part of your opponent.

Developing the ability to anticipate your opponent's intentions is key to an effective defense. Pay close attention to his body language, footwork, and attack patterns to identify movements that precede or telegraph his next move. Often, an opponent will attack just to test your response so that he can attempt to exploit any opening or vulnerability he perceives in your defense with his next attack. However, by cultivating a defensive mindset along with a strong, guarded position, you should be ready and prepared to protect yourself.

Of course, you should maintain safe fencing distance and stay just outside of your opponent's Circe of Death. From this position you'll have more time to respond to his attacks by evading, blocking, or parrying. Keep in mind that the ultimate goal of your defense is to provide you with a solid foundation from which you can effectively counterattack and defeat your opponent.

Evasion

While you can use your footwork to stay out of range of your opponent's attacks, moving too far can leave you out of range to counterattack fast. Leaning back out of range, a technique called fading, allows you to avoid your opponent's attack but stay in range, standing just at the edge of your striking zone. When you fade, an unanticipated miss can throw your opponent off balance and leave him exposed and vulnerable. As soon as his attack passes by, immediately lean back *into* range and counterattack to an exposed target.

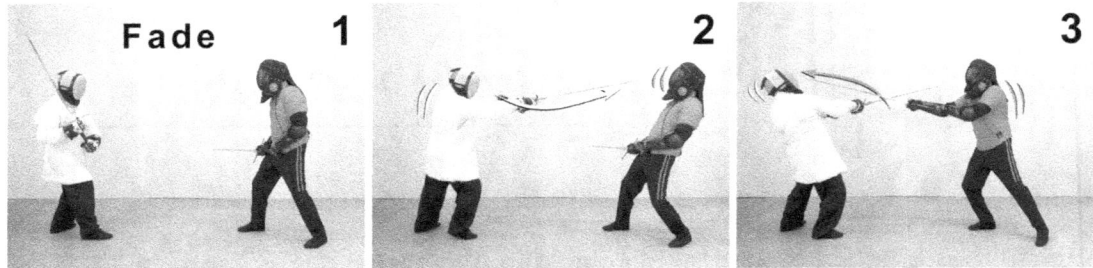

Fade: Begin by hovering just at the edge of your opponent's effective range, watching for any signs of a telegraph (1). When the opponent swings, lean back just out of range, causing him to miss his intended target (2). Immediately lean back into range, striking your opponent with the tip of your sword (3).

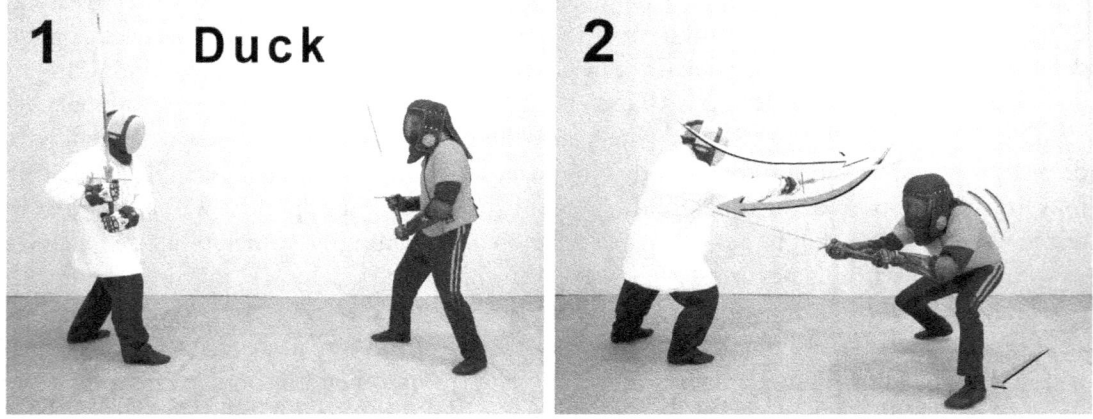

Ducking: Draw a strike by exposing your head. Hold your position until your opponent is fully committed to the angle of his attack (1). Step to your left and duck under his strike, simultaneously countering with a horizontal cut across his abdomen as his sword goes by (2).

Escape Route: When ducking a number 1 downward diagonal strike, you need to move into the acceleration zone, where the angle of the strike gives you space to maneuver, as opposed to moving into the deceleration zone, where the tip of the sword gets closer and closer to the ground, and eventually cuts off any avenue of escape.

Blocking

Blocking involves using your sword to intercept and absorb the energy of the opponent's attack. Use the full length of your blade to make a wall, or roof, between you and your opponent's sword, aiming specifically for both your swords to meet at the center of your blade. If you are at long range, your swords should meet at the weaker part of your opponent's sword, closer to his tip and your hilt, to make the center of your blade stronger in comparison. Blocking with the lower part of your blade may be even stronger than using the center; however, it puts your hands closer to the opponent, which makes them easier for him to target.

Stopping an incoming force requires the application of an equal and opposite force. Let's say your opponent generates force by swinging his sword. Swinging back in an attempt to block his attack requires greater timing than just meeting his attack with a static block. Therefore, avoid swinging to block your opponent's blade. Rather, meet the incoming force with a well-timed *pulse* that you deliver through your sword into the opponent's blade. A pulse is a slight, solid forward push into your block created by momentary tightening of the muscles in your arms, torso, and legs to create a strong, aligned structure at the moment of impact.

Correct positioning in a block is attained when your swords meet at a perpendicular angle, bringing the opponent's sword to a complete and sudden stop. Stopping his sword robs him of momentum, momentarily opening lines of attack for you to utilize while at the same time preventing him from using the leftover momentum from a failed strike to quickly recover and attack again.

174 THE ART AND SCIENCE OF SWORD FIGHTING

The Six Blocks: The high outside block (1), high inside block (2), middle outside block (3), middle inside block (4), low outside block (5), and low inside block (6).

High Blocks

High blocks defend your head and shoulders against downward strikes. They can be performed with the tip of your sword pointing either upward or downward. In downward pointing blocks, position your sword over your head with the hilt held slightly higher than the tip. You can block with your hands held on the left or right side of your body, but they should not be held over your head because they would then be in your opponent's assumed strike zone. Check your position in a mirror to make sure that you are covering your head with your sword and that your hands are off to one side.

Outside and inside high blocks.

Middle-Level Blocks

Middle blocks are primarily used to defend against horizontal attacks aimed for the center of your body, waist up. In a middle-level block, your sword is held vertically along your side, creating a wall between the opponent's sword and your body. The middle block can be performed with the tip of the sword facing up or down. The position of your middle block is usually determined by the initial position your sword happens to be in at the moment the attack is made. If your sword tip is already facing down and lower than the hilt, then block with the tip down since this will provide maximum protection at the earliest moment. Naturally, then, if your sword is pointing upward, you simply block with your tip up. You can increase the strength of your blocks by turning your body slightly into the technique, aligning your centerline with the point of engagement.

Outside and inside middle blocks.

Low Blocks

The low block is generally employed to defend against attacks aimed at your lower body, below the waist. Like the middle block, the low block forms a wall on either side of your body. However, unlike the middle block, the low block can only be performed with the tip of the sword facing downward. Low blocks are really only effective to about knee level, because a strong strike aimed below the knee will usually meet the weak part of your long sword blade and blow through your block. Therefore, a better solution is usually to move your lead foot back out of range. When you block, remember to make sure that your crossguard is aligned to catch the opponent's blade.

Outside and inside low blocks.

Practice your blocks by yourself in front of a mirror to observe your movement and perfect your positioning. Start from a guard position, then visualize your opponent attacking you with a strong cut and move to block it. Freeze and observe your final blocking position. If you see any part of your body exposed on the other side of your sword, you know you are vulnerable to being cut there and can make the appropriate adjustments. Practice until you feel confident blocking high, middle, and low on both your left and right sides.

Next, practice blocking an opponent's strikes. As always, begin this practice slowly. Block just far enough that the target is fully covered, taking care not overextend your block. Ideally, you should seek to intercept the weak part of your opponent's blade with the strong part of yours, about a third of the way down the blade from the crossguard, which also keeps your hand safely out of your opponent's strike zone. Practice meeting each incoming strike with a short, sharp pulse that kills the momentum of the incoming blow as well. Methodically analyze your practice blocks for strengths and weaknesses until you know you are getting them right.

> Don't just practice until you get it right.
> Practice until you can't get it wrong.
> —Andrea Pirlo

Counterattacking

Defense and offense are closely linked in sword fighting. A good defense sets the stage for effective counterattacking, an important part of your offense. Defending effectively creates momentary openings in your opponent's defenses that you must be ready to exploit with quick counterstrikes.

The following drill will help you to learn to see openings and to practice counterattacking. Before starting, though, it is important to commit to having a learner's mindset and to moving on a one-two count for training purposes, or you will not progress as well. Start by having your training partner strike at you and move to block the strike. Once your block is complete, have your partner hold their position momentarily before you riposte, or counterattack, to an open target. While your partner freezes, process your situation, decide your next move, and execute it. Have your partner strike you again and freeze again after you block it. Analyze your new situation and riposte to an open target. If you practice in this manner over and over again, the time you require to decide where to riposte and with what counter will lessen and lessen. For a competitive sword match you need only shorten the timing of your riposte to a half beat so that your counter lands before the opponent can defend. However, for the sake of training, use a predictable, steady tempo in order to concentrate on making clean strikes and blocks.

Counterattacking against a High Inside Strike: Your opponent makes a committed number 1 downward diagonal strike from right to left. You respond with a high inside block (1). Immediately counterattack to his exposed head before he can recover his guard (2).

Counter Attacking against a Middle Inside Strike: Your opponent makes a committed number 3 horizontal strike to your left side. You respond with a middle-level inside block (1). Immediately counterattack to his exposed head before he can recover his guard (2).

Blocking/Riposte Drills

As with the short sword, develop your blocking skills by alternate blocking and striking with a partner in a prearranged pattern. Begin with high strikes and high blocks. One partner strikes first, while the other blocks and then ripostes, striking back at the same level, allowing both partners to attack and defend. The proper evolution of the exercise is to start by blocking and striking to only one side of the body before training on the other side. This way you can focus on building a strong, reliable block without the additional cognitive task of having to detect what side the attack is coming from.

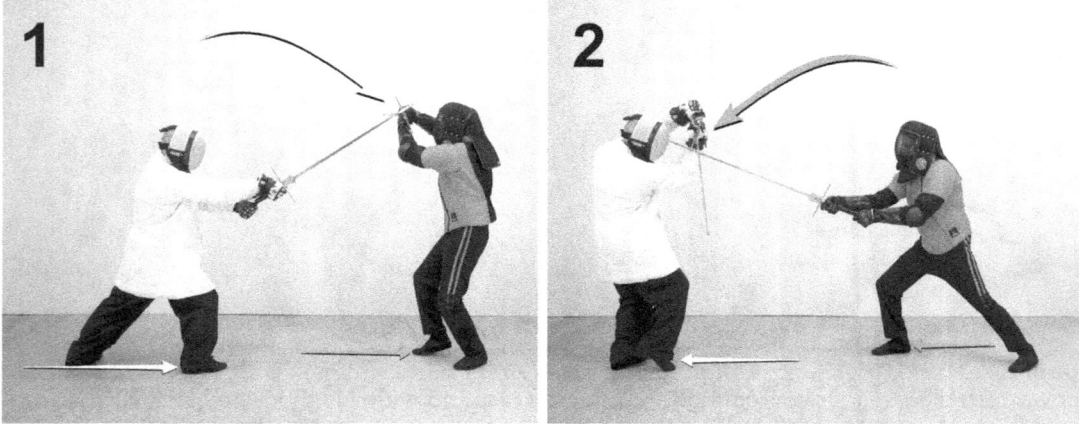

High Blocking/Riposte Drill: The opponent steps in with a high strike. Respond by retreating with a high block (1). Riposte by stepping forward with a high strike of your own, to which the opponent responds with a high block. (2). Repeat the sequence in continuous flow.

Next, combine the two drills in a prearranged pattern to learn what the attack looks like when it is delivered from both the left and from the right. In the final stage of the drill, you employ this skill to defend to either side at random, in a free-flowing manner. Remember, this is a drill, not a fight, so the emphasis is on perfecting your technique, not scoring on your training partner. Focus on developing good form throughout the drill and being certain to return your sword to a solid guard position between each strike and block. This pattern of training is a good habit to ingrain into body memory, even though it is lost when your riposte flows directly from your blocking position. Your techniques will grow precise and your ability to see the battle ground will expand and get better and better.

Next, repeat the drill using mid-level horizontal cuts and middle blocks. Keep your blocking movements as economical as possible, meaning that if the tip of your sword is pointing up when the opponent strikes, keep it up as you block, and vise-versa. Attempting to switch from a tip-up to a tip-down position mid-block leaves you momentarily exposed and unable to block at all.

Then, perform the same drill using only low strikes and low blocks. Start striking and blocking on only one side. Once you feel comfortable on one side, drill the low block and strike on the opposite side. When these drills become easy, alternate the strikes in a prearranged fashion. Finally, functionalize your low block by defending against low strikes delivered to either side at random.

Once you have developed your ability to block strikes coming at one level, it's time to learn to defend against attacks directed at two different levels, such as a high followed by a middle or a middle followed by a low. Once you are comfortable defending against two consecutive attacks, have your practice partner attack with multiple strikes to different levels, first only on one side of the body, then on the other. Next, alternate strikes to either side before moving on to stage four of the drill, striking at random.

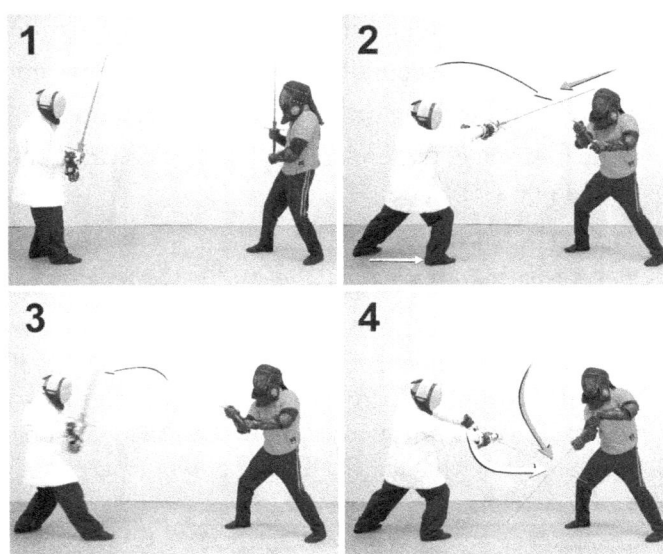

Double Level Blocking/Riposte Drill (High/Low): Begin facing your opponent, both of you in high guard (1). Your opponent steps forward and strikes for your head. Respond with a high block (2). Your opponent immediately retracts his sword (3) and flows into a low strike, which you counter with a low block (4). Recover to ready positions, reverse roles, and repeat.

Combine all three drills by alternating cuts and blocks with a partner to any level. Again, repeat the pattern of training on one side, then the other side before trying both at the same time. Being strict and systematic using this prescribed pattern helps you focus on building a strong, reliable block without the additional cognitive task of having to read what side the attack is coming from. Start from the top, high/middle/low. Then reverse and practice blocking strikes aimed low/middle/high. Create different variations of this drill by changing the order of the blocks. As before, train one side, then the other, before alternating sides in a prearranged pattern. Freestyle practice should be reserved only as a final, culminating activity.

When blocking, strive to intercept the opponent's sword with the middle of your sword on a perpendicular angle to absorb the energy of his strike and bring his sword to a complete stop. Blocking at a 90 degrees angle also acts to maximize your blocking surface, giving you a higher percentage of success blocking your opponent's attack. Be aware and remember that blocking closer to the hilt may be stronger but also brings your hand closer to the opponent's blade.

Practice the basic blocking drill below until you can calmly observe the opponent's movements and quickly identify from which side he will be striking and at what level. Once you can comfortably stand your ground and not flinch when your partner swings at you, you will begin to move with more confidence, strength, and success. When that growth occurs, it is time to add your feet. Practice good footwork by stepping into and out of range, as well as stepping around in a circular pattern as you strike and block.

To summarize, the different versions of the blocking drill are:
1. Downward strike/roof block
2. Horizontal strike/wall block (tip up or down)
3. Leg strike/low block (tip down)
4. Double level (high/middle, middle/low, or high/low)
5. Triple level (low/middle/high, high/middle/low, middle/low/high, or middle/high/low)
6. Freestyle blocking drill (any level at random)

The four stages of developing your blocks with two-man drills is to train each version:
1. On one side
2. On the opposite side
3. Alternating/prearranged
4. Either side at random

Remember to shoot for the Goldilocks Zone! An 80-percent success rate usually results in optimal learning. When you succeed less than that you tend to get discouraged and learning slows down. If you succeed more than that, you don't learn as much because you are not being adequately challenged. Therefore, your partner should strive to attack at a rate where you get hit about one time in five. Sometimes it will be more, and sometimes less; however, remember, it is always a good proportion to encourage personal growth. Of course, you and your partner should use enough control that when you do land a hit, you do no injury.

Block with the Edge or the Flat?

As we mentioned during this same discussion in part one, edge-on-edge contact should be the primary blocking method. First, the mechanics of the hand and arm are much stronger when blocking with the edge than with the flat. Second, crossguards are aligned with the edge of the blade, so if you were to block with the flat and your opponent's sword ran up your blade, there would be nothing to prevent it from cutting your hand (of course, side rings could be added to accentuate the crossguard). That said, as mentioned earlier, the flat edge can still be used successfully in everything from binds, to beats, to parries.

We also debunked the argument that you should not block with the edge of your blade because it may get damaged. In a swordfight, the reality is that you need to attack, and when you do, your opponent is going to block. When he does, you should not give up proper edge alignment at the last second in a misguided attempt at preserving your blade edge. Accept the fact that, not only is your sword going to collide with your opponent's blade, it is also going to impact his armor, and any metal-on-metal contact is also likely to damage the edge of *your* sword. Swords are consumables. Expect that they will get notched, bent, or even broken.

Another important lesson learned is that a thumbs-up grip can provide enough structure to make blocking with the flat of your blade mechanically sound. Blocking with the flat of your blade presents a greater blocking surface. This broader contact won't catch like edge-on-edge contact and allows you to more easily slide along the opponent's blade. These abilities can be useful for performing certain parries and other techniques. Of course, there are exceptions to every rule.

Jamming Blocks

As you learned in Part 1, jamming requires that you take the initiative away from your opponent by moving into his attack, catching it in the acceleration zone (see Level 2). The ability to jam an opponent's technique requires predicting your opponent's intentions and moving into his strike quickly, without hesitation. Jamming attacks are an important prerequisite skill for performing single-tempo master strokes, a technique that we will examine in Level 8.

If your attacker chambers for a forehand strike, circle in to his right side with your left foot. If the opponent is chambered for a backhand strike, angle in to his left with your right foot. In both cases, when you angle into the opponent, keep your centerline aligned with the line of combat. Since the act of jamming the opponent's strike often carries you into close range, you can use your sword to block while you use your free hand to trap the opponent's weapon hand.

You can practice jamming using all the different versions of the blocking drill mentioned above; however, instead of merely blocking, move into the attack as early as possible to jam it before it gains any significant forward momentum.

High Inside Jamming Block: Begin at the edge of your opponent's striking range, watching for him to launch his attack (1). When he does, quickly close the gap with a full step, meeting his sword while it is still in the acceleration zone (2). Slide your rear foot up to assume a strong, balanced stance as you use your sword to press against your opponent's blade (3).

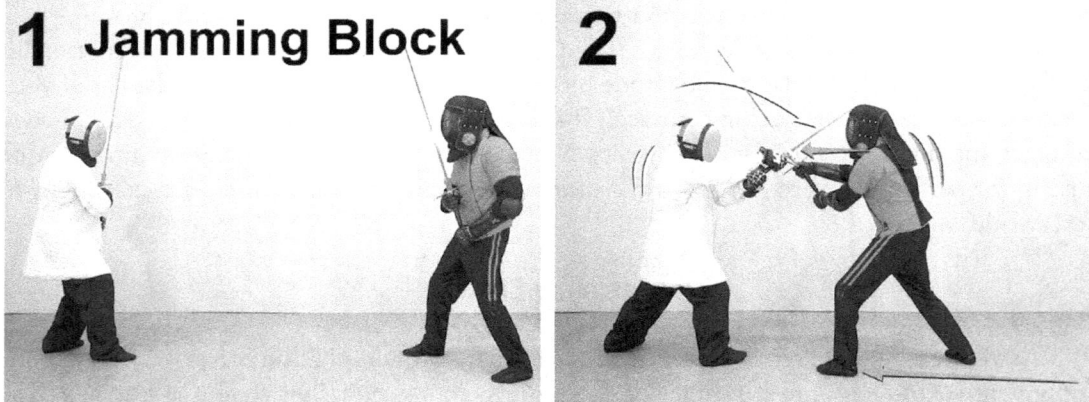

High Outside Jamming Block: Begin at the edge of your opponent's striking range, watching for him to launch his attack (1). When he does, quickly close the gap with a full step, meeting his sword while it is still in the acceleration zone (2).

Dynamic Blocking

Dynamic blocking uses circling footwork to avoid as much of the opponent's striking power as possible by moving you into the deceleration zone where his strike has begun to slow down. Your sword neutralizes the incoming attack with a short, but powerful "pulse strike."

The overhead block is actually somewhere between a block and a parry. Sometimes the opponent's weapon impacts nearly perpendicular to your sword. In such a case, the incoming force is brought almost to a complete stop. If the opponent's sword impacts your sword on a greater angle, it tends to glance off and be safely redirected to the side. Because the opponent's weapon keeps moving, the technique is a parry, not a textbook example of a block.

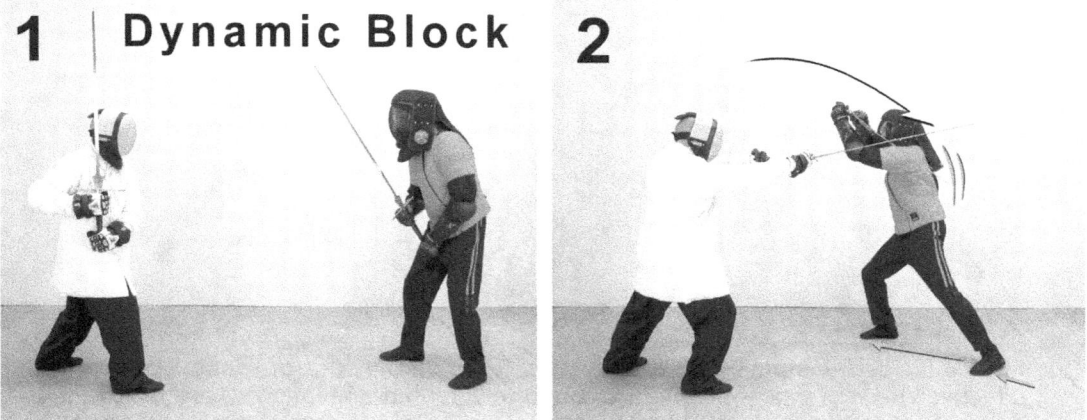

High Inside Dynamic Block: Hover on the edge of your opponent's effective striking range, watching for him to telegraph his intentions (1). When the opponent attacks with a number 1 downward diagonal strike for your head, step off to your right, moving into his deceleration zone as you perform a high block (2).

Middle Inside Dynamic Block and Riposte: Hover on the edge of your opponent's effective striking range, watching for him to telegraph his intentions (1). When the opponent attacks with a number 3 horizontal strike, take a large step off to your right, moving into his deceleration zone (2). Block his strike with a middle-level inside block (3). Counter with a horizontal strike to his head (4).

Parrying

In addition to blocking, you can also parry with your long sword. Parrying involves deflecting or redirecting your opponent's attack away from you with your sword. Once you have achieved blade-to-blade contact with your opponent's sword, use the strong part of your blade to momentarily gain control of and manipulate the path of his weapon from its original, intended course of attack. While it is possible to parry after a block, once you have stopped the opponent's sword, it takes time and energy to get it moving again. It is better to deflect his sword while it is still in motion. On the other hand, a good parry can add unexpected force to the opponent's strike, carrying his sword further than intended. You should only parry, therefore, as far as you need to expose an open line of attack. Over-parrying can leave you exposed and out of position to quickly riposte. Once you have parried the opponent's sword, you must quickly strike to an open target before he can regain his guard. We will address parrying in greater detail in Level 7.

Tres-Tres Drill

Tres-tres, the blocking and striking flow drill that you learned in Part 1, is easily adapted for the long sword. Practicing tres-tres with the long sword will help you train your range, distancing, footwork, blocking, and striking.

Start by standing at maximum fighting range, just outside of your opponent's Circle of Death. Attack by lunging forward and move out of range when defending by pulling your front foot back into a cat stance. Push off with the ball of the front foot, not your heel. The moves should flow smoothly from one into the other.

Tres-Tres Solo Drill *(description on following page)*

Tres-Tres Solo Drill (previous page): Start from a middle guard position (not shown). (1) Defend by dropping the tip of your sword and performing a right to left low block as you retreat your front foot into a cat stance. In the final position, your sword is held vertically, thumbs down, with your right palm facing outward (toward the opponent) as though you were blocking a strike to your right leg. (2) Counterattack by stepping forward into a right lunge stance as you rotate your sword in a shallow arc targeting your opponent's lead shoulder. It is important that you move from the wrists to keep the arc of your strike as direct as possible. (3) Withdraw your right foot into a right cat stance as you perform a high roof block with the long sword held over your head. The handle should be on your right with the tip angled downward slightly to your left. (4) Step forward into a right lunge stance with a low cut from right to left, aiming for the opponent's lead knee. However, do not strike through the target. Rather, stop as soon as you sense that your opponent has successfully blocked your strike. (5) Push off with the ball of your front foot and contract your adductors to withdraw your right foot into a right cat stance as you perform a middle-level wing or window block with your sword held over your right (lead) shoulder, with the tip angled downward behind you. (6) Step forward into a right lunge stance with a vertical downward strike to the opponent's head. (1) Repeat the series, beginning again with move 1.

Once you have completed one revolution of the drill, the last move simply flows back into the beginning while the pattern repeats: low, middle, high; attack, defend, attack. Practicing the drill over and over again allows you to do massive repetitions of the strikes and blocks, as well as helping you develop quick lunging and retreating footwork. As your skill with the drill increases, you can include different footwork patterns such as circling. You can also experiment with changing the range, flowing from long through middle to close range and back again. Your ultimate goal is to be able to apply these blocks and counters in a free-fighting situation.

LEVEL 6: LONG SWORD DEFENSE 187

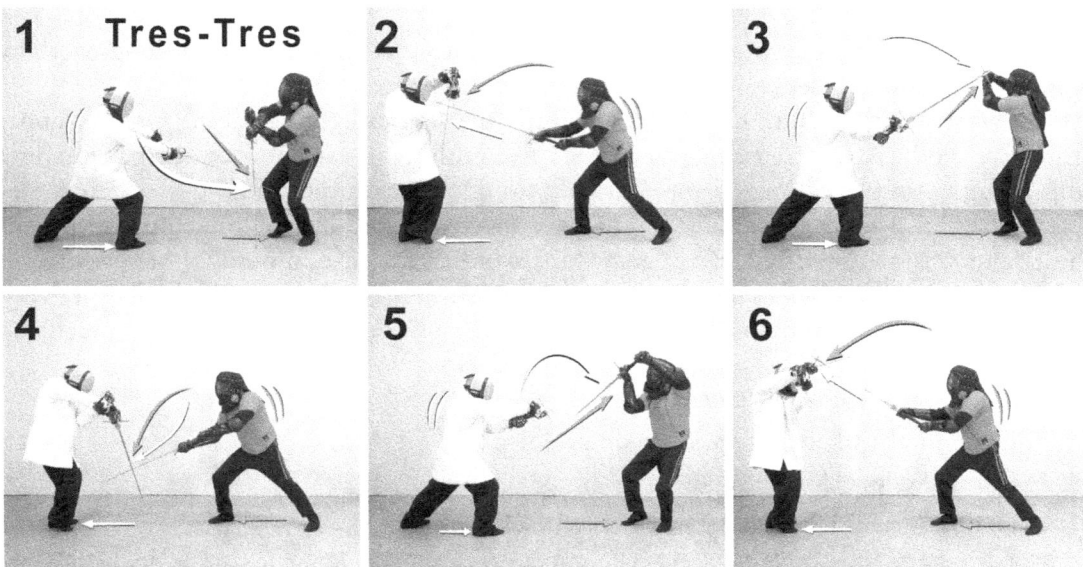

Tres-Tres with a Partner.

Tres-Tres with a Partner Step by Step

A (left): Attack with a low downward diagonal strike to the inside of B's lead knee.

B (right): Defend low with a right to left low block, with your left palm up (1).

B: Attack to the middle level with a vertical downward strike targeting the right shoulder.

A: Defend by withdrawing to a wing block, an inverted block over your right shoulder (2).

A: Attack high with a vertical downward strike to B's head.

B: Defend high with a roof block, tip over your left shoulder (3).

Reverse roles and repeat.

B: Attack low with a downward diagonal strike to the inside of A's lead knee.

A: Defend low with a right to left inverted block, palm facing out (4).

A: Attack middle with a vertical downward half strike to the right shoulder.

B: Defend middle by withdrawing to a right wing block (5).

B: Attack high with a #7 vertical downward strike to A's head.

A: Defend high with a roof block, tip over your left shoulder (6).

Reverse roles and repeat.

Level 6 Workout

This 60-to-90-minute workout is designed to improve your skills with the long sword by combining a strong defense with an effective offensive flow.

1. Warm-Up: 15–20 minutes. Start with five minutes of light stretching for your upper and lower body. After stretching, do three to five minutes of cardio work, such as jumping rope, jogging in place, doing jumping jacks, etc. Do your cardio until you feel tired, and your heartrate is elevated. Follow up with five more minutes of light stretching until your heart rate returns to normal. Next, grab your sword and do five minutes of basic footwork while practicing your blocks, parries, cuts, and thrusts. Start slowly then gradually speed up.

2. Targeting/Distancing/Control: 30–45 minutes. Spend a few minutes practicing each of the six different versions of the blocking drill:

1. Downward strike/roof block
2. Horizontal strike/wall block (tip up or down)
3. Leg strike/low block (tip down)
4. Double level (high/middle, middle/low, or high/low)
5. Triple level (low/middle/high, high/middle/low, middle/low/high, or middle/high/low)
6. Freestyle blocking drill (any level, randomly)

Utilize the four stages of development to methodically train each version:

1. First practice on only one side, throwing a single strike and performing a single block.
2. Next, practice on the opposite side, repeating the same techniques.
3. When you feel comfortable with these, begin alternating sides in a prearranged pattern.
4. Finally, strike to either side at random.

3. Footwork and Flow: 10–15 minutes. Practice the tres-tres fencing flow drill with a partner. Begin outside of your opponent's circle of death and use proper footwork to control the measure, lunging into range to attack and retreating out of range, into a cat stance, as you defend. When you are more comfortable with the drill, start incorporating different footwork patterns, such as circling, as well as flowing from long range to middle, and even close range.

4. Cool Down: 5–10 minutes. Take a few minutes to take your body from "Fight or Flight" into "Rest and Digest." Now is the time to use static stretching to increase your flexibility and to break up the lactic acid that has accumulated in your muscles.

5. Follow-Up: When you are done, record each of your workouts in a training log. Include how long you trained and a short synopsis of the material you covered in the session. Set a goal for yourself, such as performing the above workout ten times before moving on to Level 7. Stay motivated. You are doing great! Be consistent and work hard. Every practice improves your skills and deepens your understanding of sword fighting!

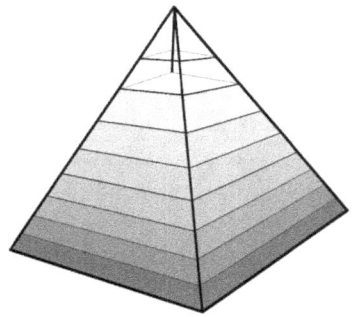

LEVEL 7:
Long Sword Fencing

Back in Level 3, you learned the basics of fencing with a short sword. We are going to build upon those skills to quickly teach you the ins and outs of fencing with a long sword. You'll find that the concepts are basically the same, although the mechanics of performing them with a two-handed sword are slightly different.

As their names suggest, the primary distinction lies in how the swords are held. While the single-handed sword is designed to be wielded with one hand, a long sword has room on the grip for two hands. Wielding the sword with two hands provides increased control, leverage, and power. Two-handed swords also generally have longer blades and, therefore, greater range that requires more deliberate footwork and larger movements to control. Longer blades tend to be heavier, however, requiring more strength to wield effectively.

Controlling the Centerline

Remember, using a true guard to control the centerline puts you in a strong defensive position while simultaneously putting your opponent under imminent threat. Keeping the tip of your sword pointed directly at his face puts him on the defensive, preventing him from entering striking range without having to first either move or get around your sword. If your opponent gives up the center to deliver an arcing strike, he opens a line of attack between the tip of your sword and his face or body. Quickly lunge or step forward with a straight thrust while his sword is still in the acceleration zone.

Engagement and the Bind

By assuming a true guard with the tip of your sword pointing directly at your opponent's face, you force him to contend with this immediate threat by engaging your sword. Once you have found the opponent's blade, your swords are engaged in a bind, if only for a moment.

At middle range, cross the strong part of your sword over the weak part of your opponent's blade to achieve an advantageous bind. This contact allows you to manipulate his blade, simultaneously smothering his attack while opening lines of attack for yourself. At close range, the strong parts of your blades cross, placing you in a heavy bind. In this position you are each able to exert equal force upon the other's sword.

Heavy pressure in the bind is generally discouraged as it prevents you from sensing your opponent's intentions. Light pressure, on the other hand, allows you to sense any pressure that your opponent may exert upon your blade. These tactile clues can reveal your opponent's intentions before you can visually perceive any physical motion. Since you are within striking range, you must not leave any open lines that would allow him to land a simple quick thrust. If your opponent's sword is on the left side of your blade, close his primary lines of attack by positioning your blade slightly to your left, with your point aimed at his left shoulder, creating a wall on your left side with your sword. Likewise, if his blade is on the right side of yours, move your sword slightly to create a defensive wall on your right side, aiming your tip at his right shoulder. Your goal is to simultaneously limit your opponent's ability to attack or defend while creating an open line of attack for you to strike or thrust with your own sword.

You can also get into binds as a result of blocking an attack or having an attack blocked. Most binding with two-handed swords starts in this fashion, either through provocation or as the result of responding to a strike, whereas with a single-handed sword, it is best to seek to actively gain the opponent's blade. In this case, however, you don't seek the opponent's blade. Instead, you simply attack or look to block an incoming attack. The increased mass of the long swords allows you to turn this momentary contact into sustained cohesion between the blades. Once established, your next priority will be to ensure that you quickly move to gain your opponent's blade.

Gaining the Opponent's Blade

As with the short sword, gaining control over your opponent's sword begins with proper positioning of your blade. Position your sword so that more of your blade is over less of theirs. This puts the strong part of your sword against the weaker part of theirs, giving you a mechanical advantage. Utilize the force of gravity by positioning your blade over the top of your opponent's blade. Keep your point on target to provide a threat as well as to set up for a thrust.

Avoid touching blades too early, as this can alert your opponent as to your intentions. When possible, simply float your blade over your opponent's until you are positioned to launch your attack. When it comes time to engage the opponent's sword, press with your true edge against the flat of his blade. This not only maximizes your power but aligns your crossguard to catch your opponent's blade.

LEVEL 7: LONG SWORD FENCING

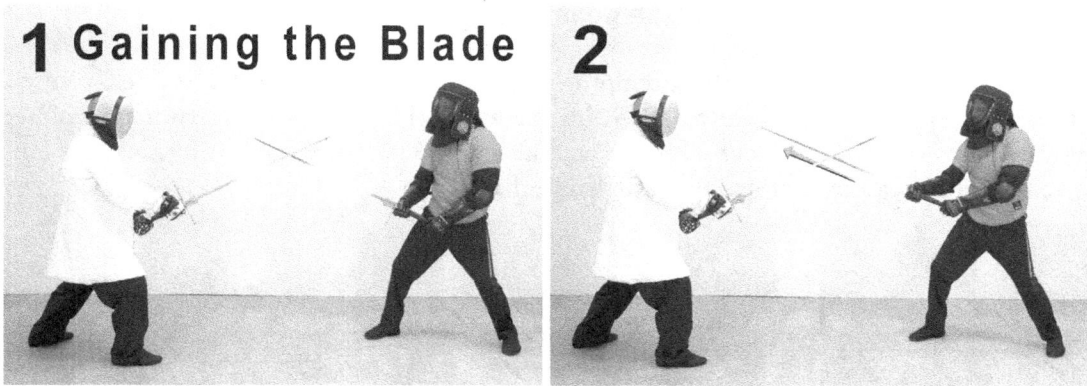

Gaining the Blade: You have engaged your opponent's blade with roughly equal amounts of your swords crossing (1). Extend your arms slightly, allowing your sword to slip past your opponent's blade without moving it until more of your blade is crossing over less of his, providing you with a mechanical advantage (2).

Glide

In the glide, you are already in perfect position to thrust while simultaneously checking your opponent's blade. No manipulation of his sword in necessary, and yet he should momentarily be unable to counterattack. The instant you have gained your opponent's blade, quickly thrust straight forward without pulling back or losing cohesion with his blade. As you thrust forward into the gap, your blade glides along the opponent's blade, checking his sword with the edge of your blade as you drive the tip of your sword into his body.

Glide: You have engaged your opponent's blade and you are both vying to control the center. You see that he is not sufficiently protecting his centerline leaving an open line of attack (1). Extend your arms, followed by a press off your rear leg, allowing your sword to skim past your opponent's blade without moving it (2).

The Cone of Defense

Your opponent will naturally attempt to get around your defense. As he does, you will need to reposition your sword to check his blade, all the while keeping your tip pointed toward him to maintain a constant threat. This can be accomplished using the four long sword guard positions that make up the Cone of Defense.

To describe the Cone of Defense more easily and clearly, we will compare its positions of defense to the numbers on a clock face. Quadrant 1 describes your right high gate, anywhere between 12 and 3 o'clock. It is defended by assuming a right hanging guard (right ox). Quadrant 2, your right low gate position, extends from 3 to 6 o'clock, and it is defended with a right middle guard (right plow). Moving your sword to the left places you in quadrant 3, which is defended with a left middle guard (left plow). Quadrant 4 is your left high gate, and it is defended with a left hanging guard (left ox).

Remember when we discussed whether it was better to block with the edge or the flat of the blade? Using the Cone of Defense is one of those times where you can still be mechanically sound blocking with the flat of the blade.

Developing a strong Cone of Defense is an important prerequisite skill to learning and employing the single tempo master cuts presented later in Level 8.

LEVEL 7: LONG SWORD FENCING 193

Cone of Defense—Quadrant 1: You have engaged your opponent's sword to the outside of your blade in middle guard (1). As your opponent thrusts forward, raise your sword to the outside, countering with position 1 (2). Extend your arms, using your sword to check your opponent's blade as you step forward, striking him with the tip (3).

Cone of Defense—Quadrant 2: You have engaged your opponent's sword to the outside of your blade in middle guard when he thrusts forward. Counter his thrust with position 2 (1). Extend your arms, checking his blade as you lean forward, striking him in the face with the tip (3).

Cone of Defense—Quadrant 3: You have blocked your opponent's sword to the inside of your blade in middle guard, countering his strike with position 3 (1). Immediately extend your arms, checking your opponent's blade as you lean forward, thrusting him in the face (3).

Cone of Defense—Quadrant 4: You have engaged your opponent's blade to the inside in middle guard (1). As the opponent thrusts forward, raise your arms to the inside, countering his thrust with position 4 (2). Extend your arms, using your sword to check your opponent's blade as you lean in and thrust forward, striking him with the tip (3).

Press

The press is similar to the glide, but you are using pressure to displace your opponent's blade while maintaining contact with it in order to control it. The action borders on binding, a skill we will look at in the next level. From an engaged position, extend your sword arm to intercept the weak part of your opponent's blade with the middle part of yours. This gives you a mechanical advantage in leverage that allows you to push the opponent's sword sideways as you thrust into the resulting opening.

When you press the opponent's blade, it is common for him to press back in return. If you are expecting this, you can use his own energy against him. For example, you press the opponent's sword, and he presses back to reclaim the line, but you make a change of engagement, circling under the pressure of his sword to suddenly and unexpectedly pop up on the opposite side of his sword and glide forward with a thrust that drives the tip of your sword into him.

Press: You have engaged and gained your opponent's blade (1). Extend your arms as you step forward with your rear leg, using your sword to push your opponent's blade off center as you thrust forward, striking him with the tip (2).

Beat

Beating is the action of striking the opponent's blade in order to disrupt his defenses and open up a viable line of attack. Because you have two hands powering the motion, a beat with a long sword is much stronger than a beat with a short sword. To beat the opponent's sword, hit it laterally with a quick, sharp strike. Strike to the weakest part of the opponent's blade for maximum effect, hitting as close to the tip of his sword as possible. Hitting near the hands doesn't work as well because the sword is stronger structurally there, so the strike results in less movement of the opponent's sword. Don't overcommit when executing a beat, since you will have but an instant to take advantage of the opening you created. Optimally, after a beat your sword will be pointed directly at the target, ready to thrust forward.

Beat: You have engaged your opponent's blade, and you are both vying for center (1). Use a short, sharp pulse to knock your opponent's blade off center (2). Immediately thrust forward, striking him with the tip before he can reclaim the center (3).

Change of Engagement

A change of engagement, also called a cut around, allows you to circle around your opponent's sword in order to create an open line of attack. It is used when your sword makes contact with your opponent's sword, and he pushes against your sword in an effort to control You can make a Change of Engagement by cutting under or cutting over the opponent's sword.

To execute a cut under, you must be sensitive to changes in pressure on your sword. As soon as you feel your opponent's sword pressing on yours, relax and make a tight circular motion with the tip of your sword under his blade to take the centerline. To make the tight circular motion, pull up on the pommel to drop the tip of your sword under your opponent's blade, then push on the pommel to raise your tip, suddenly popping up on the other side. Immediately strike or thrust into the gap before your opponent can reclaim the line.

Cut Under: Your opponent is applying lateral pressure against your blade (1). Lower the tip of your sword, letting him slip past your blade (2). Immediately thrust forward, striking him with the tip before he can recover (3).

Cut Over

The cut over is similar to the cut under except that, instead of passing under your opponent's blade, you go over the tip of his sword instead. It is used when your sword is close to the tip of your opponent's sword, making it shorter and thereby faster to pass over his sword than under it. In this common move, you feel a little pressure against your blade first, then remove your sword by lifting the tip, thereby letting the opponent's blade move laterally, which opens a vertical line of attack.

The cut over is used whenever the tip of your opponent's sword is close to your blade, making it more economical to pass over his tip with your blade than passing under his blade with your tip. Press down on the pommel of your sword, raising the blade just enough to clear the tip of his sword, then pull up on the pommel to deliver a strike or thrust along the open line before your opponent can parry your attack.

Cut Over: You've gained the opponent's blade, and he is applying lateral pressure in an attempt to hold the center (1). Raise the tip of your sword, letting his blade slip under yours (2). Immediately thrust forward, striking him with the tip before he can recover (3).

Double Change

The double change consists of a combination or two of consecutive changes of engagement performed in quick succession. Your first change is actually a feint. It causes the opponent to over-block in an attempt to protect his threatened line. When he does, you perform a second change, returning to your original line of attack. Don't worry about making contact with the opponent's sword between changes. If you counter quickly with a thrust or strike, your opponent will have trouble blocking or reclaiming the center.

Double Change: Your opponent is applying lateral pressure against your blade, so you cut under his blade (1). The opponent recovers quickly and reclaims the center, but now he is applying lateral pressure against your blade in the opposite direction (2). Respond by cutting under his blade again (3). Immediately thrust forward, striking him with the tip before he can recover (4).

Parry

While blocking stops the opponent's sword, parrying redirects the opponent's sword off its intended line of attack. It is exceptionally useful against thrusts. While it is possible to parry after a block, once you have stopped the opponent's sword, it takes time and energy to get it moving again. It is better, therefore, to deflect his sword while it is still in motion. Once you have parried the opponent's sword, you must quickly strike to an open target before he can regain his guard.

Be aware and careful, though, because without your meaning to, a good parry can backfire. A wary opponent may be able to redirect his strike, using your own force to help power a second strike to an open target.

Since the human body is taller than it is wide, parry laterally, to the sides, as opposed to vertically. If you were to parry a thrust upward from below, you risk parrying his thrust into your own face. It is much safer to parry to the sides, which allows you to redirect the strike clear of your body with the smallest motion, since your body is thinner than it is tall.

Parry with the middle of your blade but avoid parrying with the flat. By parrying with the edge, you maximize the amount of pressure you can exert on your opponent's sword. Only parry as far as you need to in order to expose an open line of attack. Over-parrying can leave you exposed and out of position to quickly counterattack.

A semi-circular parry moves the opponent's blade from the middle line to the low line, or vice-versa. For example, you are engaged with the opponent's blade in a middle outside guard. Parry the opponent's blade in a clockwise circle, downward to the outside.

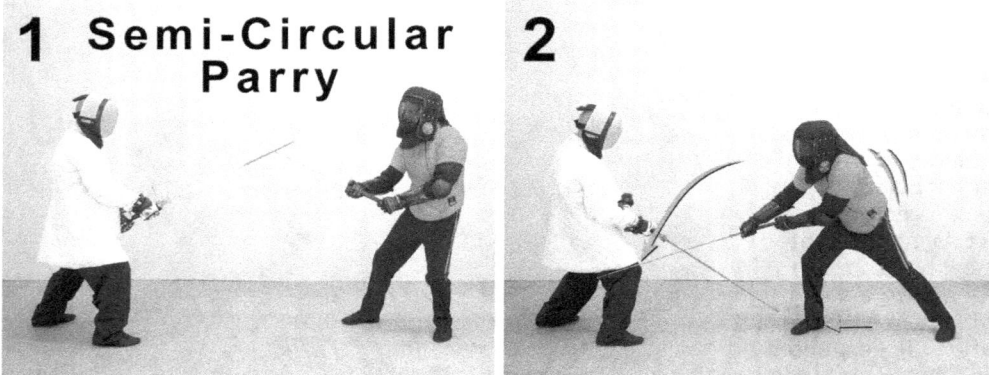

High-to-Low Semi-Circular Parry: You've gained the opponent's blade (1). Drop the tip of your sword as you lunge forward, striking him in the knee (2).

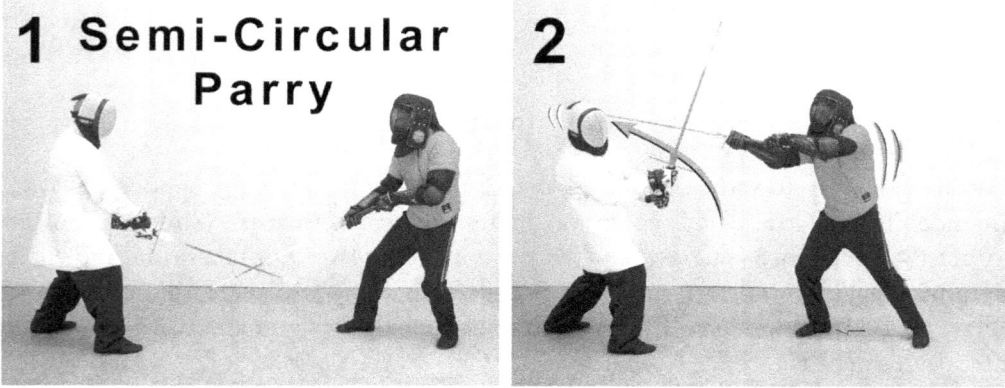

Low-to-High Semi-Circular Parry: You've engaged the opponent's blade in low guard (1). Step forward, gaining your opponent's blade as you raise your sword in a counterclockwise half circle, striking him in the head (2).

A circular parry redirects the opponent's sword in a complete circle, returning to the original line without ever losing cohesion. However, by pressing your sword forward as you make the circular parry, by the time your sword returns to the original line, you should be in a more advantageous position to land an attack.

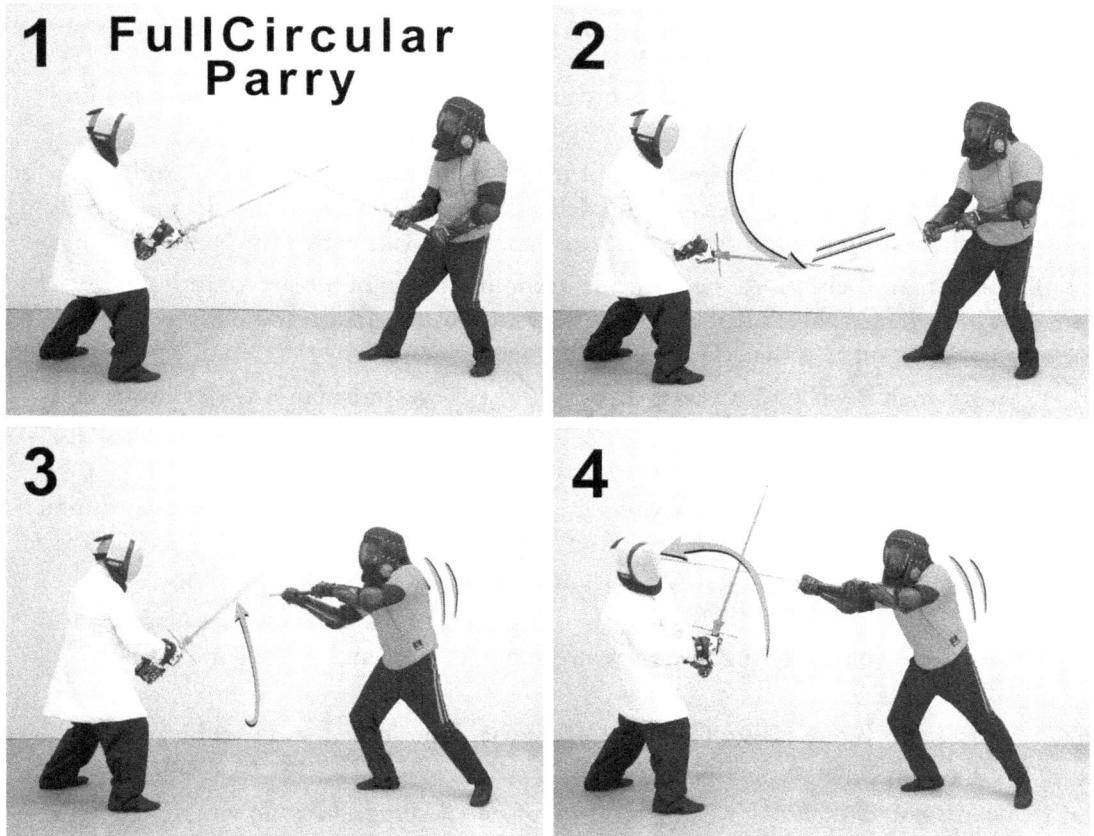

Circular Parry: You've gained the opponent's blade on the inside in middle guard (1). Press your sword down in a counterclockwise arc (2). Lean in as you continue the circle, pressing his blade ahead of your own (3). Complete the circular parry with a focused strike to the head (4).

A Sample Bout

As we observed previously, sword fighting can be likened to a game of physical chess. Again, while there are practically infinite combinations of possibilities that could play out, the following example will provide you with a good sampling of a skilled exchange. By working through it with a partner, you may gain new and clearer understanding of the strategies and tactics used when fighting with the long sword.

1. Swordsman A faces off against Swordsman B, beginning well out of, both holding their swords in a right high guard.
2. As the fighters approach the edge of the Circle of Death, Swordsman A suddenly draws back his sword, steps in, and delivers a number 1 downward diagonal strike aimed at Swordsman B's left side. Swordsman B blocks with a tip-up high left block.
3. Swordsman B checks A's sword while dropping the tip of his sword until it points at Swordsman A's face. He then thrusts forward. Swordsman A responds by parrying this thrust off to his left.
4. Swordsman B wheels his sword overhead to strike Swordsman A with a horizontal strike to the right side of his head, which Swordsman A counters with a tip-up high block.
5. Swordman A performs a clockwise semi-circular parry, targeting B's legs. Swordsman B retreats, and the fighters end up in middle guard with the swords crossed on the inside.
6. Swordsman A makes a change of engagement to an outside position, then extends his arm to gain control of B's blade by crossing more of his blade over B's blade than B has over A's blade, giving Swordsman A more leverage and hence a mechanical advantage.
7. Swordsman B moves into Cone of Defense hand position 1 and uses his edge to redirect A's blade to the right.
8. Swordsman B thrusts forward, and Swordsman A responds by flowing into a high block.
9. Swordsman B cuts around A's sword, taking the inside line, and lunges forward with a thrust to A's chest.
10. Swordsman A defends with the Cone of Defense hand position 3, redirecting Swordsman B's thrust to the inside, and driving the tip of his sword into B's face.

Level 7 Workout

This 60-to-90-minute workout is designed to develop your fencing skills with a two-handed long sword.

1. Warm-Up: 15–20 minutes. Start with five minutes of light stretching for your upper and lower body. Follow this with five minutes of cardio work, such as jumping rope, jogging in place, doing jumping jacks, etc. Try to maintain a high activity level until you feel tired and your heartrate becomes elevated. Then, do five more minutes of light stretching until your heart rate returns to normal. Next, grab your sword and work through some basic footwork while you practice your blocks, parries, cuts, and thrusts, first slowly then gradually speeding up.

2. The Cone of Defense: 10–15 minutes
Drill 1: Practice all four hand positions.
Drill 2: Lunge forward moving from position 2 to position 3.
Drill 3: Clear a stationary sword while lunging, moving from 2 to 3.
Drill 4: Clear a thrust while lunging, moving from 2 to 3.
Drill 5: Same as Drill 4 but clear the thrust and stab your partner at the same time.

Begin moving slowly until you have the mechanics of the technique correct, then gradually add speed and power. While you might be tempted to train without full gear, especially when you are going slowly, it is recommended that you suit up for safety.

3. Fencing Drills: 20–25 minutes. Work through the various techniques presented in Level 7 with a partner. Start by practicing gaining your partner's blade. Once engaged, gently play for control of the center line using the glide and press. Take turns playing the part of the aggressor, thrusting forward when you see an opening causing the defender to move and protect the open line. Remember, the goal is to drill and develop good habits, not score points on an opponent. Sometimes your thrust will land; other times it won't. Shoot for the Goldilocks zone of a 75–80 percent success rate. Missing one in four or five actually promotes learning and makes you better. Start moving slowly, gradually increasing the speed and intensity. Work together to maximize your mutual learning experiences. Switch roles and repeat.

Next, take turns practicing the change of engagement. This could be in the form of a cut over or a cut under the opponent's blade, depending on the positioning of the swords. Then practice the double change, while your partner defends. Your opponent should retreat as you advance to maintain correct fencing distance. Reverse roles and repeat the drill.

Then, practice using the beat to open a line of attack, while your partner attempts to defend. Reverse roles and repeat the drill.

Finally, put all the techniques together, using each to best effect as the situation arises, being sure that both you and your partner practice being the attacker and defender, deciding together when to change roles. Remember, these are drills, not sparring, so keep the focus on developing your technique rather than scoring points. The idea is to practice many repetitions with the focus on developing optimal techniques. If you are worried about scoring and being scored upon, you cannot focus on learning and performing the techniques to the best of your ability.

4. Sparring: 10–15 minutes. The only way to know what techniques work best under what conditions is to test them out against a non-compliant opponent. Maintain a strong defense at all times, then focus on analyzing your opponent's defense and exploiting his weaknesses to land specific moves. Even though you should be wearing full safety equipment when you spar, you should still control the strength of your strikes and take care not to injure your training partner. A good guideline is to not hit your partner any harder than you want to be hit.

5. Cool Down: 5–10 minutes. Take a few minutes to take your body's autonomic nervous system from "Fight or Flight" into "Rest and Digest." Now is the time to use static stretching to increase your flexibility and break up the lactic acid that has accumulated in your muscles.

6. Follow-Up: When you are done, record each of your workouts in a training log. Include how long you trained and a short synopsis of the material you covered in the session. Set a goal for yourself, such as performing the above workout ten times before moving on to Level 8. Just think about how far you have come! Stay motivated, remain disciplined, be consistent, and keep working hard.

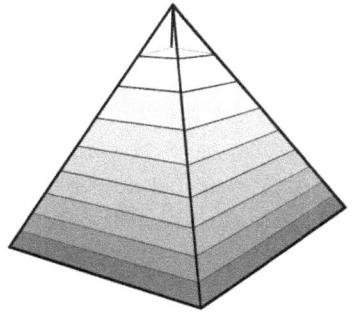

LEVEL 8:
Advanced Long Sword

Before you train advanced long sword techniques, you should have trained hard and often to put into place a deep understanding of the fundamental techniques and principles presented in Levels 5, 6, and 7. The workouts should have honed your skills in areas such as footwork, timing, distance management, and blade control. This foundational base is necessary for advanced long sword training, which involves a more sophisticated level of training and understanding.

Again, if this all sounds familiar, that is by design. As we've seen in the previous two levels, fighting with the long sword and fighting with the short sword share many commonalities. Just as Levels 5 and 6, Long Sword Offense and Long Sword Defense, were reprises of Levels 1 and 2, Level 8 reads much like Level 4. By applying the same principles you learned with the short sword to the long sword, we can streamline your learning. More versatile applications of techniques make for less memorization, which equates to more efficient and effective mastery.

Long Range

When the objective is to hit your opponent and not get hit back, trained combatants will naturally stand at their maximum striking range to minimize the chances of being struck while staying close enough to attack. Effective long-range combinations require quick, efficient footwork and proper target prioritization. At this long range, it makes sense to strike at the nearest vulnerable targets, usually the hands and lead leg. Targeting the edges is a key element of the outside game.

When targeting the leg, aim for the lead knee. Be ready to attack as soon as he moves into your circle. To keep your opponent from being able to simply step back out of range of your strike, try to anticipate his advance. If you can catch him mid-stride as he enters, it will be difficult for him to withdraw his leg before your strike lands. Remember that attacking your opponent's low line leaves your high line open and your head exposed. Therefore, it is essential to strike at maximum range to avoid any counter cut. As always, be prepared to capitalize on the success or failure of your initial strike. If your strike misses, be prepared to maintain the initiative by flowing directly into a second attack. If your attack is successful, quickly move back out of range to avoid your opponent's counterattack.

When targeting the hand, full strikes can leave you exposed should your attack fail. Therefore, use half strikes when attacking the hand. Returning quickly to your original guarded position minimizes the amount of time you are exposed. If your first cut misses, you can use a double strike to make a second, unexpected attack to the same target. If your opponent avoided your strike by pulling his hands back and out of range, compensate by leaning in slightly farther with your second strike.

A hand strike usually requires less power to harm to your opponent than a head or body shot, yet it still has the ability to end the confrontation. However, landing a hand strike can be difficult to accomplish because the opponent's hands can move quickly. Rather than chasing the opponent's hands around trying to hit them, increase your chances by waiting for him to commit to a strike instead. You will not only then know where the opponent's hands should be at a given time, but, because he is committed to the attack, it will be difficult for him to avoid your counterstrike. Furthermore, if you strike his hand straight on as he is swinging at you, the resulting forces will be far greater than if you had hit his hand when it was stationary. Keep in mind that merely striking the opponent's weapon hand may not be enough to end the confrontation. Be prepared to either continue striking or quickly move safely out of range after striking his hands.

The ability to strike the hands successfully and consistently requires that you be able to read your opponent, see his attack coming, and plot the trajectory of your sword to his hand almost instantaneously in your head. Developing these skills takes practice.

Outside Game: Hover at the edge of your opponent's Circle of Death, watching for him to telegraph his attack (1). As he strikes for your head, evade by fading back out of range of his strike and simultaneously hit his hands (2).

The Three-Step Rule

You already learned about baiting and drawing in Part 1. The Three-Step Rule builds on these strategies by providing you with an easy-to-remember formula to subtly and successfully set up your opponent:

1) Leave an opening your opponent cannot resist.
2) Wait until he is committed to his attack.
3) Counter where you know he will be open.

The key to using the Three-Step Rule lies in hours of committed slow practice with a partner training how to create openings, recognize when an opponent is committed to his attack, and know what attack you should use back. Leave openings and have your partner attack as he would in combat, but at half speed. React and counterattack at half speed as well. Moving slowly allows you to concentrate on refining your technique, as opposed to moving quickly and instinctively which does not allow for analysis and evaluation during the execution, which is when the most progress and improvement takes place. Use this time to learn how to see, feel, and flow. Speed will come later of its own accord, and, when it does, your techniques will flow quickly without the appearance of being hurried or rushed.

For example, since a right to left diagonal strike is the habitual methods of attack, there is a very good chance that you can draw a right high strike by leaving your head exposed. Your opponent will strike fast and hard when he takes this bait, and he may take it the instant it is offered. So, don't get caught sleeping! Be prepared to evade or block the instant your opponent moves to take the strike. Once you have neutralized his attack, immediately counterattack while his sword is still out of position, and he is recovering from his failed attack.

Three-Step Rule: Bait your opponent by exposing your head, offering him a target he cannot resist (1). When he moves to strike, hold your position until he is fully committed to his attack, then suddenly duck his strike, hitting his hands as his sword goes by (2).

Feinting

As we learned in Part 1, a feint is a fake attack intended to ensure your opponent is incapable of dealing with your real attack, which is ready to go right behind the feint. The most basic feint is something along the lines of "fake left, go right," but even making the most basic of feints work in sparring takes practice. Here are some guidelines to keep in mind when feinting:

1) Any feint should also be a real attack.

2) Your opponent must feel threatened by your feint.

3) Your feint should not leave you vulnerable to a double hit.

First and foremost, any feint you throw should also be a real attack. If you stick to only one guideline, this is the one. You miss a good opportunity to strike your opponent if your feint does not continue into a real attack. Furthermore, if you feint and your opponent does not react to it, he will still have time to respond by either blocking your true attack, or worse, by countering with a simple direct attack while you are bouncing between semi-attacks.

The key to feinting is to make your opponent respond to your initial move in a way that makes your real attack more likely to succeed. If he just sits there, secure in his knowledge that you are only trying to fake him out, your feints will be meaningless. However, if all your feints are also real attacks, whenever your opponent does not defend against the feint, it is exactly the same as if he did not defend against your attack. In order for your feint to be effective, your opponent must perceive and feel threatened by it first and then be pulled into action in response to it. If your opponent does not perceive your action as threatening to him, he will probably not react. Therefore, make your initial movements obvious enough that your opponent sees what you are doing and has time to respond. When he is committed to his response, change directions mid-swing, striking him from a new, open angle before he can recover and respond.

Finally, your feint should not leave you vulnerable to a double hit. Protecting yourself from a double hit takes some foresight and anticipation. If the opponent does not fall for your feint, they might simply attack you at the same time. You must be prepared for this possibility, or you risk a double hit. Be aware, as well, that the opponent may also attack within the space you create if you take too long to switch between your feint and your intended hit. Remember that most feints are not done with any sort of engagement between your blades. When fighting in absence of the blade, your risk of a double hit is already sharply increased. Switching attacks mid-motion further increases the likelihood of your opponent launching a *heedless* attack. A heedless attack occurs when your opponent does not know or does not care what the consequences of his attack will be on himself, which often results in mutual hits.

When you have found and engaged your opponent's blade, you are fighting with *cohesion*, meaning the blades are touching, allowing you to feel your opponent's intentions through their sword. This cohesion makes feints much more difficult, as the tactile feedback between you and your opponent is much more direct. Rather than disengage to attempt a feint, it would be better to work to gain your opponent's blade though winding (explained later in this chapter), pushing, and the like. A correct attack and understanding how to wind in your bind will generally get you a lot further than feinting. Many successful sword fighters feint rarely, if at all, for this very reason—feinting can be risky in comparison to fighting with cohesion.

Feinting: Begin squared off in high guard (1). Since the opponent's sword is on the right side of his body, strike to his left side (2). If he does not move to block in time, strike him, but if he does move to block, quickly wheel around his block to strike his right side while his sword is out of position (3).

Programming

The human mind can be very predictable. Our brains have a natural tendency to look for patterns, and you can use this knowledge to trick your opponent into doing what you want him to do. This is called programming. Programming is an exceptional method of setting up your techniques and maximizing the probability of eluding your opponent's defenses in order to land a decisive, disabling strike. Programming is accomplished by first getting your opponent to expect a certain attack and then quickly changing your attack halfway through the technique.

To begin programming, deliver a strike to any open target. If it is blocked, retreat to your ready position, only to attack the same target again in exactly the same manner a moment later. Make note of how your opponent counters your technique and quickly determine where he is open in that instant. The third time you attack, your opponent will subconsciously expect the same attack you have thrown twice previously. Use that expectation to your advantage by feinting with the initial technique and striking where your opponent has left himself open.

Again, proper timing is important. You must remain committed to your feint until you perceive that the opponent has committed to a specific defense before you quickly and smoothly change your strike to an unexpected, and therefore an undefended, one. Do not strike on a 1–2 practice count as this allows your opponent an opportunity to adjust and counter your technique. Instead, strike on the half-beat... meaning not counting 1–2, but 1–1.5!

Programming: Begin squared off in high guard (1). Since the opponent's sword is on the right side of his body, strike to his left side. If he does not move to block in time, strike him (2), then quickly recover (3). Strike the same target, expecting that he will now move to block (4). When he does, quickly wheel around to strike his right side (5). When he moves to block his right side, wheel your sword around to strike him on his left side while his sword is out of position (6).

Trick Guards

As you learned in Part 1, the following ready positions are not designed to offer you protection. Instead, they are well-laid traps that rely on deception, earning them the name "trick guards." Rather than start from one of these positions, allowing your opponent the opportunity to study your position and figure out your plan, it is better to adopt an alternate ready position suddenly in the midst of combat. In the heat of the moment, your opponent is far more likely to get greedy and take the bait.

Low Guard

One of the most deceptive ready positions is the low guard, commonly referred to as a fool's guard, so named because it leaves your entire body seemingly exposed to attack, but, as the saying goes, only fools rush in. In reality, the tip of your sword is close to your opponent in this guard. Assume a fool's guard by dropping the tip of your sword in front of you. Once your opponent begins stepping forward, he is committed to moving in that direction until he can replant his foot. Therefore, as the opponent advances to attack, press down on the pommel to quickly raise the tip of your sword into a thrust. If your timing is good, you can catch him midstride, hitting him square in the chest or face, killing his momentum and disrupting his attack.

Low Guard: Set-up (1) and execution (2).

Low Guard: Lure the opponent in by suddenly and unexpectedly dropping the tip of your sword in the midst of combat (1). As he takes the bait and begins to strike, catch him in the acceleration zone, lunging forward with a thrust to the face (2).

Rear Low Guard

The rear low guard, often called a tail guard, is assumed by dropping the tip of your sword down and behind you. This position appears to leave you defenseless; however, as in each of the trick guards, this is seldom the case so long as you have good timing and are able to control distance. Be ready to step forward with your rear foot to close the gap or to quickly step back with your front foot to maintain proper distancing should the opponent rush you. Both maneuvers place you in a strong position to effectively attack your opponent.

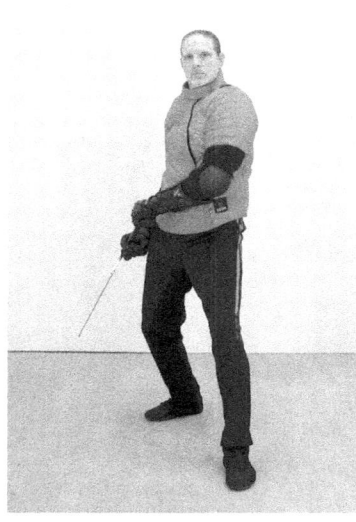
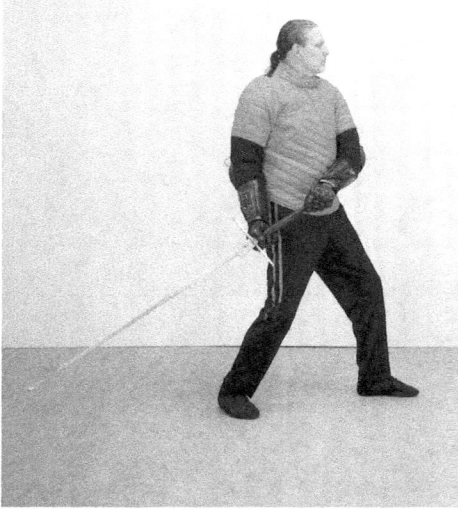

Rear Low Guard

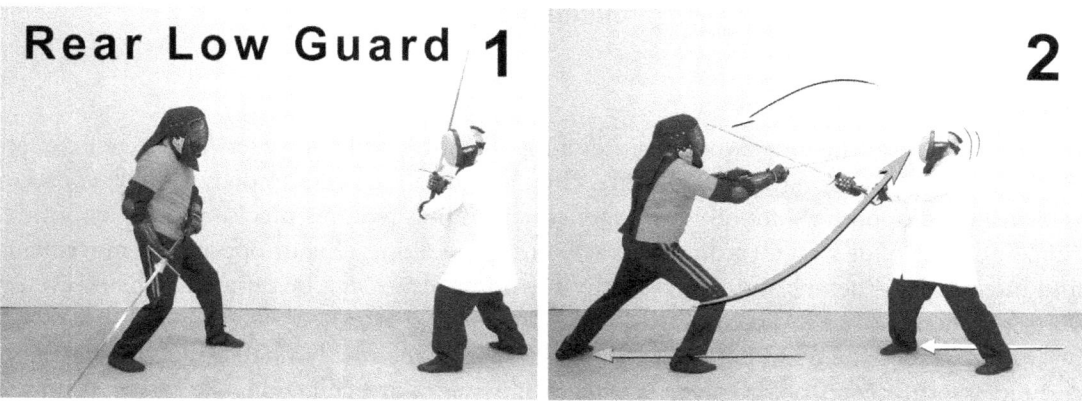

Rear Low Guard: Lure the opponent in by suddenly and unexpectedly dropping the tip of your sword down and behind you (1). As he takes the bait and steps in to strike, step back to maintain distance as you make a sweeping number 5 strike, an upward diagonal strike, to the face (2).

Rear High Guard

The rear high guard, also called a wrath guard, is assumed by leaning your body away from the opponent as you chamber your sword to your right side, resting on your upper arm with the tip pointing back a little behind you. This position can be used to launch a powerful overhand strike. Begin the movement by rotating your body to generate momentum with the sword. As you do, assume a strong, upright posture, and realign your center with your opponent. From here, your sword leads your body as you either step forward with your rear foot to close the gap, or quickly step back with your front foot to maintain proper distancing if the opponent rushes you. Both maneuvers place you in a strong position to effectively attack your opponent with a number 1 strike, cutting downward diagonally from right to left.

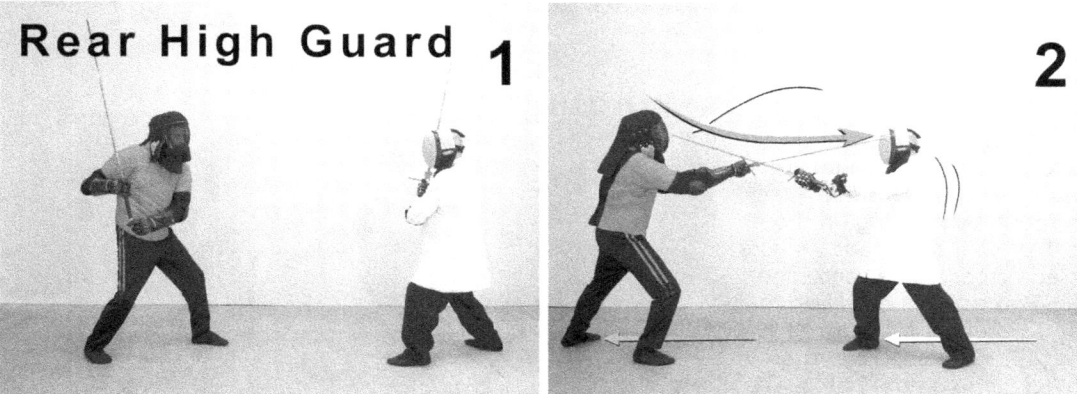

Rear High Guard: Lure the opponent in by suddenly and unexpectedly switching to a left lead with your sword held behind you (1). As he takes the bait and steps in to strike, step back to maintain distance as you make a number 3, right-to-left horizontal strike to the head (2).

Middle Range

Winding

Winding with the long sword requires a high level of skill and practice to execute effectively. It involves rotating your sword in a circular motion in order to deliver quick consecutive strikes to opposite sides of your opponent. Winding requires precise timing, coordination, and control of your sword, as well as an understanding of your opponent's movements and intentions. When performed correctly, a winding attack can be difficult to block even if your opponent knows it is coming.

Develop accurate winding on the Meyer's Square. Open with a half strike on any angle, stopping at the center of the target and withdrawing your blade along the original line of attack. Without returning to or flowing through a guarded position, wheel the tip of your sword 360 degrees and perform a full strike from the opposite angle along the same line. Next, develop winding with speed and power by training on a pell or tire dummy.

Helicopter attack is a term used to describe a series of consecutive high horizontal winding strikes that deliver quick multiple attacks to opposite sides. A helicopter strike can be even more effective when paired with footwork patterns, such as circling.

Winding: Using a thumb grip to stabilize the blade, swing your sword in a horizontal arc over your head from left to right (1). Complete the rotation by pivoting on the ball of your right foot, as your blade crosses the centerline (2). Return in an overhead horizontal arc from right to left (3). Complete the rotation by pivoting on the ball of your left foot, as your blade crosses the centerline (4).

LEVEL 8: ADVANCED LONG SWORD   213

Winding: Starting from a high guard (1). The winding strike starts on your right side, the left of our opponent, and swings around overhead to your left side, the right side of the opponent's head (2) or to the right side (3). Follow up either strike with the other, striking quickly to the opposite side (horizontal arrows).

You can also use winding to immediately follow-up on a blocked attack. When your opponent blocks your sword, his sword is not only committed to protecting one side of his body, but he is also likely to be momentarily moving or applying pressure away from his centerline. This provides you with an opportunity to suddenly wheel your sword to unexpectedly attack from the opposite angle. As soon as you recognize that your initial attack is about to be blocked, turn your strike into a half strike, pulling back along the original line of attack. However, instead of withdrawing your sword to a guarded position, quickly rotate the blade in a full circle, attacking 180 degrees from your original angle of attack.

Defensively, you can use a winding strike to break a helicopter attack. As your opponent attacks, you block his first attack, but as he wheels around for a second strike, drop the tip of your sword to deliver a short winding strike under your opponent's blade. This winding strike will close his line of attack and catch his sword with the strong part of your blade, as you simultaneously arc the tip of your sword into the pocket of your opponent's neck. If you err high, you will still hit him in the head, and, if your strike comes in low, your strike should hit somewhere on his shoulder. The end result is a dynamic hanging block performed with a simultaneous winding strike.

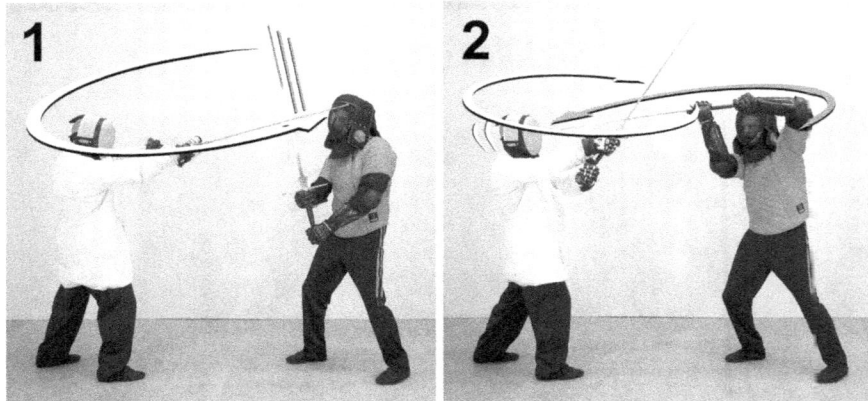

Winding Under: Use a winding strike to break a helicopter attack. As your opponent attacks, you block his first attack (1). As he wheels around for a second winding strike, drop the tip of your sword to deliver a short winding strike under your opponent's blade, closing his line of attack and catching his sword with the strong part of your blade as you simultaneously arc the tip of your sword into the side of his head (2).

Master Cuts (and Thrusts)

As we learned in Part 1, master cuts are techniques that defend against your opponent's attack while simultaneously attacking him with a cut or thrust to an open line. Master cuts are executed in such a way that you cut into his sword with the lower half of your blade and simultaneously attack him with the upper half of your blade. Although these two actions are performed as a single motion, it is imperative that your primary focus be checking your opponent's sword to neutralize his attack before committing to an attack of your own.

Highline Master Cut

You already got an introduction to this technique when you learned how to use a winding strike to break a helicopter attack. Whereas that technique was part of a block/riposte combination, the winding strike can also be applied as a single master strike against an overhead attack. As your opponent launches a right to left downward attack (strike #1), assume a thumbs-up grip as you raise the hilt of your sword into a left hanging guard to intercept the incoming strike with your forte, blocking with the back of the blade, or false edge. Simultaneously, wheel the tip of your sword into the pocket of your opponent's neck. If you should err high, you will still hit his head; err low and you will hit his shoulder. If the opponent evades by moving back, maintain the initiative by flowing directly into a thrusting attack.

LEVEL 8: ADVANCED LONG SWORD

High Master Cut: You face off against your opponent in high guard (1). As the opponent strikes for your head, step off to the side with your right foot, blocking his sword as you simultaneously strike him in the head (2).

Midline Master Cut

The midline master cut intercepts the opponent's sword between his neck and waist level, blocking and striking simultaneously with a single angle 1 strike. Begin by standing at the edge of your opponent's effective striking range and relax your guard, as you lean your head forward, ever so slightly, to invite an attack. Offer your opponent a clear shot at your left high line, psychologically encouraging him to attack using a number 1 strike, a textbook application of the Three-Step Rule. When the opponent takes the bait, step off to your right into his deceleration zone. Checking the opponent's sword with your forte, or strong part of the sword, simultaneously strike a vulnerable target area on the opponent using the foible or distal end of your blade. Striking with the end of the sword closer to the tip allows you to utilize the full range of your sword, while maximizing the length of the lever, which also increases the force of your strike.

Just as there are master cuts, there are also master thrusts. The idea is the same, simultaneous attack and defense, only now your attack is more linear, resulting in a stab with the tip rather than cut with the edge of the blade. Master cuts can also be used to defend your low line.

Midline Master Cut: You face off against your opponent, with your sword chambered at your left hip (1). As the opponent strikes for your head, thrust forward, blocking his sword as you simultaneously strike him in the head (2).

Low Master Cut: You face off against your opponent, with your sword chambered in high guard (1). As the opponent strikes for lead leg, step forward with a low cut, blocking his sword as you simultaneously strike his lead knee (2).

Half-Swording

Half-swording is a historical fencing technique that was commonly used during the Medieval and Renaissance periods, particularly in Europe. It involves gripping the sword hilt with one hand while gripping the blade with your other hand, essentially splitting the sword into two sections, thus the name "half-swording." By gripping the blade, you increase your tip control, allowing you to stab into the gaps in an opponent's armor.

Half-swording was primarily used when fighting in armor, especially in situations where thrusting techniques were more effective than cutting. By grabbing the blade, the swordsman could better direct the point of the sword through the gaps in an opponent's armor, targeting vulnerable areas like the inside of the joints or the visor slit in the helmet.

LEVEL 8: ADVANCED LONG SWORD 217

Half-Swording: Start at measure, hovering at the edge of your opponent's Circle of Death, watching for him to telegraph his next move (1). As he pulls his sword back to strike, drop the tip of your sword, grasping the blade with your left hand (2). Shuffle forward as you block high with the center of your sword (3). Redirect the opponent's blade off to your right, channeling it into your crossguard as you stab forward with the tip of your sword (4).

Half-Sword Takedown: Start at the edge of your opponent's striking range (1). Suddenly close the gap, dropping the tip of your sword to the side, catching the blade with your left hand (2). Jam the opponent's sword with a perpendicular check (3). Maintain cohesion as you pivot to your left, striking the opponent with the pommel of your sword (4). Place your lead foot behind the opponent's lead heel to keep him from stepping backward, as you hook your pommel over his shoulder (5). Pivot your hips from left to right, knocking your opponent to the ground (6).

Attempted Murder!

In 2004, I attended Live Steel Fight Academy's annual tournament. I brought my armor, a combination of boiled leather and plate, and suited up for an exhibition match against Joe McLaughlin. Joe and I were both assistant instructors at the time. It was a sunny day, and we were decked out in full Medieval armor, going at it pretty good with blunt long swords. At one point, I saw Joe release his grip and move to half-sword, which was not unusual, but then he switched his grip again. So, he was now holding the blade with the hilt high over his head. I admit that I was not expecting it when he suddenly brought it crashing down on me. I moved to block, and his blade slid down to my crossguard. Normally, this would just stop his blade, but instead, *his* crossguard, which was pointed down like the tip of a pickaxe, extended well past my crossguard to transfer all of the energy of his strike into the top of my right hand. To this day, I am thankful that I was wearing steel clamshell gauntlets in that fight, because that strike hurt even through them. If I had been wearing hockey or lacrosse gloves, I am sure I would have been out for the rest of the day, if not on my way to the hospital. Such was my introduction to the *murder stroke*!

This photo was taken just moments before Joe McLaughlin (left) landed his murder stroke on me.

Murder Stroke

While half-swording is usually performed by holding the hilt of the sword and the blade, a quick grip switch with your right hand, from the hilt to the distal end of the blade, suddenly puts the long sword in an upside-down position with the hilt now at the far end of the blade. The idea is to use the weight of the sword handle like the head of a hammer to deliver a very powerful blow, striking with the end of the crossguard. Condensing all of the energy of the strike into a very small area increases greatly the force of the impact, to the point where it can be felt even through heavy armor. (Ask me how I know!)

LEVEL 8: ADVANCED LONG SWORD

Murder Stroke: Begin at the edge of your effective striking range (1). Drop the tip of your sword counterclockwise, catching the blade in your left hand (2). Continue rotating the sword as you step forward, switching your right hand to the blade as well (3). As you finish your step forward, swing your sword downward, striking your opponent with the crossguard (4).

In-Fighting

You are in close range when you can touch any part of your opponent's body with your free hand. This range opens up new avenues of attack, including immobilizing and disarming the opponent, but first you need to learn how to work the bind.

The Bind

As we learned in Part 1, the bind refers to contact between the swords. When your forte is crossing the weak part of your opponent's blade, you are in a light bind. This contact gives you more leverage than your opponent, allowing you to control the flow of the action. When the strong parts of your blades cross, you are into a heavy bind, where you can each exert equal force upon the other's sword.

Unlike the unrealistic heavy binds that you see in the movies, where the combatants have a conversation while their blades are locked between them, in reality this position only lasts an instant. However, there are some techniques that can *only* be performed in that instance, including striking with the pommel of your sword, striking with your free hand, grabbing, disarming, kicking, and foot sweeping.

High Bind: You are facing off against your opponent, both of you in high guard (1). As the opponent swings for your head, step forward and block his strike with the strong part of your sword. You are now locked in a high bind (2).

Striking with One Hand

When in close range, you can release one hand to suddenly and unexpectedly strike your opponent. You will probably only get one shot, so you'll need to make it count. This means not only knowing how to hit, but precisely where to hit for maximum effect.

If your opponent is wearing a helmet, punching is not a good option. However, a tiger claw could be used to grab the opponent's helmet through the visor slit, giving you momentary control of his head. Where the head goes, the body will follow, so you can use this control to unbalance your opponent and force him to the ground

If your opponent were unarmored, striking his eyes with sufficient force not only temporarily blinds him, but would also result in his turning away, breaking his structure and allowing you to land a finishing blow with your sword. Of course, you should never actually poke your training partner in the eye. It is only safe to land the strike when you are wearing masks to protect your faces, but recognize that, just like a cut or thrust to the face, a successful eye poke could bring a fight to a quick end.

LEVEL 8: ADVANCED LONG SWORD

Tiger Claw: You are facing your opponent, both in high guard (1). You each deliver a number 1 strike and end in a bind (2). Drop your tip, rotating your sword clockwise to parry your opponent's sword down to your right (3). Maintaining your check on the opponent's sword with your right hand, use your left hand to deliver a splayed finger tiger claw strike to the eyes (4).

Grabbing

When in the bind, you can release your grip on your sword with one hand and use it to grab your opponent. Grabbing gives you a point of contact on your opponent's body that allows you to push and pull him in order to disrupt his balance and control his actions. This grab can be particularly effective when combined with a foot sweep or attack with your sword.

Pommel Strike

Pommel strikes can be effective in close combat situations where there isn't enough space to use your sword's blade effectively. A sudden strike with the pommel can surprise and stun an opponent, making them more vulnerable to follow-up attacks. While executing the pommel strike, it is important to check your opponent's sword. This check can be done either by using your free hand to grab and control his weapon hand or by maintaining cohesion between the blades, being sure to check the opponent's sword throughout the movement.

222 THE ART AND SCIENCE OF SWORD FIGHTING

Pommel Strike: Begin at range in high guard (1). As the opponent strikes, step in and block his strike, ending in a high bind (2). Reach up and grab his right wrist with your left hand as you rotate your sword around your opponent's blade (3). Pull his arms down as you drive the pommel into his face (4).

Disarming

Taking an opponent's sword in combat is a difficult task that requires skill and timing. First, you must use your sword to bind your opponent's sword and control his movements while disarming him. Once this bind has been achieved, reach out and grab the opponent's sword by the hilt between the opponent's hands. This grab is easiest when blocking to the outside of your body. When blocking to the inside, you can reach either under your sword, in the case of a high block, or over your sword when blocking low. Once you have a hold on your opponent's sword, pull or twist it from his grip as you either cut him with your sword, or use your blade-on-blade pressure to assist you in completing the disarm. The specific technique you employ will, of course, depend on the type of sword your opponent is using and the situational circumstances.

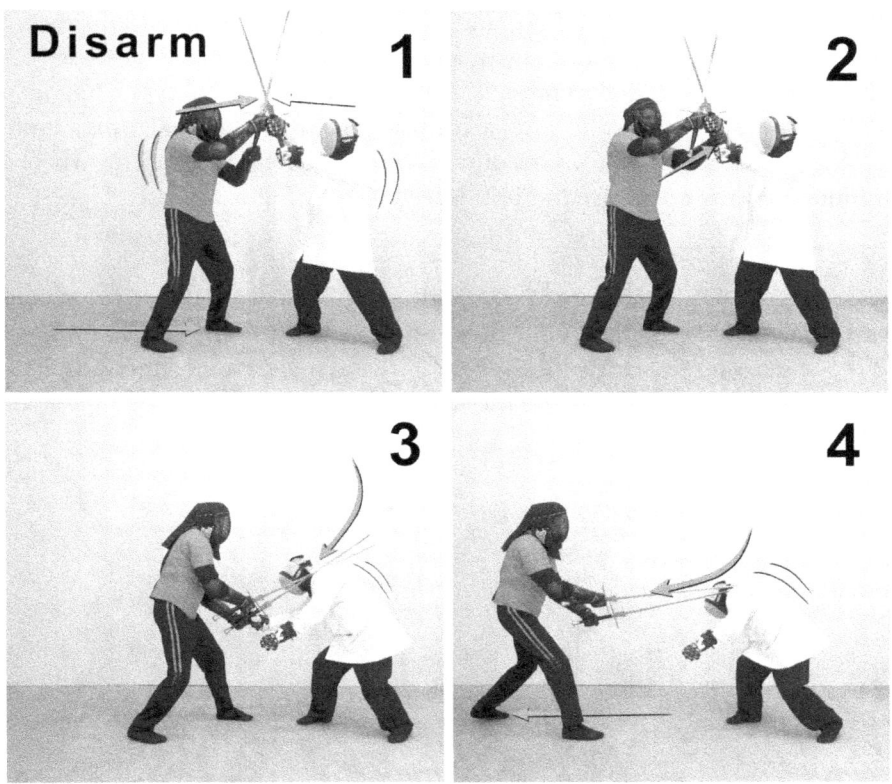

Disarm: Close the gap with a full step, running your swords together into a high bind (1). Quickly use your left hand to grasp the handle of the opponent's sword between his hands (2). Pull the opponent's sword down as you use your sword to press his blade back upon him (3). Finish by stepping back, cutting the opponent with both swords (4).

Kicking

As we mentioned in Part 1, kicking in a swordfight is generally not recommended when fighting at long or even middle range because your leg and foot would be vulnerable to being cut. That being said, there are situations where kicking is useful, especially when your opponent is close and your swords are in a heavy bind. At my school, we have a saying, "The first person to remember that they can kick will win the bind." While this is obviously not always true, kicks are reliable tools when in the bind.

To prevent telegraphing, keep your hips and shoulders the same height throughout the kick. Move smoothly and quickly, using your whole body to generate power, especially your hips. Remain relaxed until the precise moment of impact. Keep your supporting leg bent slightly, with your foot flat on the floor and eyes on your opponent at all times. Pull your kicks back as quickly as possible and regain a stable, balanced stance.

While a kick is seldom a fight ender, it is often enough to break your opponent's focus, disrupt their structure, or break the bind, all of which helps you up to deliver a more effective follow-up attack with your sword. Of course, you must use good control when practicing these techniques, taking great care to not injure your training partner.

Knee Kick

Use your knee to attack the opponent's thigh, groin, or solar plexus. Thrust your knee up and forward into the target, using your hips. Raise your leg swiftly and strongly, thrusting your fully bent knee up and forward into the target. At the same time, bring your hands down sharply to pull your attacker into the strike. Use the spring of your supporting leg and hip to add power to the technique.

Knee Kick: You're locked in a bind, with wrists grabbed (1). Pull the opponent forward as you drive your knee up fast and strong into his midsection (2).

Front Kick

The front kick can be used to attack the groin. To execute a front kick, shift your body's center of gravity directly over your supporting foot and raise your kicking knee on a line between your hip and your intended target. Flow smoothly through this position, straightening your leg with a strong snapping motion. Thrust your hips forward slightly to add range and power to your kick. Keep your ankle straight and fully extended, pointing your toes and striking with the instep (top of your foot) and shin. Your opponent's thighs will naturally funnel your kick into his groin.

LEVEL 8: ADVANCED LONG SWORD 225

Front Kick: You've come into a high bind and grabbed your opponent's wrist, but he has grabbed you back (1). Deliver a front kick to the opponent's groin with the top of your foot (2).

Stamping Kick

Stamping kicks are typically used to attack your opponent's knees and disable his locomotor system. To chamber for a stamping kick, raise your knee into a ready position with your foot fully flexed, ankle bent with your toes pulled back toward your shin. The kick can be performed at any angle, to the front, sides, or behind you. While you can strike with your heel, turning your foot and striking with the outer edge of your foot provides you with a broader striking surface, making it easier to strike the knee, shin, or instep of your attacker. After striking the target, you should either withdraw your knee quickly, or continue through your target, either blowing out his knee or scraping your foot down his shin to stomp powerfully on his foot.

Stamping Kick: You find yourself locked in a bind, grabbing each other's wrists (1). Your opponent is too far away for a knee kick, but raise your knee in much the same way, in preparation for a strong stamping kick (2). Turn your toes out, striking his knee with the bottom of your foot, taking care to not hurt your training partner (3).

Foot Sweeps and Takedowns

An unexpected foot sweep can suddenly sway the odds in you favor. Foot sweeps create openings by disrupting your opponent's balance by attacking their stance. You can use your front or rear leg to attack your opponent's lead foot, sweeping with the arch, instep, or heel of your foot. Swing your leg in a shallow arc, skimming the ground lightly with your foot, to intercept your opponent's foot just below the ankle. To successfully sweep an opponent, he should first be off-balanced, so it is important to set-up your foot sweep carefully. Be prepared to quickly follow up on your opponent's momentary loss of balance. For safety, only sweep to the back of your opponent's leg, never to the front. When training, be sure your partner knows how and is prepared to fall. Do not practice sweeps that are above your partner's falling capabilities.

Instep and Arch Sweep

Begin with you and your opponent facing each other in right stances with your swords locked in a heavy outside bind. Bring your left (rear) foot forward in a shallow arc to intercept your opponent's right (lead) foot from the outside and behind as you simultaneously grasp your opponent's right shoulder with your left hand. Contact the base of your opponent's right foot sharply with the instep (top) or arch (bottom) of your left foot, sweeping it up and across your opponent's body while pulling your opponent's shoulder in the opposite direction of the sweep. Use the opportunity you've created to win the bind.

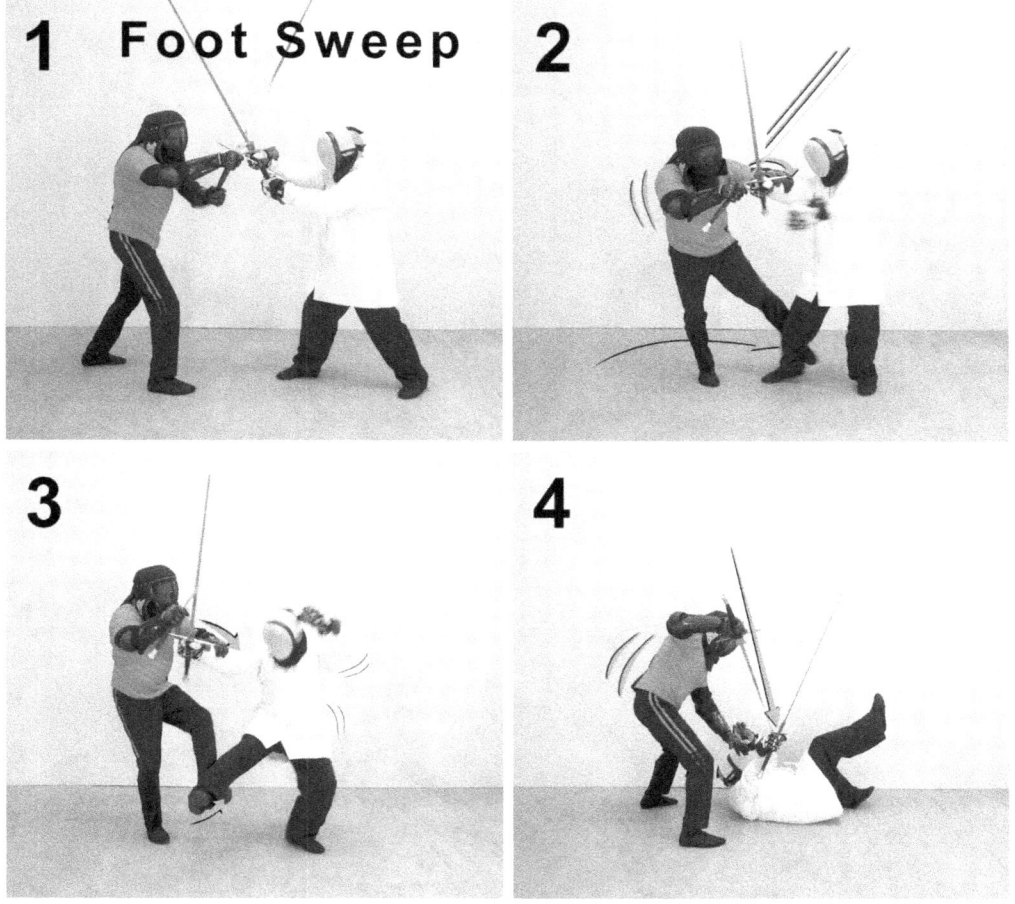

Foot Sweep: You've come into a high bind (1). Grab your opponent's arm with your left hand as you sweep your left foot forward (2). Contact the Achilles tendon of the opponent's lead leg with the top or bottom of your foot, sweeping his foot off the ground as you pull on his arm in the opposite direction (3). Continue checking his weapon hand as he falls, stabbing him before he can recover (4).

Foot Pin

While not technically a sweep, the foot pin is a subtle trick that you can use to momentarily disrupt your opponent's footwork. The idea is to step forward naturally, inconspicuously placing your lead foot on top of your opponent's. This is not a stomping motion, just a subtle little toe cover that throws off his next step. When he tries to step, his foot won't move, throwing him off-balance and opening him up to a quick attack.

Foot Pin: You've come into a high bind (1). Step through and place your left foot on top of your opponent's lead foot (2). Shove him backward using both arms (3). Immediately step back and strike while he is still recovering his balance (4).

Sparring

Only through experience accumulated through hours of sparring can you begin to understand the intricacies of fighting with the long sword. Sparring provides you with a never-ending series of challenges that you must analyze and then strategize to overcome. Long sword sparring in full protective gear is physically demanding, but also a great way to improve your physical fitness level while enjoying the thrill of simulated combat.

For safety, wear all of your protective gear. Just as it took time to feel comfortable sparring with the single-handed sword, sparring with the long sword may feel awkward at first. Your experience with the short sword should tell you that all you need to do is stick with it. Expect that your techniques may not work well at first. Expect that you *will* get hit. Perhaps often. Sometimes it will hurt. Deal with it. If you need to, upgrade your armor, but remain open to the thrill that comes with training in combat sports, the satisfaction of overcoming hardships, and the confidence that comes with knowing that your techniques actually work.

In sparring you can use foam swords, bamboo shinai, wooden wasters, or blunt metal long swords. Check to see how hard the swords hit, taking into consideration the protective gear you are wearing. Discuss with your sparring partner the level of control with which you are both comfortable. If your swords do not flex in the thrust, you should consider banning hard thrusts or thrusts to the face.

Sparring does not always mean free fighting at full speed and power. What are your goals for this sparring session? Are you sparring to develop specific skill sets, such as defending your low line or defending then counterattacking? What level of intensity are you comfortable with? Agree on a set of rules to maintain safety and promote effective training. You might decide to limit attacks to specific target areas (e.g., only leg attacks or only strikes to the body will score). Decide ahead of time if foot sweeps and takedowns are allowed. These rules can be changed between rounds to add variety to your sparring.

Level 8 Workout

This 60-to-90-minute workout is designed to round out your swordsmanship with a two-handed sword.

1. Warm-Up: 15–20 minutes. Start with five minutes of light stretching for your upper and lower body. Follow this with five minutes of cardio work such as jumping rope, jogging in place, doing jumping jacks, etc. Go until you feel tired and your heartrate is elevated, then five more minutes of light stretching until your heart rate returns to normal. Next, grab your sword and work through some basic footwork while you practice your blocks, parries, cuts, and thrusts, first slowly then gradually speeding up.

2. Long Range: 10–15 minutes. Work through the various long-range techniques presented in Level 6 with a partner. Practice targeting the edges, baiting, and drawing using the trick guards. Begin moving slowly until you have the mechanics of the technique correct, then gradually add speed and power. While you might be tempted to train without full gear, especially when you are going slowly, it is recommended that you still wear your gloves and mask for safety.

3. Middle Range: 10–15 minutes. Stand across from your partner in true guards at middle range, with your swords engaged and both playing gently for the center. Practice thrusting forward when you see an opening, while your training partner moves to defend the open line. Remember, the goal is to drill and develop good habits, not score points on an opponent. Sometimes your thrust will land, other times it won't. When it doesn't, flow directly into a counterattack. Work together to maximize your mutual learning experiences. Switch roles and repeat.

4. Close Range: 10–15 minutes. Work through the close-range techniques presented in Level 8 with your training partner. Practice coming into the bind, and then working to resolve the bind in your favor. As always, begin moving slowly until you have the mechanics of the technique correct, then gradually add speed and power to your practice, taking care not to injure your training partner.

5. Sparring: 10–15 minutes. The moment of Truth! The only way to know what techniques work best under what conditions is to test them out against a non-compliant opponent. Maintain a strong defense at all times, then focus on analyzing your opponent's defense and exploiting his weaknesses to land specific moves. Even though you should be wearing full safety equipment when you spar, you should still control the strength of your strikes and take care not to injure your training partner. This is a good time to pull out your boffer swords (see Appendix 4 at the end of this book). Whatever weapons you are using, it is always a good guideline to not hit anyone any harder than you would want to be hit.

6. Cool Down: 5–10 minutes. Take a few minutes to take your body from "Fight or Flight" into "Rest and Digest." Now is the time to use static stretching to increase your flexibility and break up the lactic acid that has accumulated in your muscles.

LEVEL 9:
Great Sword

Because the bastard sword can be used with one hand or two, it did not warrant its own section in this book. However, the great sword, while similar to the long sword, is different enough that it deserves some special attention. The good news is that, after all your training in first short sword and then long sword, we are able to cover the topic thoroughly in a single level.

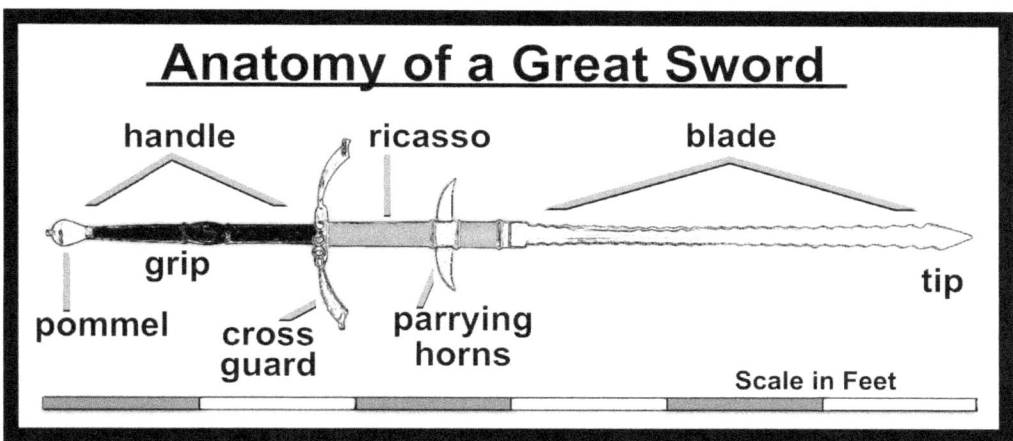

Anatomy of a Great Sword

The most obvious characteristic of a great sword is its remarkable length. A great sword, like a staff or polearm, can be about as long as the wielder is tall. Any longer and it would become unwieldy and not able to be used like a sword. Instead, it would have more in common with, and thus be employed like, a long spear.

To manipulate the long and usually heavy blade of a great sword, your hands need to be spaced far apart to provide you with good leverage. For this reason, the handle of a great sword can take up a third of the overall length. The handle is further extended by the ricasso, an unsharpened part of the blade that was sometimes wrapped in leather. In addition to an oversized crossguard to protect your hands on the handle, great swords are often equipped with parrying horns. These horns protect your hands when you are gripping the ricasso.

Some great swords, particularly German battle swords, were equipped with wavy blades that served as psychological weapons and status symbols. In addition to its impressive size, a great sword, especially one with a flamed blade, can be an intimidating weapon that may strike fear into your opponent, possibly helping you to win the encounter before the fight even begins. While the serrations do not help much in chopping, when drawn either forward or backward across a target, each wave catches and focuses the energy of your cut into the curved edge. This sawing motion is aided by the excessive weight of the weapon. Conversely, it can be argued that serrations on the blade would only serve to drag and slow the momentum of your strike. In either case, since the long blade of the great sword lends itself to being grabbed by an opponent, the serrated edge acts as a good deterrent.

However fierce they might have been, the fact is that serrated blades on great swords were rarely used in combat, mostly because they were very expensive and difficult to produce and maintain. Furthermore, while the serrations may aid in cutting, every curve on the blade provides a potential weak spot, making them more prone to breaking and, therefore, less reliable than a straight blade. This design weakness is why great swords with *flamberge* blades were usually reserved for bodyguards, ceremonies, and parade grounds.

Grip

You hold a great sword similarly to how you hold a long sword, but the grip is much wider. Your non-dominant hand grips just above the pommel, while your dominant hand grasps behind the crossguard. Your hand can be placed thumb facing up, toward the sword tip (1), or facing down, toward the pommel. You should not feel overly committed to either grip. Rather, switch your grips as is necessary to best utilize the weapon given the circumstances.

For a wider grip, move your lead hand to just behind the parrying horns, using either the thumb (2) or pinky side of the hand leading. This grip (3) is akin to half-swording with a long sword. As in half-swording, your grip on the weapon is so wide that cross-handling, that is, crossing your arms as you often do when normally wielding a long sword, can place you in a weak position to either attack or defend. While you will certainly flow through crossed-hand positions when blocking and striking, when gripping the ricasso, strive to maintain a strong open position that allows you to quickly and easily manipulate your sword.

Stances and Footwork

The predominant stances used in conjunction with the great sword are the back stance and forward stance. To provide a stable, balanced position that allows for precise execution, keep your dominant foot in front to correspond with your lead hand. Leading with your off foot does not lend itself to optimal body mechanics, due to your wide grip on the weapon. If you wanted to switch leads, the best solution would be to change your grip on the sword at the same time that you switched your stance; however, since both hands need to switch positions, this is neither an easy nor a fast maneuver.

Therefore, in the interest of maintaining a consistent lead, avoid making full passing steps that would switch your stance from a right leading stance to a left leading stance. (As always, simply reverse these directions if you are left hand dominant, or when practicing with your off-hand grip, which is a very good thing to do!)

Of course, there are exceptions to every rule. There are times when a passing step is necessary and appropriate, such as when following through on a big swing, when retreating, or when closing the gap between you and your opponent. Historically, great swords were often employed against spears and polearms. If you needed to get past the point in a hurry, you would use passing steps to quickly charge in, and use the parrying horns and crossguards for protection as you did. Once inside the effective striking range of the longer polearms, a man armed with a great sword could inflict tremendous damage, both physically and psychologically, when breaking the pike lines so that regular infantry could penetrate and follow behind.

Cat Stance

Lunge

Guards

The guards with the great sword are very similar to those used with the long sword. However, because you have an exceptionally wide grip when wielding the great sword, you'll want to avoid crossing your arms or leading with your off-foot. These limitations are why there are fewer guards and stances that work well in conjunction with the great sword.

Middle and Hanging Guard

The middle guard is the same with the great sword as it is with a long sword, except that you only assume it on one side. With a long sword, you can easily switch your lead because crossing your hands has little effect on your ability to wield the sword effectively. However, due to the longer handle and wider grip, crossing your arms with the great sword puts you in a weak position, unable to attack or defend effectively. In the strong stance, your off hand is held down by your rear hip, with the tip of your sword pointed toward the opponent's face. This stance provides a strong defense while loading your sword for a thrusting attack. Raise the handle, and the middle guard becomes a hanging guard. Raise the tip, and the middle guard becomes a high guard.

Middle Guard **Hanging Guard**

High Guard

High Guard

The high guard is a loaded position. Your sword is withdrawn, chambered with the tip pointing up, ready to strike. This puts you in a good position to deliver powerful downward strikes. The high guard does not require much lateral space, especially when used to deliver repeated downward strikes. This lack of need for a lot of lateral space provides you with a strong offense that gets even stronger when combined with thrusting from middle guard.

Basic Strikes

By now, you should be very familiar with the basic striking pattern. Performing the strikes with the great sword teaches you how to manipulate the weapon, attack from all angles, and make each strike flow smoothly into the next. The basic pattern provides you with the foundational skills for all strikes using the great sword, as well as how not to hit the ground. When cutting downward, you have to stop the mass of the sword before it hits the ground, potentially damaging your weapon and costing you the fight. When cutting upward, as in strike 8, the ground prevents you from loading deeply, and the weight of the sword works against the force of gravity, making the strike slow and difficult to generate power.

LEVEL 9: GREAT SWORD   235

Practice each strike until you can perform it with grace and power. Practice striking with both the true and false edge. After you are proficient with the basic pattern, you'll want to practice the strikes in different, short combinations. The Meyer's Square is the perfect piece of training equipment to extend your training.

Your strongest strike is going to be an angle 1, slicing diagonally downward from right to left with the true edge. This strike starts in a right high guard (1A) and cuts diagonally downward from right to left, ending in a left low guard (1B).

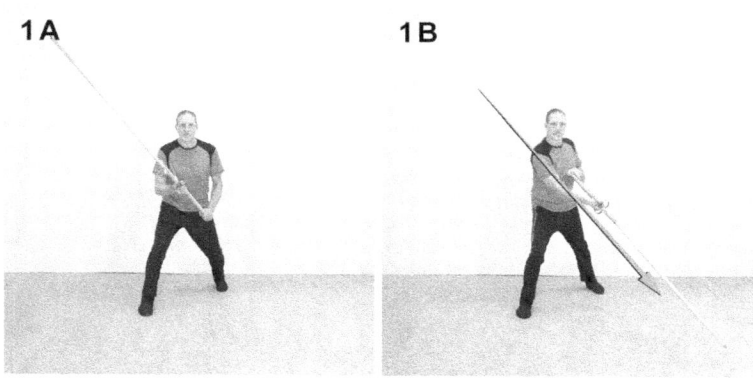

Flow through the low guard position into a left high guard in order to set you up for the second strike (2A). Pull the pommel upward with your rear hand as you push downward with your lead hand to perform a descending cut from left to right with the true edge (2B).

Immediately upon completing the second cut, flow into a right middle-level loaded guard, loaded for strike 3 (3A). Strike 3 is a horizontal cut from right to left made with the true edge (3B).

Set up a return strike with the true edge by flipping the sword over, into a left middle-level loaded position (4A). Strike 4 returns along the same line, cutting from left to right (4B).

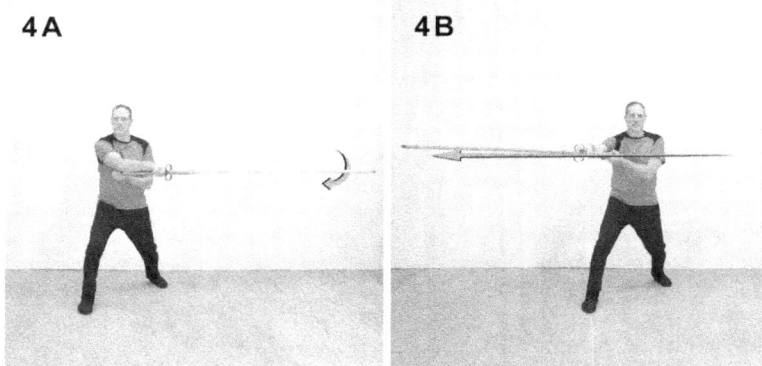

Set up strike 5 by dropping the tip of your sword into a right low guard (5A). Strike 5 is an ascending cut from right to left, made with the true edge (5B).

Immediately after strike 5, use the remaining momentum to carry your sword around, dropping the tip into a left low guard (6A). Strike 6 is an ascending cut from left to right made with the true edge (6B).

LEVEL 9: GREAT SWORD 237

Flow into a high guard with the tip of your sword pointed to the sky, loading you for strike 7 (7A). Drop the tip, making a vertical downward cut, ending in a low guard (7B).

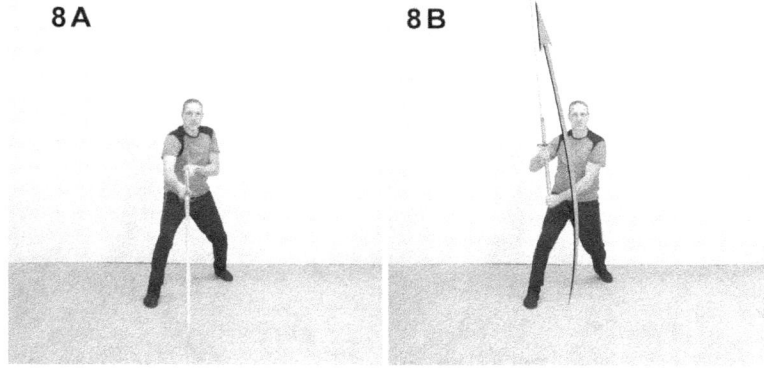

Begin from a low guard (8A). Lift the tip by pulling upward with your lead hand while pressing downward on the pommel with your back hand (8B).

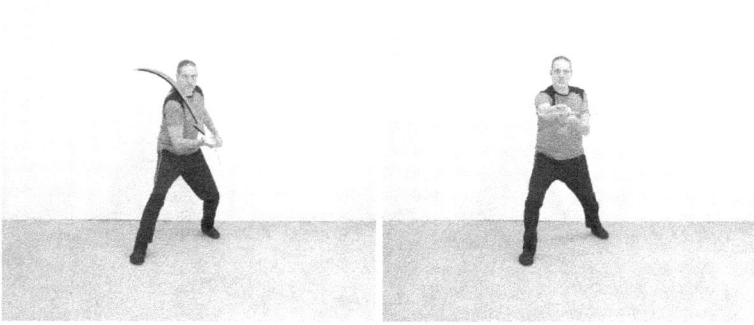

Shift into a back stance as you withdraw the hilt to your left hip with the tip pointing directly at your opponent (9A). Shift into forward stance as you thrust forward (9B). Immediately withdraw to a guarded or ready position.

Half Strikes

Your strongest strike is going to be an angle 1, slicing diagonally downward from right to left with the true edge. This strike starts in a right high guard (1) and ends in an extended middle guard (2). You can then reverse the motion of the cut, slicing back along the same line, cutting upward diagonally from left to right with the false edge, ending in a right high guard (3).

An abbreviated version of this cut allows you to better occupy the centerline. The obvious take-away is that it is harder to generate power, but the fact that you are hardly straying from the middle guard position allows you to occupy and control the center.

Half Strike

Double Strikes

Double Strike

If you miss your target, you can use the weight of the great sword to your advantage by continuing your swing, looping around for a second pass along the same angle. Let's examine an angle 1 double strike as an example. This strike starts in a right high guard (1). Shift into forward stance as you slice diagonally downward from right to left with the true edge (2). Seeing your opponent has evaded your strike causing you to miss your target, keep your hands in front of you as you loop the sword around for another strike (3). Complete the double strike with a second cut along the same angle (4). This strike is especially effective when combined with advancing footwork, such as a shuffle forward or gathering step

While at first twirling may seem like just a flashy exercise, it is actually an important part of training. Figure eights help you become familiar the great sword, and they teach you how to manipulate the great sword. A quick twirl, called a flurry, can be used to confuse an opponent by disguising your intentions and setting you up for unexpected angles of attack. A figure eight can be used to parry an opponent's weapon before quickly striking with the other end.

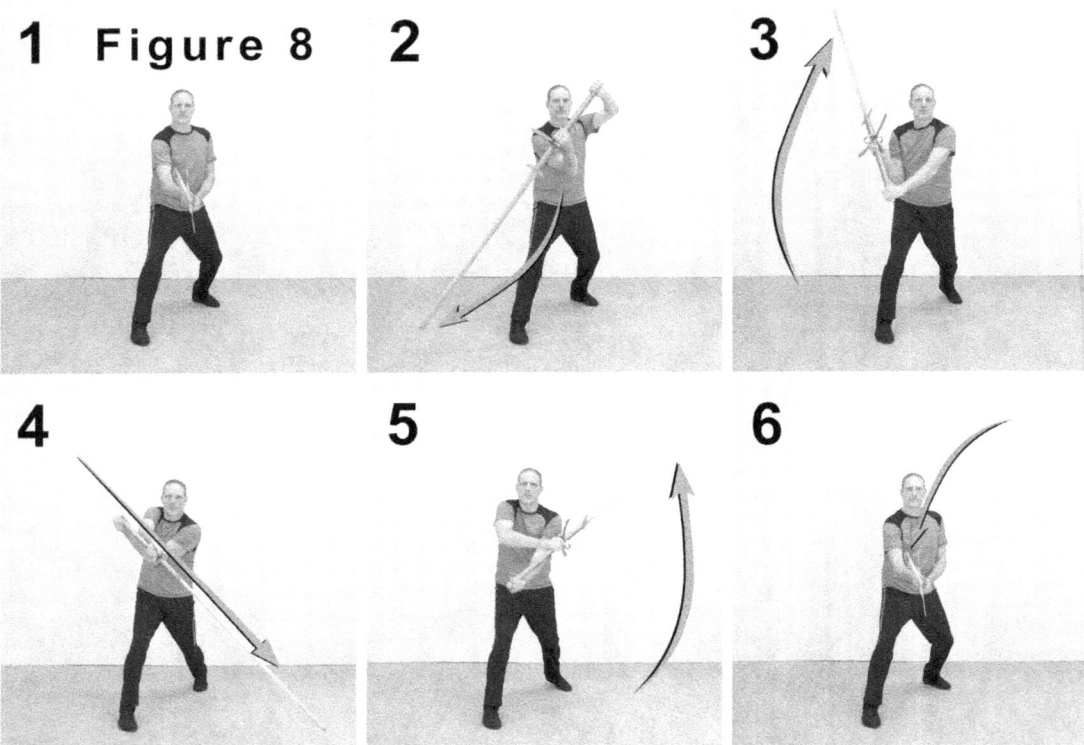

The simple downward figure eight consists of two consecutive strikes with the sword. Begin from a middle guard (1). Drop the tip of your sword back and to your right (2). Bring your left arm across your body and begin sweeping the tip up and forward (3) into a right to left downward diagonal strike (4). Continue the motion of the sword, bringing the tip upward on your left side (5). Finish with a left-to-right downward diagonal strike with the tip, finishing in middle guard (6). Repeat the motions, practicing them until you can perform all the strikes smoothly, flowing them seamlessly into one fluid motion.

Upward figure-eights can be a little more difficult at first, but with practice they can be just as smooth and fast as your downward figure-eights. When first learning this twirl, begin doing downward figure-eights, then slow down and finally stop your motion. Reverse the direction of your sword, backtracking along the same path, only now in an upward direction, alternating striking diagonally upward from left to right and from right to left.

Upward Figure 8

Defense

The great sword was designed primarily to contend with polearms, such as spears, halberds, and pole-hammers. However, it is effective against other weapons, too, including short and long swords. From the middle guard, you can block quickly to either side by moving the handle of your sword to the left or right. Whenever possible, keep your tip oriented on your opponent to set yourself up for a quick thrusting counterattack. If your tip is withdrawn, you should be chambered to make a cutting attack.

The length of your blade should prevent your opponent from attacking your legs. Any attempt to exploit a low line of attack should be met with a forward thrust with your tip or a downward cut with the blade. However, if your opponent does get in range for a low line attack, you can block by raising the pommel of your sword, pivoting on your lead hand to quickly drop the tip to close the line.

In addition to parrying and blocking with the blade, you can catch the opponent's weapon with the parrying horns. Strikes that make it past the horns should get caught by the oversized crossguard. Once your opponent's attack has been blocked, maintain cohesion with his blade, pivoting at the point of contact to lever the blade of your sword into the opponent.

Great Sword Blocks: These basic blocking positions will allow you to defend against attacks coming in from almost any angle.

LEVEL 9: GREAT SWORD   243

Cone of Defense

You can use the Cone of Defense effectively with the great sword. The angles and hand positions are basically the same as if you were wielding a long sword, but the increased length of the blade dramatically increases the range, making the technique even more effective.

The Great Sword Cone of Defense: Here you can see the different blocking positions that are used to cover quadrants 1 to 4.

Trick Guards

Because the great sword is so long, it is inherently slower in comparison to a short or long sword. This drawback makes deceiving your opponent an even more important skill to have in your arsenal of great sword techniques. When performed correctly, these simple tricks can confound your opponent.

A Hard-Learned Lesson

My first match against a great sword left a lasting impression on me. While training with some friends in the SCA (Society for Creative Anachronism), I once fought a teenage kid who wore minimal armor and wielded the most ridiculous sword I had ever seen. It was made from thick rattan, as all our weapons were, but it was over six feet long with a two-foot crossguard. At the time, I could not take him seriously. He just stood there before me with that stupid sword slung over his shoulder. I was sure I was going to tear this kid up. I was thinking that someone should ring a school bell, because class was about to be called to session. The only thing is, I didn't realize that I was the one who was about to get schooled!

First, I found out why he wore so little armor: I couldn't get close enough to hit him. Every time I tried to close the gap with my normal-length long sword, the kid would fall back and drop a brutally hard strike on me. It was so fast that the first few hits rang off my helmet before I could get up an effective block. Then, he started targeting my hands. I was wearing a really nice pair of steel clamshell gauntlets; however, after only a few strikes, I could hardly hold my sword and had to yield the fight.

Whenever I get my butt kicked, I like to analyze why. Then, I get practicing. I figure that if a technique is good enough to beat me, then it will probably work on most others. I study my opponent's technique, come to understand it, and then I work hard to hone it and add it to my arsenal. I call the technique the young warrior used to defeat me the *high rear guard*.

Some members of the SCA group that I was training with the day I first fought against a great sword.

High Rear Guard

The high rear guard is performed in much the same way as with the long sword, but now with greater range. This will require a change in timing as well as distancing.

If the opponent approaches cautiously, you can advance on him by stepping forward with your right foot to close the gap unexpectedly as you strike diagonally downward.

If the opponent rushes in to close the gap, retreat by stepping backward with your left foot into a right stance, giving just enough ground to maintain proper distancing for a focused strike with your sword. Keep the staff in contact with your shoulder for as long as possible as you execute the strike, using your shoulder to get the sword moving quickly. Finish the strike by pushing forward simultaneously with your right hand as you pull back sharply with your left.

High Rear Guard: Lead with your left foot as you stand just out of range of your opponent, holding your sword over your right shoulder (1). When the opponent rushes in to close the gap, step backward with your left foot into a right stance, delivering a powerful angle 1 strike with your sword, putting you in a good position to follow up with a thrust to the head (2).

Low Rear Guard

The low rear guard, commonly called a tail guard, is assumed by dropping the tip of your sword down and behind you. Like the high rear guard, this position appears to leave you defenseless; however, as with each of the trick guards, this is seldom the case so long as you have good timing and are able to control the distance. Be ready to step forward with your rear foot to close the gap or to quickly step back with your front foot to maintain proper distancing, should the opponent rush you. Both maneuvers place you in a strong position to effectively attack your opponent's ankle, knee, groin, ribs, or head. Use both hands to quickly bring your sword into play, pushing forward with your lead hand as you pull back on the pommel with your off hand.

Low Rear Guard: Lead with your left foot as you stand just out of range of your opponent, holding your sword low behind you (1). When the opponent rushes in to close the gap, step backward with your left foot into a right stance, delivering a powerful angle 5 strike with your sword (2).

Close-Range Techniques

When facing a great sword, any opponent with a shorter weapon will quickly realize that he will need to pass your blade in order to attack you. One of the weaknesses of the great sword is that the extreme length and weight of the blade make it relatively slow. When you pull back to strike, it takes time to stop the sword, reverse its motion, and get it started again. If you leave a big enough gap, an opponent with good timing can check your sword and enter to take advantage of another weakness of the great sword, its limited capabilities at close range. Therefore, you should have a surprise in store for any swordsman that is skilled enough to get past the blade of your great sword.

By now, you should see that many techniques performed with the long sword translate easily to the great sword. Since the close-range techniques, such as kicks, foot sweeps, and takedowns, will look almost identical, I will not repeat them again here. It is enough to know that, once you have developed the strength and skill needed to wield the great sword proficiently, you will be able to adapt most long sword techniques for use with the larger sword.

Pommel Strikes

The strike with the weighted pommel of a great sword is a powerful, close-range attack that can literally stop a man dead in his tracks. In this technique, you can strike from the side or thrust from the front. To thrust, first raise your sword high over your shoulder, with the tip pointing behind you, allowing you to drive the pommel firmly into your target. As with all thrusting techniques, pull your strike back quickly and reset, ready to defend or attack again. Often times, you can even land a cut as you retreat.

The overhand pommel thrust relies on good timing and sure footwork to land successfully. If the opponent is charging you, the technique can be performed stationary, using the opponent's forward momentum to maximize the power of your pommel strike. In either case, take care to exercise good control, because pommel strikes can really pack a punch.

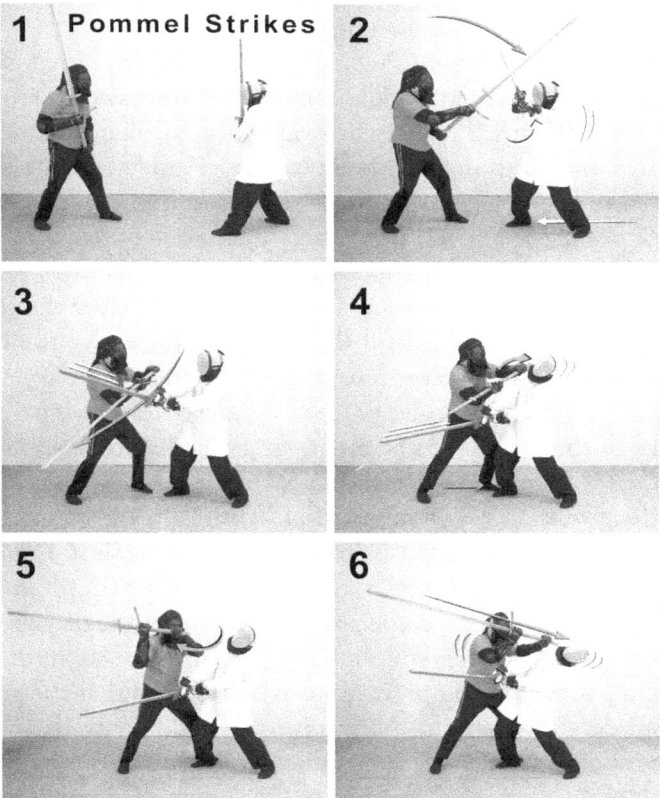

Pommel Strikes: You find yourself squared off against an opponent armed with a long sword (1). The opponent senses your vertical strike and charges forward, blocking your strike with a roof block (2). Drop the tip and raise the pommel, parrying the opponent's sword off to your right (3). Drive the pommel into the opponent's face (4). Continue through the target, raising your sword high over your shoulder with the tip pointing behind you (5). Thrust the pommel straight into your opponent's face (6).

Level 9 Workout

This 60-to-90-minute workout is designed to develop proficiency with the great sword.

1. Warm-Up: 15–20 minutes. Start with five minutes of light stretching for your upper and lower body. Next, grab your sword and work through some basic footwork while you practice your cuts, thrusts, figure-eights, blocks, and parries with the great sword. Start slowly, then gradually speed up.

2. Long Range: 10–15 minutes. Work through the various long-range techniques presented in Level 9 with a partner. Practice targeting the edges. Bait and draw using the trick guards. When the opponent attacks, block and counter. Begin moving slowly until you have the mechanics of the technique correct, then gradually add speed and power. While you might be tempted to train without full gear, especially when you are going slowly, it is recommended that you still wear your gloves and a mask for safety. If you don't have a partner, you can still practice these techniques to a pell or to the air.

3. Middle Range: 10–15 minutes. Practice fencing with your great sword. Stand across from your partner in true guards at middle range, with your swords engaged, and both of you playing gently for the center. Practice thrusting forward when you see an opening, while your training partner moves to defend the open line. Remember, the goal is to drill and develop good habits, not score points on your opponent. Sometimes your strike will land; other times it won't. When it doesn't, flow directly into a counterattack. Work together to maximize your mutual learning experiences. Switch roles and repeat.

4. Close Range: 10–15 minutes. Allow your opponent to close the range and jam your attack. Practice coming into the bind and then working to resolve the bind in your favor. Work through your kicks, foot sweeps, foot pins, free hand strikes, pommel strikes, grabbing, and takedowns with your training partner. As always, begin moving slowly until you have the mechanics of the technique correct, then gradually add speed and power to your practice, taking care not to injure your training partner.

5. Sparring: 10–15 minutes. The moment of Truth! The only way to know what techniques work best under what conditions is to test them out against a non-compliant opponent. Maintain a strong defense at all times, then focus on analyzing your opponent's defense and exploiting his weaknesses to land specific moves. Even though you should be wearing full safety equipment when you spar, you should still control the strength of your strikes and take care not to injure your training partner, keeping in mind that the great sword is heavy and so requires considerable strength to bring it to a quick, controlled stop. This is a good time to pull out your boffer swords (see Appendix 4 at the end of this book). Whatever weapons you are using, it is always a good guideline to not hit anyone any harder than you would want to be hit.

6. Cool Down: 5–10 minutes. Take a few minutes to take your body from "Fight or Flight" into "Rest and Digest." Now is the time to use static stretching to increase your flexibility and break up the lactic acid that has accumulated in your muscles.

Acknowledgments

I would like to thank the following people who had a special impact on my sword training over the years (please forgive me if I have overlooked anybody): Sir Chuck Bennett, Knight of the S.C.A. and my first western quarter staff Rob Walters, my first long sword instructor; Steve Wolk, who introduced me to the Filipino martial arts; Master Bao Ngo, for his past teachings and continued guidance, both in the martial arts and life in general; Sensei Joe Montague, who introduced me to the bokken; Sir Dave Dickey, founder of Live Steel Fight Academy and creator of the Three-Step Rule; and Xia Chongyi, founder of the Taiji Fencing League, who taught me the art of sword stealing.

Special thanks to: my wife Kathy, for supporting all my crazy obsessions; Doctorae Joe McLaughlin, my Live Steel brother and cofounder of Modern Gladiatorial Arts (MGA), for his exceptional insight and help in editing this book; Noah Dingler, who crafted the amazing great sword wasters featured in Level 9; Madeline Crouse, Carol Riley, Dalton Weber, Derek Fair, and Kyle Edwards, who all helped with various aspects of editing the manuscript; Brian Lesyk for demonstrating all the techniques with me; and, last but not least, Andrea Hilborn for dedicating so much time and energy to shooting the photos and videos for all my different books and video series.

Models: Joe Varady, Brian Lesyk
Photo Credits: Andrea Hilborn, Joe Varady
Cover Photo: Andrea Hilborn

Expand Your Horizons

This book, especially when used in conjunction with the video series of the same name, can provide you with an excellent foundation for learning to sword fight. However, the complex nature of the activity makes it hard to beat in-person lessons with a qualified instructor. That is why I recommend that, in order to continue your sword fighting journey, you seek out a fencing or HEMA club. HEMA groups are not the only option. For example, I learned a lot training with the Taiji Fencing League. My advice is to attend any gatherings that offer seminars and workshops on sword fighting, regardless of style. Just rack up experience!

Taiji Fencing League Grand Champion
2015–2017 (Retired Undefeated)

Appendix 1: Sword Fighting Equipment Suppliers

There are many commercial vendors who produce and sell products for sword fighting. To get you started, here is a list of ten reputable suppliers including descriptions of their services as promoted online.

Arms and Armor (www.arms-n-armor.com) "At Arms and Armor we hand-make a full range of historically accurate European weapons from the past thousand years."

Castille Armory (www.castillearmory.com) "Castille Armory creates world class swords and accessories for a discerning clientele." "Highest quality sparring and tourney grade combat weapons."

Federschwert (www.federschwert.com) "Federschwert provides Historical European Martial Arts / HEMA gear, equipment and supplies in the US."

HEMA Gear Canada (https://hemagearcanada.com) "We are an online distribution store created to support Canadian and North American artisans. Our goal is to offer a platform for Canadian or North American historical fencing products to be sold."

HEMA Supplies (www.hemasupplies.com) "HEMA Supplies provides quality imported equipment to the United States HEMA communities."

Kult of Athena (kultofathena.com) "Kult Of Athena offers a huge selection of swords and other weapons from the ancient Bronze Age up until the first World War."

Leon Paul USA (www.leonpaulusa.com) "Established in 1921, Leon Paul is the only fencing company run by Olympic Fencers. We offer innovative fencing gear at the forefront of technology."

Purpleheart Armory (www.woodenswords.com) "We offer the largest selection of Historical European Martial Arts (HEMA) equipment in the United States."

SPES USA (www.histfenc.us) "Our company is pleased to offer you the highest quality gear and fencing equipment."

Superior Fencing (www.supfen.com) "We offer affordable prices with high quality HEMA Protective Gear and shipping all over the world."

Appendix 2: Instructional Resources on YouTube

We live in an amazing age where you can easily access the teachings of many fantastic instructors teaching different styles from all around the world. I am always watching videos to help expand my horizons and deepen my understanding of sword fighting. Here are ten YouTube channels I enjoy watching:

Academy of Historical Fencing Here you will find all manner of videos relating to the practice of historical European swordsmanship, from lessons to equipment reviews, sparring footage and articles.

Björn Rüther Björn Rüther is a German historical fencer who specializes in Joachim Meyer, but his channel will provide lots of concepts that apply to all aspects of swordsmanship.

Blood and Iron HEMA Blood and Iron Martial Arts is one of Canada's leading schools in Western martial arts.

Dequitem German historical fencing and amazing armored fight scenes.

Dreynschlag Focusing on the Liechtenauer tradition using various weapons including sword, dagger, polearms, etc.

Schildwache Potsdam Historical fencing videos featuring Martin, a HEMA instructor at the University of Potsdam in Germany.

Schola Gladiatoria Matt Easton of Schola Gladiatoria covers fencing, combat sports and martial arts, antique swords, militaria and weapons, armor, sword reviews, movie and TV fights.

Shadiversity A fun channel about swords, armor, and Medieval history.

Skallagrim Educational entertainment focused mainly on historical arms and armor, as well as knives/tools, firearms, bows, and crossbows.

VCU HEMA The official channel of Virginia Commonwealth University's HEMA Club, the first collegiate sponsored HEMA club. Website: https://hemaclubatvcu.tidyhq.com/. Check out their gear recommendations!

Appendix 3: Test Cutting

Over the centuries, test cutting has been a common way to evaluate the effectiveness of swords and swordsmanship. *Tameshigiri* is a 17th century Japanese term that literally means, "test cutting." Today, test cutting continues to be a staple exercise in many arts involving swordsmanship. It is a staple exercise because cutting with a sharp sword not only helps you refine your technique; it can lead to a deeper understanding of the dynamics and potential consequences of swordplay. Test cutting involves using a sharp sword to slice through various materials, such as plastic jugs and bottles, foam pool noodles, gourds, vines, sticks, bamboo, straw bundles, rolled tatami mats, and lumps of clay. Cutting with a live blade helps you evaluate the effectiveness of your technique, specifically blade alignment and cutting power. Test cutting requires extensive training, as it demands a combination of physical skill, mental focus, and knowledge of proper cutting alignment and mechanics.

If you have never cut before, it is recommended that you find a practitioner in your area or a seminar that has qualified people to train you before attempting to cut with sharp swords.

Typically, in HEMA, a practitioner is not allowed to use "sharps," as they are called, until the basic handling procedures and cutting techniques are taught and reviewed by a qualified instructor. This time frame is usually six months. Even after training for six months, only the most basic of cuts are performed until the practitioner is deemed skilled enough to perform the more advanced techniques. The purpose of tameshigiri is not to simply cut successfully, but to evaluate the biomechanics, edge alignment, and timing of striking with a live sword. Later on, the practice is also a test of the practitioner's skill in sharpening weapons properly, since a dull weapon will not cut effectively and gives non-constructive feedback.

First, you'll need a sharp sword. When selecting a live blade for test cutting, it's important to consider several factors to ensure you make a safe purchase. First, decide what type of sword suits your interests best, such as katana, long sword, or rapier. Prices of swords can vary greatly and depends on the type, quality, and craftsmanship of the sword. Research customer reviews and seek recommendations from knowledgeable individuals to ensure a sword's quality. The least expensive swords suitable for light cutting practice are apt to be made from carbon steel or stainless steel (such as 440, 154, or VG10). They are designed to withstand light to moderate cutting. However, for superior hardness, edge retention, and durability, you will want a sword constructed from high carbon steel (such as 1060 or 1095) or specialized sword steel (such as T10 or L6). Additionally, you'll want to make sure the sword has a full tang (the part of the blade that extends into the handle), as this is the part of the blade most susceptible to breakage. Whenever possible, handle the sword before buying it to assess its grip, balance, and overall feel.

Once you have your sword, you'll need to select an appropriate target. Recyclable plastic jugs and bottles are a good place to start. These are often easily available and usually free. In my house, every empty plastic bottle, from milk to laundry detergent, gets rinsed, filled with water, and placed in the garage, to be sliced with a sword at a later date. Pool noodles are relatively inexpensive and also readily available, especially during the summer months. If you know of and have access to a bamboo grove, there is usually plenty of green bamboo that needs to be trimmed back. While you could cut the stalks *in situ*, it is usually more convenient and economical to place precut sections in a bamboo holder made from a piece of pipe that has been solidly anchored in the ground. Straw mats called *tatami* were first used in the traditional Japanese sword arts to provide a target that more accurately simulates a human body. The rolled mats are usually soaked in water to provide the proper consistency. Occasionally, a stalk of green bamboo is inserted in the center of the mat to represent a bone.

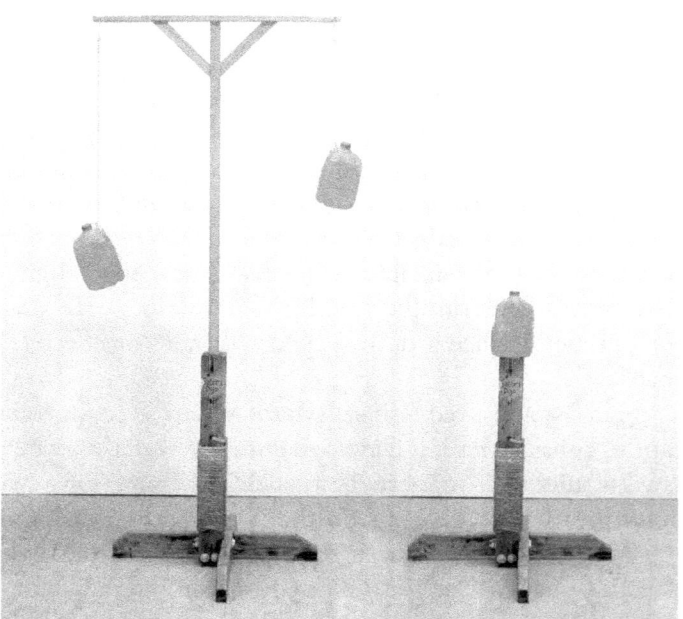

Stands for supporting jugs for slicing with a sword.

Whatever material you choose to cut, it is absolutely essential to have a controlled environment that is safe, one cleared of obstacles and bystanders. To minimize the risk of accidents or injuries, bystanders should not only stand well away from the cutting area but should be able to anticipate where an errant sword might fly, in the off chance that it should it slip out of your grip, and stay clear of that area as well. Your target can be set on a platform or suspended by a cord or string.

Once you are confident that the designated cutting area is safe, chamber your sword into a loaded ready position. Focus your attention on your target. Like a golfer setting up his shot, take time to make a few controlled trial passes, either stopping just short of your target or purposely missing altogether. Once you are satisfied that everything is as perfect as you can make it, execute your cut with a swift and controlled motion. It is essential that you maintain a firm grip on your sword so that it does not fly out of your hands after the cut or if you should miss. Make the cut with your whole body, not just your arms, using your hips to generate maximum power and accuracy during your cut. After the cut is complete, do not immediately drop your guard. Rather, finish in a strong, balanced stance, maintaining a state of focused awareness for a few seconds after completing your technique. Keep your body relaxed, yet alert, ready to attack again. In the Japanese martial arts, this state is called *zanshin*, meaning "lingering mind" or "remaining mind."

Every cut gives you immediate feedback on your technique. Clean cuts give you an idea of the potential damage that might be inflicted by a similar strike on a live target. Imperfect cuts, when analyzed purposefully, can tell you what changes you need to make in your technique. Failures to cut cleanly are usually the result of insufficient power, incorrect edge alignment, or improper follow through. Proper edge alignment is crucial for making a clean cut, and test cutting allows you to test and see the results of your edge alignment. Since curved swords have an asymmetrical blade, the weight distribution helps you to sense this proper edge alignment more easily than you can with a symmetrical straight blade.

Remember, live blades are dangerous weapons, so handle them responsibly and with respect, *always*. Like a firearm, you'll want to secure them when not in use. Never leave real swords where untrained individuals, especially children, can access them. Familiarize yourself with the laws regulating sword ownership and use in your area to ensure you comply with your local laws.

A six-jug horizontal cut with a katana.

Appendix 4: Make Your Own Padded Swords

Foam padded swords, sometimes referred to as *boffer* swords, are good for light sparring with minimal protective gear. However, they generally lack the weight and heft of a real sword, and so do not make very good trainers. Not only do they lack the feel of the genuine article, but most padded swords are not designed to hold up to intensive training against anything other than a padded weapon. Their weaker, hollow plastic cores can't stand up to hard collisions against more dense and heavier wooden or synthetic swords. The one advantage of boffer swords is that they tend to stick together in the bind like sharp blades would, making them good for developing particular skills related to binding.

You can build durable, inexpensive padded swords from easily obtained materials. The design presented here features a PVC core covered completely with closed-cell pipe insulation, and thick foam striking caps on the tips. The entire sword is covered in a smooth layer of duct tape.

When constructing padded weapons, it is important to know a little about PVC. Polyvinyl chloride is a readily available and relatively inexpensive product that comes in two general forms. One is called rigid PVC (RPVC) or unplasticized PVC (uPVC). This type of PVC tends to be brittle and is unsuitable for padded weapons construction. On the other hand, regular PVC is softer and more flexible than uPVC due to the addition of plasticizers. Flexible PVC is used in construction and is commonly available at most hardware stores. It's preferrable for making swords.

Different types of PVC and plastic pipe (left). Always submit a sample to the crush test to see if it is suitable for padded weapons construction (right).

To test if the PVC you are using is the right one for a padded sword, take a short length and apply the crush test. Put your sample into a vice or strike it with a heavy hammer on a hard surface. Plasticized PVC will fold and compress, while brittle PVC will shatter. You might want to wrap the end of your test piece with a paper towel to keep shards from flying, and for easy clean up. Always wear eye protection while testing your PVC. And, remember, only use impact-resistant PVC in your padded weapons construction!

Start with 3/4-inch interior diameter PVC pipe (one-inch exterior diameter). Using the plans provided, cut the pipe into pieces. Sand the ends to remove any sharp edges. You will need four-way connectors to build the crossguards. Connect the pieces using PVC cement. Use end caps to close the open ends on the handle and crossguards, but not the tip as you want to minimize the weight on the distal end of the blade.

Next, carefully cover the entire length of the sword with closed-cell pipe insulation. Cut this layer even with the tip, and then cut several foam disks the same diameter as the foam padding. Affix at least three of these disks on the end, using strips of duct tape, to create a padded thrusting tip. Cover the end of the PVC with a few layers of duct tape to prevent it from cutting into the foam.

Carefully wrap the entire length with duct tape. You can wrap the handle tightly for a better grip, but make sure not to compress the foam covering the blade any more than necessary. A tightly wrapped blade will not allow the foam to absorb the impact of a strike, and it will hurt more than a sword that has been loosely wrapped. When done, inspect your new boffer sword carefully to be sure that the entire length is adequately padded and that it has no rough edges that might cause abrasions.

Finally, test your sword with your partner. Hit softly at first, gradually working up to harder and harder strikes in order for you and your sparring partner to get a feel for how hard you can fight safely with the padded weapons you made. Again, these weapons are designed for light sparring against other similarly constructed padded weapons. When employed properly and with good control, combatants should be safe wearing minimal protective gear, such as light gloves, a mask, and a cup.

Make Your Own
Padded Short Sword

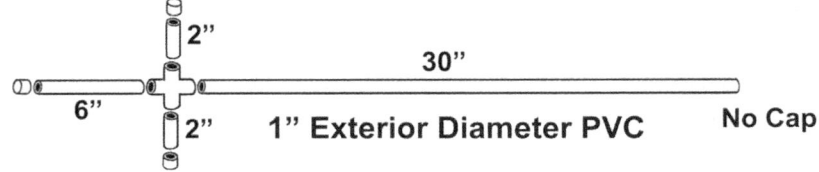

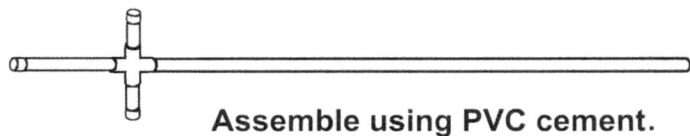

Assemble using PVC cement.

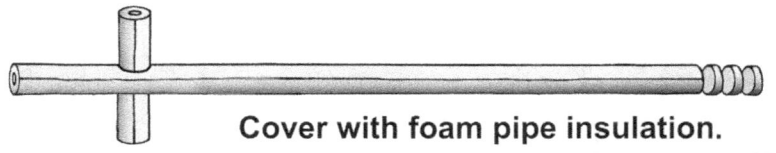

Cover with foam pipe insulation.
Overall length with thrusting tip: approx. 40"

Wrap carefully with duct tape.

The result should be proportional
to a standard short sword.

APPENDICES 259

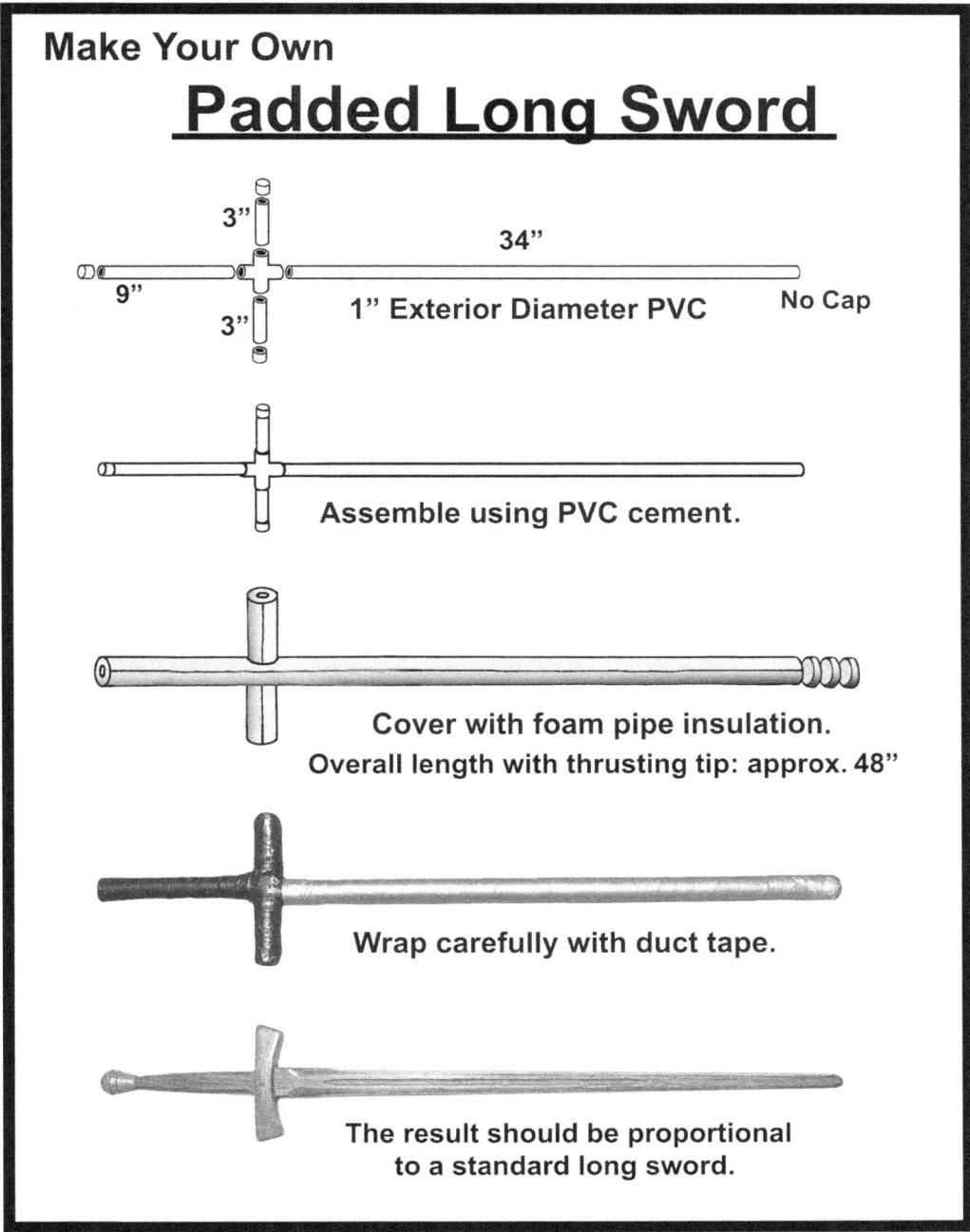

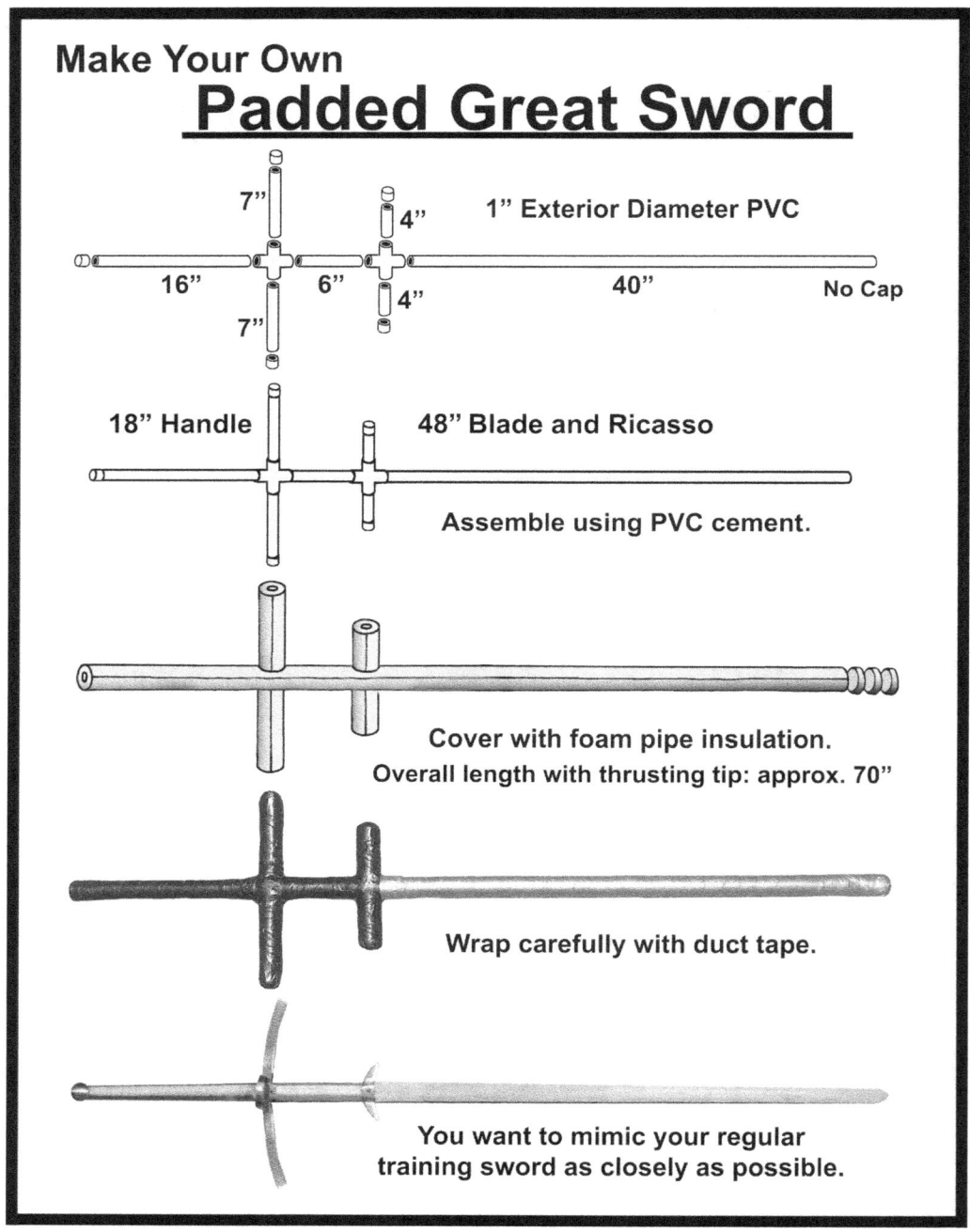

About the Author
Grandmaster Joe Varady, M.Ed.
Black Belt, 7th Degree

Joe Varady began his formal martial arts training in 1986. Over the past three decades, he has cross trained in Eastern martial arts, such as karate, tae kwon do, judo, wing chun, and eskrima, as well as various Western martial arts, including boxing, fencing, long sword, sword and shield, poleaxe, and various methods of armored fighting. Joe is also a trained educator with a master's degree in elementary education.

Joe currently spreads his martial arts knowledge as the head instructor of two programs: Satori Dojo, a traditional martial arts school, founded by Master Joe in 1994, and Modern Gladiatorial Arts, an eclectic weapons system co-founded with Doctore Joe McLaughlin, in 2014. Both programs are located in Joe's hometown of Phoenixville, Pennsylvania. Master Joe is also an active member of the Universal Systems of Martial Arts Organization, a fellowship that provides practitioners of different styles of martial arts with an open forum for sharing techniques and principles. Joe was inducted into the Philadelphia Historic Martial Arts Society Hall of Fame in July 2016. In 2021, with more than thirty-five years in the martial arts, Master Joe was promoted to Grandmaster, 7th degree, at the age of fifty-two. A year later, in 2022, Joe was inducted into the Pennsylvania Karate Hall of Fame.

In addition to *The Art and Science of Sword Fighting*, Joe Varady is the author of three other book and video series, *The Art and Science of Staff Fighting* (2016), *The Art and Science of Stick Fighting* (2020), and *The Art and Science of Self Defense* (2022). All book and video series are available worldwide through YMAA Publication Center of wherever fine books are sold.

Joe Varady's Sword Training Highlights

1990–2000 Trained armored combat with various SCA groups

2003–2009 Assistant Instructor at Live Steel Fight Academy, Pottstown, PA

2005   Live Steel Fight Academy Grand Champion
Won five out of eight events, including long sword, dagger, rapier and dagger

2006   Live Steel Fight Academy Grand Champion
Won four out of six events, including long sword, bastard sword, sword and shield

2007   Live Steel Fight Academy Grand Champion
Won four out of six events, including long sword and rapier and dagger

2014   Universal Systems of Martial Arts Organization Competitor of the Year

2014   Co-founded Modern Gladiatorial Arts

2015   Taiji Fencing League Northeast Champion

2015   Taiji Fencing League Grand Champion

2016   Inducted into the Philadelphia Historic Martial Arts Hall of Fame

2016   Taiji Fencing League Grand Champion

2017   Inducted into the Action Martial Arts Magazine Hall of Fame

2022   Inducted into the Pennsylvania Karate Hall of Fame

2005 Live Steel Fight Academy Grand Champion

BOOKS FROM YMAA

101 REFLECTIONS ON TAI CHI CHUAN
108 INSIGHTS INTO TAI CHI CHUAN
A WOMAN'S QIGONG GUIDE
ADVANCING IN TAE KWON DO
ANALYSIS OF GENUINE KARATE
ANALYSIS OF GENUINE KARATE 2
ANALYSIS OF SHAOLIN CHIN NA 2ND ED
ANCIENT CHINESE WEAPONS
ART AND SCIENCE OF STAFF FIGHTING
THE ART AND SCIENCE OF SELF-DEFENSE
ART AND SCIENCE OF STICK FIGHTING
ART OF HOJO UNDO
ARTHRITIS RELIEF
BACK PAIN RELIEF
BAGUAZHANG
BRAIN FITNESS
CHIN NA IN GROUND FIGHTING
CHINESE FAST WRESTLING
CHINESE FITNESS
CHINESE TUI NA MASSAGE
COMPLETE MARTIAL ARTIST
COMPREHENSIVE APPLICATIONS OF SHAOLIN CHIN NA
CONFLICT COMMUNICATION
DAO DE JING: A QIGONG INTERPRETATION
DAO IN ACTION
DEFENSIVE TACTICS
DIRTY GROUND
DR. WU'S HEAD MASSAGE
ESSENCE OF SHAOLIN WHITE CRANE
EXPLORING TAI CHI
FACING VIOLENCE
FIGHT LIKE A PHYSICIST
THE FIGHTER'S BODY
FIGHTER'S FACT BOOK 1&2
FIGHTING THE PAIN RESISTANT ATTACKER
FIRST DEFENSE
FORCE DECISIONS: A CITIZENS GUIDE
INSIDE TAI CHI
JUDO ADVANTAGE
JUJI GATAME ENCYCLOPEDIA
KARATE SCIENCE
KEPPAN
KRAV MAGA COMBATIVES
KRAV MAGA FUNDAMENTAL STRATEGIES
KRAV MAGA PROFESSIONAL TACTICS
KRAV MAGA WEAPON DEFENSES
LITTLE BLACK BOOK OF VIOLENCE
LIUHEBAFA FIVE CHARACTER SECRETS
MARTIAL ARTS OF VIETNAM
MARTIAL ARTS INSTRUCTION
MARTIAL WAY AND ITS VIRTUES
MEDITATIONS ON VIOLENCE
MERIDIAN QIGONG EXERCISES
MINDFUL EXERCISE
MIND INSIDE TAI CHI
MIND INSIDE YANG STYLE TAI CHI CHUAN
NORTHERN SHAOLIN SWORD
OKINAWA'S COMPLETE KARATE SYSTEM: ISSHIN RYU
PRINCIPLES OF TRADITIONAL CHINESE MEDICINE
PROTECTOR ETHIC
QIGONG FOR HEALTH & MARTIAL ARTS
QIGONG FOR TREATING COMMON AILMENTS
QIGONG MASSAGE
QIGONG MEDITATION: EMBRYONIC BREATHING
QIGONG GRAND CIRCULATION
QIGONG MEDITATION: SMALL CIRCULATION
QIGONG, THE SECRET OF YOUTH: DA MO'S CLASSICS
ROOT OF CHINESE QIGONG
SAMBO ENCYCLOPEDIA
SCALING FORCE
SELF-DEFENSE FOR WOMEN
SHIN GI TAI: KARATE TRAINING
SIMPLE CHINESE MEDICINE
SIMPLE QIGONG EXERCISES FOR HEALTH, 3RD ED.
SIMPLIFIED TAI CHI CHUAN, 2ND ED.
SOLO TRAINING 1&2
SPOTTING DANGER BEFORE IT SPOTS YOU
SPOTTING DANGER BEFORE IT SPOTS YOUR KIDS
SPOTTING DANGER BEFORE IT SPOTS YOUR TEENS
SPOTTING DANGER FOR TRAVELERS
SUMO FOR MIXED MARTIAL ARTS
SUNRISE TAI CHI
SURVIVING ARMED ASSAULTS
TAE KWON DO: THE KOREAN MARTIAL ART
TAEKWONDO BLACK BELT POOMSAE
TAEKWONDO: A PATH TO EXCELLENCE
TAEKWONDO: ANCIENT WISDOM
TAEKWONDO: DEFENSE AGAINST WEAPONS
TAEKWONDO: SPIRIT AND PRACTICE
TAI CHI BALL QIGONG: FOR HEALTH AND MARTIAL ARTS
TAI CHI BALL QIGONG
THE TAI CHI BOOK
TAI CHI CHIN NA
TAI CHI CHUAN CLASSICAL YANG STYLE
TAI CHI CHUAN MARTIAL APPLICATIONS
TAI CHI CHUAN MARTIAL POWER
TAI CHI CONCEPTS AND EXPERIMENTS
TAI CHI DYNAMICS
TAI CHI FOR DEPRESSION
TAI CHI IN 10 WEEKS
TAI CHI PUSH HANDS
TAI CHI QIGONG
TAI CHI SECRETS OF THE ANCIENT MASTERS
TAI CHI SECRETS OF THE WU & LI STYLES
TAI CHI SECRETS OF THE WU STYLE
TAI CHI SECRETS OF THE YANG STYLE
TAI CHI SWORD: CLASSICAL YANG STYLE
TAI CHI SWORD FOR BEGINNERS
TAI CHI WALKING
TAI CHI CHUAN THEORY OF DR. YANG, JWING-MING
FIGHTING ARTS
TRADITIONAL CHINESE HEALTH SECRETS
TRADITIONAL TAEKWONDO
TRAINING FOR SUDDEN VIOLENCE
TRIANGLE HOLD ENCYCLOPEDIA
TRUE WELLNESS SERIES (MIND, HEART, GUT)
WARRIOR'S MANIFESTO
WAY OF KATA
WAY OF SANCHIN KATA
WAY TO BLACK BELT
WESTERN HERBS FOR MARTIAL ARTISTS
WILD GOOSE QIGONG
WING CHUN IN-DEPTH
WINNING FIGHTS
XINGYIQUAN

AND MANY MORE . . .

VIDEOS FROM YMAA

ANALYSIS OF SHAOLIN CHIN NA
ART AND SCIENCE OF SELF DEFENSE
ART AND SCIENCE OF STAFF FIGHTING
ART AND SCIENCE STICK FIGHTING
BAGUA FOR BEGINNERS 1 & 2
BAGUAZHANG: EMEI BAGUAZHANG
BEGINNER QIGONG FOR WOMEN 1 & 2
BEGINNER TAI CHI FOR HEALTH
BREATH MEDICINE
BIOENERGY TRAINING 1&2
CHEN TAI CHI CANNON FIST
CHEN TAI CHI FIRST FORM
CHEN TAI CHI FOR BEGINNERS
CHIN NA IN-DEPTH SERIES
FACING VIOLENCE: 7 THINGS A MARTIAL ARTIST MUST KNOW
FIVE ANIMAL SPORTS
FIVE ELEMENTS ENERGY BALANCE
HEALER WITHIN: MEDICAL QIGONG
INFIGHTING
INTRODUCTION TO QI GONG FOR BEGINNERS
JOINT LOCKS
KNIFE DEFENSE
KUNG FU BODY CONDITIONING 1 & 2
KUNG FU FOR KIDS AND TEENS SERIES
MERIDIAN QIGONG
NEIGONG FOR MARTIAL ARTS
NORTHERN SHAOLIN SWORD
QI GONG 30-DAY CHALLENGE
QI GONG FOR ANXIETY
QI GONG FOR ARMS, WRISTS, AND HANDS
QIGONG FOR BEGINNERS: FRAGRANCE
QI GONG FOR BETTER BALANCE
QI GONG FOR BETTER BREATHING
QI GONG FOR CANCER
QI GONG FOR DEPRESSION
QI GONG FOR ENERGY AND VITALITY
QI GONG FOR HEADACHES
QIGONG FOR HEALTH: HEALING QIGONG
QIGONG FOR HEALTH: IMMUNE SYSTEM
QI GONG FOR THE HEALTHY HEART
QI GONG FOR HEALTHY JOINTS
QI GONG FOR HIGH BLOOD PRESSURE
QIGONG FOR LONGEVITY
QI GONG FOR STRONG BONES
QI GONG FOR THE UPPER BACK AND NECK
QIGONG FOR WOMEN WITH DAISY LEE
QIGONG FLOW FOR STRESS & ANXIETY RELIEF
QIGONG GRAND CIRCULATION
QIGONG MASSAGE
QIGONG MINDFULNESS IN MOTION
QI GONG—THE SEATED WORKOUT
QIGONG: 15 MINUTES TO HEALTH
SABER FUNDAMENTAL TRAINING
SAI TRAINING AND SEQUENCES
SANCHIN KATA: TRADITIONAL TRAINING FOR KARATE POWER
SCALING FORCE
SEARCHING FOR SUPERHUMANS
SHAOLIN KUNG FU FUNDAMENTAL TRAINING: COURSES 1 & 2
SHAOLIN LONG FIST KUNG FU BEGINNER—INTERMEDIATE—ADVANCED SERIES
SHAOLIN SABER: BASIC SEQUENCES
SHAOLIN STAFF: BASIC SEQUENCES
SHAOLIN WHITE CRANE GONG FU BASIC TRAINING SERIES
SHUAI JIAO: KUNG FU WRESTLING
SIMPLE QIGONG EXERCISES FOR HEALTH
SIMPLE QIGONG EXERCISES FOR ARTHRITIS RELIEF
SIMPLE QIGONG EXERCISES FOR BACK PAIN RELIEF
SIMPLIFIED TAI CHI CHUAN: 24 & 48 POSTURES

SIMPLIFIED TAI CHI FOR BEGINNERS 48
SPOTTING DANGER BEFORE IT SPOTS YOU
SPOTTING DANGER FOR KIDS
SPOTTING DANGER FOR TEENS
SUN TAI CHI
SWORD: FUNDAMENTAL TRAINING
TAEKWONDO KORYO POOMSAE
TAI CHI BALL QIGONG SERIES
TAI CHI BALL WORKOUT FOR BEGINNERS
TAI CHI CHUAN CLASSICAL YANG STYLE
TAI CHI FIGHTING SET
TAI CHI FIT: 24 FORM
TAI CHI FIT: ALZHEIMER'S PREVENTION
TAI CHI FIT: CANCER PREVENTION
TAI CHI FIT FOR VETERANS
TAI CHI FIT: FOR WOMEN
TAI CHI FIT: FLOW
TAI CHI FIT: FUSION BAMBOO
TAI CHI FIT: FUSION FIRE
TAI CHI FIT: FUSION IRON
TAI CHI FIT: HEALTHY BACK SEATED WORKOUT
TAI CHI FIT: HEALTHY HEART WORKOUT
TAI CHI FIT IN PARADISE
TAI CHI FIT: OVER 50
TAI CHI FIT OVER 50: BALANCE EXERCISES
TAI CHI FIT OVER 50: SEATED WORKOUT
TAI CHI FIT OVER 60: GENTLE EXERCISES
TAI CHI FIT OVER 60: HEALTHY JOINTS
TAI CHI FIT OVER 60: LIVE LONGER
TAI CHI FIT: STRENGTH
TAI CHI FIT: TO GO
TAI CHI FOR WOMEN
TAI CHI FUSION: FIRE
TAI CHI QIGONG
TAI CHI PRINCIPLES FOR HEALTHY AGING
TAI CHI PUSHING HANDS SERIES
TAI CHI SWORD: CLASSICAL YANG STYLE
TAI CHI SWORD FOR BEGINNERS
TAI CHI SYMBOL: YIN YANG STICKING HANDS
TAIJI & SHAOLIN STAFF: FUNDAMENTAL TRAINING
TAIJI CHIN NA IN-DEPTH
TAIJI 37 POSTURES MARTIAL APPLICATIONS
TAIJI SABER CLASSICAL YANG STYLE
TAIJI WRESTLING
TRAINING FOR SUDDEN VIOLENCE
UNDERSTANDING QIGONG SERIES
WATER STYLE FOR BEGINNERS
WHITE CRANE HARD & SOFT QIGONG
YANG TAI CHI FOR BEGINNERS
YOQI: MICROCOSMIC ORBIT QIGONG
YOQI QIGONG FOR A HAPPY HEART
YOQI:QIGONG FLOW FOR HAPPY MIND
YOQI:QIGONG FLOW FOR INTERNAL ALCHEMY
YOQI QIGONG FOR HAPPY SPLEEN & STOMACH
YOQI QIGONG FOR HAPPY KIDNEYS
YOQI QIGONG FLOW FOR HAPPY LUNGS
YOQI QIGONG FLOW FOR STRESS RELIEF
YOQI: QIGONG FLOW TO BOOST IMMUNE SYSTEM
YOQI SIX HEALING SOUNDS
YOQI: YIN YOGA 1
WU TAI CHI FOR BEGINNERS
WUDANG KUNG FU: FUNDAMENTAL TRAINING
WUDANG SWORD
WUDANG TAIJIQUAN
XINGYIQUAN
YANG TAI CHI FOR BEGINNERS

AND MANY MORE . . .

more products available from . . .

YMAA Publication Center, Inc. 楊氏東方文化出版中心

1-800-669-8892 • info@ymaa.com • www.ymaa.com

www.ingramcontent.com/pod-product-compliance
Lightning Source LLC
Chambersburg PA
CBHW081427070526
44586CB00020B/2515